STOP SIGNS

Recognizing, Avoiding, and Escaping Abusive Relationships

LYNN FAIRWEATHER, MSW

SEAL PRESS

STOP SIGNS
Recognizing, Avoiding, and Escaping Abusive Relationships

Copyright © 2012 by Lynn Fairweather, MSW

Published by
Seal Press
A Member of the Perseus Books Group
1700 Fourth Street
Berkeley, California

Library of Congress Cataloging-in-Publication Data

Fairweather, Lynn, 1974-
    Stop signs : recognizing, avoiding, and escaping abusive relationships /
Lynn Fairweather.
        p. cm.
    Includes bibliographical references and index.
    ISBN 978-1-58005-387-7
    1. Intimate partner violence—United States. 2. Abused women—United States. 3.
Psychological abuse—United States. 4. Intimate partner violence. 5. Abused women.
6. Psychological abuse. I. Title.
    HV6626.2.F335 2012
    362.82'920973--dc23
                                2011047092

10 9 8 7 6 5 4 3 2 1

Cover design by Briar Levit
Interior design by Tabitha Lahr
Printed in the United States of America
Distributed by Publishers Group West

This book is meant to empower and educate, but it is not a guarantee against abuse. While the abuse cases shared in this book are true, some details and names have been changed to protect personal rights and identities.

CONTENTS

Dedication

This book is dedicated to my wise and courageous grandmother June, who always knew I would be an author.

Introduction

A danger foreseen is half-avoided.
—Thomas Fuller

During the genesis of this project my intention was to write a book expressly for professionals in the domestic violence, threat assessment, and law enforcement fields. My objective was to shape the knowledge I have gathered over my twenty-year career into a concise format for practical use in helping to keep women safe. However, as I began working on it and would casually mention my progress to others, something unexpected began to happen. Dozens of women—acquaintances, colleagues, friends—approached me about intimate partner abuse. Some would speak up in front of a group, while others would wait until I was alone, either in line for the ladies room, or walking to my car after a speaking engagement. They spoke in desperate tones about themselves, their partners, their relatives, and neighbors. Some had tears in their eyes, others showed anger or fear. They wanted to know what signs to look for in an abuser, how to know if the way their boyfriend treated them was "normal," and how to keep their ex-husband from finding them. It was through these conversations that I realized everyday women were the audience I needed to reach because *the power to prevent domestic violence was more in their hands than those of the professionals* who were assigned to help them. I came to understand that the average female has valid questions and concerns for herself and her loved ones, but doesn't know who to ask. Often, we don't feel that our suspicions warrant a call to the police or a domestic abuse hotline, but we know something is wrong in some of the relationships we see or participate in. When it comes to intimate partner abuse, many women feel that they should be able to "handle it themselves" or that they should "stay out of other people's business." Yet millions of women are affected by abuse each year, with thousands of women losing their lives to violence.

According to the National Coalition Against Domestic Violence, 85 percent of abuse victims are women, and the U.S. Department of Justice tells us that three-quarters of those killed in domestic homicides are female as well.[1] Therefore, by sheer numbers the issue of intimate partner abuse is largely a matter of violence against women. In this book, we focus on intimate partner abuse between heterosexual couples. Research has shown that male-perpetrated violence occurs in roughly equal numbers in gay and straight relationships, and that abuse is somewhat less prevalent in lesbian couples, although still a present and serious concern. However, LGBTQ victims face issues heterosexual people don't, and I am not an expert in this area. For more resources and information please contact Lambda GLBT Community Services (www.lambda.org), The Network/La Red (1-617-742-4911 or www.thenetworklared.org), or the Gay Men's Domestic Violence Project (1-800-832-1901 or www.gmdvp.org).

When asked if it was possible for women to exit an abusive relationship safely, Rhodes University psychology researcher Mike Earl-Taylor said the following:

*The most effective way for women to avoid being victim-
ized by controlling male partners is not to become seriously
involved with them.*[2]

At first glance, this statement might seem condescending in its sim-
plicity, but what Mr. Earl-Taylor is saying is entirely true and isn't meant
to blame women who are in relationships with abusive partners. There is
no shame in falling for an expert con artist, but women who have done so
are at additional risk of repeating the cycle if they don't educate themselves
on proactive prevention. No matter what your past relationships were
like, it *is* possible to protect yourself and those you love through awareness
and coordinated efforts between internal and external supports.

My goal is to introduce women to a self-preservation philosophy
that encourages knowledge, empowerment, and solution-based strategies for assessing and managing risk in relationships.

There is significant protection in knowledge, and any willing
woman can learn the signs and strategies that will help to increase
her safety.

I have spent my entire professional life of nearly two decades
working directly with victims and perpetrators of domestic violence, and
during that time I have learned a great deal about the dynamics, factors,
and prevention of intimate partner abuse. I have also been the victim of
an abuser and now, as a survivor, I want to pass on what I know about
avoiding, recognizing, and escaping a nightmare that affects millions of
women each year. There are three levels of prevention through which I
will provide practical ideas and advice to help identify, avert, and safely
end potentially life-threatening relationships. In the vernacular of public
health professionals, this book is simultaneously about:

- *Primary* prevention: Stopping abuse from happening in
  the first place

- *Secondary* prevention: Self-identification of abuse while it is still at an early stage
- *Tertiary* prevention: Avoiding further harm once the problem has been recognized

While many compassionate and dedicated professionals such as police, advocates, prosecutors, and counselors are positioned to help victims of abuse, they typically enter the picture after it has already occurred. Most community discussions around prevention focus on macroefforts like tougher antiviolence laws, stronger supervision of offenders, and youth education programs. While these are all worthy endeavors, the ideas presented in this book concentrate more on personal strengths-based solutions, such as learning how to identify abusers and empowering yourself to become a less vulnerable target. I always recommend that victims of abuse seek assistance, and the following chapters will tell you exactly where to find it, but no one can fix your life for you. Your effort and courage must play a central role. This book is about saving yourself and relying on your inner strength to avoid and escape life-threatening circumstances.

The ideas I propose in this book are not meant to blame anyone for having an inefficient "abuse radar" but rather to arm women with information that can make them safer while placing the power of change back into their own hands. In her book *The Trouble with Blame* psychologist Sharon Lamb states:

> *I do wish to argue that an exclusively external view is problematic not only because it underestimates the validity of what the victim is telling us, but because of an inherent contradiction between the social forces account (which is almost always presented in its most deterministic way) and the possibilities for change. In other words if we tell*

victims that there was nothing they could have done to stop the abuse, then we make them powerless to stop it from happening again.[3]

I believe every woman can become her own hero instead of waiting for one to come along and save her. My wish for you is not obedience to my ideas or anyone else's, but rather the cultivation of an organic and self-reliant strength.

Finally, this is not a book about "male-bashing," and it does not advocate diminishing the legal or human rights of men.

During my life I have met many kind, just, gentle men for whom I have a great deal of respect and love. I believe them to be the majority and just like most women, they seek loving and healthy relationships. These are not the men I am talking about in the following chapters.

Reducing violence requires a state of true equality in society. It is for this reason that we should welcome men into the antiviolence movement and applaud the efforts of so many that have already saved thousands of lives. I encourage all men and women to stand side by side in protecting our mothers, daughters, sisters, and friends from the threat of intimate partner abuse. Never underestimate the power of collaborative hope and commitment, for only in unity can we accomplish the truly transformational.

Chapter 1

It Will Never Happen to Me:
Intimate Partner Abuse in America

We are effectively destroying ourselves by
violence masquerading as love.
—R. D. Laing

As the police car's headlights appeared around the corner, I felt all at once a sense of relief and a feeling of dread because I knew there was no turning back. Whatever happened next was out of my hands and I had no idea what the exact repercussions would be. But I was alive, and help had arrived. As the officer stepped out of the squad car and approached me, a young woman emerged from the passenger side and stood off to the edge of the driveway. She wasn't in uniform. I squinted against the bright beam of the flashlight as the officer swept it over me. When he saw the blood covering my face, hair, and clothes, his expression softened. "Who did this to you?" he asked gently. I motioned toward the house, replying in a half-whisper, "He's in there." The officer spoke into his radio for a moment, and asked me to sit down on the curb. Neighbors began to emerge from their homes, looking curious and concerned. "Who is she?" I asked, pointing to the young woman. "That's my daughter," he said. "She's on a ride-along with me tonight." Her expression wore shock, and I wanted to reassure her that I was okay, but my face hurt too much to smile. Instead, I just said, "My dad's a cop too."

It's easy to assume that since I came from a police family and worked in a domestic violence shelter, I had all the protective factors that a young woman could need to avoid becoming the victim of abuse. The truth is it doesn't matter how you were raised, what you do for a living, or how much education you've had. The probability that you may run into an abuser during your lifetime is extraordinary. Laura McCloskey, a professor at Indiana University, studied just these odds. Her team of researchers used survey responses to reveal the following likelihood: a lower-income, thirty-two-year-old woman has a 40 percent chance of being abused, regardless of her race or occupation.[1]

"The men who are out there, unfortunately, are pretty violent," McCloskey stated in the report. "The chance of getting hit by some guy you're dating, especially if you're dating low-income and unemployed men, is kind of high."

Another study revealed that younger women are particularly at risk, as females between the ages of nineteen to twenty-nine reported more violence by intimates than any other age group.[2]

So who are the victims of domestic abuse? Simply put, they are us. They are our mothers, our sisters, our best friends, our daughters, and ourselves. No one is immune to the possibility of meeting or becoming involved with an abusive partner.

According to a 1998 Commonwealth Fund survey, one-third of American women will experience physical and/or sexual violence at the hands of a current or former intimate partner during her lifetime.[3] That's a sobering fact, and while on one level it may be reassuring to know that you are not alone, it is also a sad testament to the prevalence of abuse in America. Yet if so many women are experiencing abuse, why don't we hear more about it? Shame, mostly. Domestic abuse isn't something women share easily because of the shame, guilt, and embarrassment that often surround a victim's past. Years ago, I recall opening up to a friend about my own experience, only to have her respond in disgust, "And why were you with a guy like *that?*" Her reaction made me feel stupid for ever having dated him to begin with, and even more foolish for staying with him as long as I had. It also discouraged me from sharing my experience with anyone else who knew me, for fear of appearing naïve, flawed, or even masochistic. It took me a long time to realize that the shame was not on me but on him, and on anyone who judges a woman for accidentally walking into a nightmare while trying to find a loving relationship.

Since we don't often hear survivor's stories, it may be hard to comprehend that domestic abuse is as prevalent as victim advocates suggest. But it is. For all you know, both the woman at the supermarket check-out counter *and* the woman behind you in line suffer some level of intimate partner abuse, whether it's physical, emotional, or verbal (more on types of abuse in Chapter 2). For example, when I tell people about my work as a domestic violence expert, I am still stunned by the number of women who open up to me about being victims of abuse. Hair stylists, cab drivers, police officers, waitresses, and attorneys— women from all walks of life—reveal painful secrets. Many others tell me incredible stories of survival and hope, from which they emerged stronger, wiser.

Take eighty-two-year-old Dorothy, for example, a woman I met while attending a charity function, who struck me profoundly with her honesty and courage. She told me about how she had raised four children with a violent man who beat and sexually abused everyone in the family. Back in her day, women didn't divorce and raise families on their own so she was forced to endure the daily horrors of life under his reign. Finally, one night she put sleeping pills in his drink and slipped away with the children while he was unconscious. The next few years were full of financial struggle for Dorothy and her children, food was scarce and winters were cold, but she told me she never regretted a minute of her journey. "Even if my kids were hungry, at least no one was molesting or beating them. I'd rather we all live poor than walk around in fear of that monster."

Many women never tell anyone about their abuse and the majority never report to the police—even those who do, often never see justice for their efforts. Unfortunately, they aren't getting the medical care they need either. Less than one-fifth of victims reporting an injury from intimate partner violence sought medical treatment following the injury.[4] Some cannot seek help because their abuser won't let them, or they live in a rural area far from medical care. Others don't have insurance and are concerned about the costs, while some women are afraid their medical provider will make a report to the authorities, forcing them to bring a frightening personal issue into the open before they are ready. Perhaps they are in the country illegally or have an outstanding warrant for arrest. Imagine these women sitting on their couches with bags of frozen vegetables on their bruised limbs and faces, rinsing washcloths soaked with blood in the bathroom sink. Picture what they will tell friends and family the following day, conjuring up stories of slippery staircases and errant boxes falling from shelves. All the while, never telling a soul what they've really been through.

Perhaps this woman is you.

WHAT DOES A VICTIM LOOK LIKE?

If you were to base this question on statistics alone, it might look like an episode of Cops: poor uneducated women, often minorities or women with a drug or alcohol problem. Why? Because limited statistics show us that domestic abuse disproportionately affects African American and Native American women, and those with substance abuse issues.[5, 6] But this picture may be deeply skewed, since the numbers come mainly from police departments, courts, emergency rooms, and battered women's shelters. Women without accessible wealth (which are primarily nonwhite) are more likely to use these resources than those who can afford to hire attorneys, stay in hotels, utilize private healthcare, and sell off assets in order to finance an escape. It's not that abuse doesn't happen to more affluent or middle class women, it's just that they aren't appearing in public agencies and institutions as often as minority women, where they can be accurately counted. Additionally, because of the stigma attached to domestic abuse—and the damaging stereotype that only poor, dysfunctional women are prone to victimization—many educated women do not seek help from public agencies. Thus, figures on the racial, educational, and economic backgrounds of abuse victims may be slanted to suggest that some groups of women are more or less prone to victimization than others.

Finally, it's important to note that these statistics chiefly represent physical violence cases, because verbal and emotional abuse alone is rarely reported or prosecuted. But as you'll discover in Chapter 2, verbal and emotional abuse is just as prevalent and equally damaging as physical abuse.

A similarly disturbing and hard to quantify statistic related to intimate partner abuse is the impact on children. My domestic violence work is flooded with stories of children who are often covictims of their mothers, or at least primary witnesses to unspeakable acts. I recall one case in particular where two young boys were forced to watch, film, and even participate in their father's abuse of their mother. They would cry and beg their father to stop but he insisted that they needed to "learn how to control women." Months after their mother exited the relationship, these children still talked incessantly about the abuse, the younger one admitting that he sleeps with his lights on after years of lying in a dark room, listening to his mother get beaten across the hallway.

It is estimated that in 30–60 percent of households where a child's mother is being abused, the perpetrator is also hurting the children.[7]

In addition to the risks of living in a violent home, I have known hundreds of victims who have had to contend with the child-protective system as well. In many cases, they welcomed the assistance, and with the help of dedicated caseworkers, were able to break free from years of horror in their homes. Still, in other cases, well-intentioned but

Case in Point

Sadly, the horrors children face in abusive families extend beyond the abuse itself. In one case I worked on, a six-year-old boy named Jayden was separated from both his parents when his mother lost custody after a brutal beating. The child-protection agency placed blame with the victim, stating that she acted irresponsibly by bringing her son to his father's apartment. The abuser incarcerated, Jayden ended up in a sexually violent foster care home, giving new and more awful meaning to his definition of abuse.

inexperienced caseworkers would sometimes remove children from the home, citing their mother's "failure to protect" them from an abusive partner. While they may have had the best interests of the children in mind, the caseworkers didn't understand that mom might be killed if she left without the right knowledge and support.

Studies have shown that children, even unborn babies, can be affected by witnessing domestic violence.[8] When I say that a child has "witnessed" abuse, I mean that they either saw it happen, heard it from another room, or saw the aftermath, such as broken furniture or a mother's bruised face. Even if they aren't around when the abuse occurs, children are sensitive to tension in the home and can often sense the stress between parents. They may feel sad or angry about the situation and act out in a variety of emotional and behavioral ways at home or in school. They may also blame themselves for the family

Take Action

Was violence a factor in your home as a child? Consider picking up a few books on the subject to help you understand and overcome the deeper impact it may have had on you. I recommend *Adult Children of Abusive Parents: A Healing Program for Those Who Have Been Physically, Sexually, or Emotionally Abused,* by Steven Farmer; or *Toxic Parents: Overcoming Their Hurtful Legacy and Reclaiming Your Life,* by Dr. Susan Forward

Additionally, consider seeking professional counseling to reduce your chances of repeating a generational cycle of abuse. For referrals, contact your local domestic violence shelter, victim resource center, or county mental health department. When we take steps to deal with the traumas of our past, we are better preparing ourselves to face the challenges of our future.

discord. Under this burden of guilt, they can become withdrawn and depressed. Research shows that kids who witness violence at home are more likely to fight in school, use drugs or alcohol, or attempt suicide.[9] As adults, they may become victims or abusers themselves. Studies show that witnessing violence between parents is the strongest risk factor for transmitting violent behavior from one generation to the next.[10] Fostering a healthy adult relationship is more difficult if you've never seen one up close.

SHE ASKED FOR IT, DIDN'T SHE?

Over the years, I've heard many harmful myths about intimate partner abuse from the informed and uninformed alike. Some place blame with the offender, but qualify the abhorrent behavior as being a function of something outside the abuser's control, thus diminishing his responsibility. For example, even police officers responding to calls have told me that they believe that mental health or drug and alcohol issues lie at the core of domestic violence. These are both separate and contributing matters, but neither addresses the root cause of abuse: an intense need for power and control, accompanied by a sense of entitlement to use force in gaining it (I will discuss more about the origins of abuse in later chapters).

Another common misconception is that victims are to blame because they provoke the abuser or "press his buttons." The old misogynistic fallacy, "She must have asked for it," assumes that a woman should know her place in the relationship, and if she steps out of line she should be punished. Some media sources perpetuate this myth by suggesting that trivial spousal disagreements lead to murder, as did a September 2010 CBS News report by Naimah Jabali-Nash entitled "Kentucky Tragedy: Man Kills Wife, Five Others, in Rampage Over Cold Eggs, Say Cops."[11]

While many women are sympathetic to victims of violence, some simply do not understand the dynamics of abuse. There is a grave and detrimental misconception that women are somehow emotionally flawed, weak, or otherwise "damaged" if they end up in an abusive relationship. Thus, women who put down or blame victims of abuse do so almost unconsciously, to separate themselves from "those women." Heads in the sand, they tell themselves that they will never be affected by violence because they aren't making the same mistakes they attribute to victims. They believe they are *smarter* than that. But abusive men do not walk around with a capital A stitched on their T-shirt or suit. As you'll learn in further chapters, abuse is complex and often insidious, sometimes not showing up until a victim is married to the abuser. In one previous case of mine, a smart doctoral student named Kate had married her college sweetheart. "It wasn't until I was pregnant that he began showing his true colors," she told me. "Sure, in retrospect, there were small signs—his sarcasm, growing suspicion when I stayed late at the office. A rough grab here and there, but in the three years we were together before it began, I never once thought he was anything else but a loving husband."

In the end, this form of denial separates women from one another, further isolating victims from understanding and assistance.

WHY DOESN'T SHE JUST LEAVE?

Imagine if you had to go home this evening, pack everything you could fit into a duffel bag, and leave the rest (including pets) behind, not knowing if you would ever see any of it again. Then picture taking yourself and your children away from everything familiar to stay with a group of strangers in a women's shelter. You might have to stay for weeks at a time, following restrictive safety and communal living rules, possibly quitting your job or schooling, and cutting off contact with friends and relatives to avoid detection. You would likely have to run through your savings, borrow from relatives, or go on public assistance to financially survive. Then consider hiring expensive lawyers to fight it out in court with your ex for years to come, moving to a new city, getting a new job, and starting your entire life over.

Leaving is simply far easier said than done.

If you are living in abuse, you may have been told by friends, family, coworkers, counselors, or police that you must leave that situation right away. In my experience, the most common reaction the lay public has to stories about women trapped in abusive relationships is this: "Why doesn't she just leave?" This "Dissolution Solution" fallacy is one of the most damaging of all abuse myths because it suggests that the victim could end all her problems by simply walking out the door of a dangerous relationship, when in fact an unplanned, unsupported exit can exacerbate a risky situation. But as you'll learn in this book, victims can leave. And if you're currently in an abusive relationship, you *will* leave. For many abused women, as difficult as it is, uprooting their life in the dramatic way described above is preferable to what they deal with at home, and it may be their best chance at survival. The important thing is to know *how* and *when* to leave an abuser, which we'll discuss in subsequent chapters. For now, it's critical to understand the dynamics and repercussions of "just leaving."

In some cases, radical change will not solve the problem. Instead, it can aggravate an already dangerous, unstable scenario. The period after separation is often the riskiest time for an abused woman, as her controller reacts to the loss of his "possession" and the narcissistic injury that accompanies it. When I served on a high-lethality domestic violence response team in the Pacific Northwest, almost every one of the hundreds of women we worked with had already ended the relationship with her abuser. Yet in case after case, he continued to stalk, violate, threaten, abuse, and terrorize her and her children. In a similar vein, one Michigan study found that 37.4 percent of the women with one or more violent partners said that the violence continued after separation, and 45.6 percent indicated that the violence increased.[12] Therefore, leaving often doesn't immediately stop the abuse, and in many cases, it can introduce the point of highest risk to a victim.

This misleading notion also places the responsibility for termination of violence on the wrong party. Shouldn't we instead be asking, "Why doesn't he just stop beating her?"

Case in Point

"I thought I was pretty clear with David when I told him our relationship was over. But he kept coming by, calling me, and trying to get back together. I thought he was just lovesick, that he would get over me eventually, until he started getting angry. Suddenly, every time he left a message, it centered around what a stuck-up bitch I was, how I lied to him and ruined his life. He started talking about how he wanted to see me suffer. I felt like I was going to throw up whenever the phone rang."

—Gwen, age thirty

The truth is, women choose to stay in dangerous situations for a variety of complex reasons, including fear, poverty, cultural or religious beliefs and obligations, hope for change and of course, love. Often the rationales for staying with an abusive partner are found in combinations as individual as the victims themselves.

Fortunately, most battered women do get out alive. One study found that after a year's time, 30 percent of women had left their abuser and that number rose to 70 percent after five years.[13]

In the days of our mothers and before, women seldom had the resources or social support to escape violent relationships. But today, the abuse response and prevention community is strong, with an established presence or connection to nearly every American city. The stereotype of the cowering, bruised woman who stands faithfully by her man is dying fast. Embrace hope, and remember, even the smallest effort a victim makes to strengthen herself and transform her situation, matters—especially if that victim is you. Every great journey begins with a single step.

> ### ⚠ Take Action
>
> If you are in a relationship that feels unsafe, take the first step by speaking the truth. Tell someone what is happening, preferably a person who can offer you concrete suggestions and resources in your area. Pick up your phone, any time of day or night, and call The National Domestic Violence hotline at 1-800-799-SAFE. You won't be required to tell them who you are or where you're at, but speaking with an advocate, even anonymously, can give you options you never thought existed.

WHEN VICTIMS FIGHT BACK

Sharon Cahill had had enough. The day her boyfriend attacked their four-year-old daughter after he poured hot coffee over Sharon's legs, she fought back, attacking him with a desperate flurry of punches and slaps. But Sharon's boyfriend was a foot taller, eighty pounds heavier, and far more vicious. In fact, her violent response was just what he had been waiting for. Once Sharon took a swing, her abuser cut loose on her, justifying it by saying "she came at him." He answered without mercy, picking her up and throwing her across the room, then kicking her in the head repeatedly as she lay on the floor. As she recovered in the hospital afterward with a broken arm, burns, and a concussion, Sharon wondered, "Was this my fault?"

Like the myth that a woman can "just leave," another damaging fallacy is the idea of "mutual combat," the belief that women are just as violent and abusive as men in relationships. This fable is perpetuated primarily by antifeminist activists representing "father's rights" groups and attorneys of the abusers, who contend that men are unfairly penalized in many domestic abuse cases, and that victim-assistance organizations are profiting from the prosecution of innocent men. But when we examine the facts more closely, a different picture emerges.

By definition, "use of force" in intimate partner relationships can range from a one-time shove to a consistent pattern of terrorization, coercion, mental/verbal abuse, and violent physical or sexual assaults. But according to domestic violence experts, only the latter would be defined as battering. Men and women aren't usually engaging in "mutual combat" when they physically fight because the word "mutual" insinuates that both come from an equal position of size, strength, and fighting skills. Women are often more injured in altercations because they usually have less physical size and strength and are fighting to prevent pain rather than inflict it. While male victims often present with superficial scratches and red marks, females frequently present with broken bones and severe contusions. I once heard a well-known domestic violence prosecutor remark, "If women beat men the way men beat women, hospital emergency rooms would have putting greens and sports bars inside them."

The "equal use of violence" theory, sometimes called "sexual symmetry," draws its evidence largely from statistics taken out of context, such as the female arrest rate and a measurement tool called the Conflict Tactics Scale. Both of these examples, explained below, demonstrate how statistics and flawed research disregard the real circumstances and stories behind the numbers.

The Deceptive Female Arrest Rate

In some American cities, women now represent over 20 percent of intimate partner violence arrests.[14] But while arrest rates show that women are often charged with assault, this is primarily a reflection of the "mandatory arrest" policies that many states originally adopted for the protection of battered women. Unfortunately, the law also works against them, since in most states officers must make an arrest when they have probable cause to believe that violence (or another abuse-related crime) has occurred. This is where it gets sticky, because if a woman's abuser shows injuries, she will be subject to the same laws as he would, regardless of whether she inflicted those wounds in self-defense or not. The irony here is that the law was initially implemented to prevent police from leaving a victim—assumed to be the woman—in danger by simply telling the abuser to "take a walk around the block," as they once did decades ago. Thus, whoever tells the most convincing tale of victimhood and has injuries to prove it, gets to stay behind while their partner is cuffed and booked.

Abusers, by nature, are manipulative, turning the tables when dealing with the police and finding creative ways to threaten their victims into silence. And if he has sustained even a *scratch* during the act of assaulting her, he will often play it up, complaining of the pain he is experiencing. Meanwhile, she may be far more injured but in ways he has made sure are invisible, such as striking her in the stomach. Take Tanya, a thirty-seven-year-old Portland, Oregon, mother who said that her husband would always hit her on the head because bruises there were impossible to see under her hair, and swelling was usually reduced by the time she was allowed to leave the house. "I sometimes wished he would beat me in public, just so somebody else could see that it was actually happening." she said. "I was terrified that if I called the police and they didn't believe me, the beatings would get that much worse for me after they left. I felt terrified and utterly, completely trapped."

In many cases where women have been arrested for domestic abuse, they were using force to defend themselves or their children, or to regain some semblance of control in the chaos of frequent victimization. Sometimes, women who have been previous victims of abuse will react differently to hostile behavior in a partner, even taking on the role of aggressor in a bid for self-protection. They may feel that abuse in a relationship is inevitable and seek to regain some control by striking first to "burst the tension bubble" or "get it over with." This is not to say they are justified in using violence—women who attack men without provocation are still culpable for their actions. I offer these points not to condone or excuse abuse, but to shed light on what some women feel they must do to avoid falling back into the victim's position.

Conversely, men typically use force in relationships to establish and maintain power and control over women. According to studies, they are also more likely to deny their actions, whereas women own up to physical violence more often, admitting using force when confronted by police or caseworkers—and thus setting themselves up for arrest.[15]

In reality, many women arrested for domestic violence assaults and killings are actually acting in self-defense, whether in the moment or as a reaction to an overall life-threatening situation. As Lisa Larance, coordinator of the RENEW program through Catholic Social Services in Washtenaw County, Michigan, posited: "The person who is the power-holder lays out the choices and the victim merely chooses from among them."[16]

The Appearance of Aggression

Other people who believe that women use violence in equal proportion to men point to a research instrument called the Conflict Tactics Scale, which many victim specialists agree uses a skewed lens to determine its high rate of female "abusers." This index asks subjects to reveal whether they have ever struck a partner, but it doesn't ask them *why* or what was happening at the moment. Because it doesn't take into account context, culture, or motive, we see only raw numbers that fail to tell the full story. Many abusers will complain fervently about how a woman victimized them once while leaving out all the times he attacked her. In his mind, her one slap is far more grievous than his fifty beatings.

When I served as cofacilitator of a domestic violence educational class in a women's prison, many women asked me if they should be in the group or not, because they weren't sure if they were a victim or an abuser. These women knew people had hurt them but could also recall instances in which they had struck back or struck first. Many had been arrested for domestic violence and were serving sentences on assault and even murder charges involving their intimate partners. Some felt guilty sitting in the same room with women who identified themselves as "bona fide" victims, and questioned whether they were even deserving of the information and support that the group provided. While I would have liked to talk more in depth with each of these women and hear more about their individual circumstances, time was brief in the jail group, and I was never sure whether I would see a participant again, so my cofacilitator and I would present them with a simple question to help them make sense of their experience: "If you completely stopped all the yelling, the hitting, and the conflict, what would your partner do?" If the answer is that they would stop as well and harmony would reign, then perhaps you are the abuser. But if the answer is that he would continue to relentlessly attack you, and you would be in an even more vulnerable position for not fighting back, then you are the victim.

If domestic abuse affects two to four million women annually but kills less than two thousand per year, that leaves a large majority of battered women who do not lose their lives to the violence. At least not

Case in Point

I remember working with a tough, streetwise young woman named Tanisha who seemed proud of her defensive maneuvers when we first spoke. "I don't let that bastard get away with it!" she exclaimed. "If he hits me, he knows I'm going to hit him back. I don't go off for no reason, but I'm not going to stand there and let him beat me up." While her courage was admirable, her approach was destined to end in tragedy. One night during a particularly violent argument, her abuser yelled, "You're dead now, you fucking bitch!" Tanisha picked up a kitchen knife to defend herself, and as her abuser rushed her in a football-style tackle, she thrust it forward, stabbing him in the abdomen. The next time we spoke, a thick glass wall stood between us at the county jail where Tanisha was being held for attempted murder. Her boyfriend claimed that she attacked him without provocation. "He put me here," she said. "I never had a choice."

in the traditional sense—they physically survive but are then left with two options: either remain in the abuse or leave the relationship, both of which come with their own set of unique challenges. What about the women who do remain in their situation, sometimes for decades, bearing children into such madness and suffering in silence? Sometimes the daily terror becomes too much for them and they resort to killing their abuser, either as they are being assaulted or in a maneuver of general self-defense, assassinating their partner (sometimes in his sleep) after suffering years of his horrific abuse. These numbers have decreased since the 1970s, due to the growing strength and efficacy of the battered women's advocacy movement and an improvement in the criminal justice response to domestic abuse. However, hundreds of women remain in prison to this day for murders that were actually self-defense. Sometimes victims kill themselves because they feel there is no other way out and don't want to give power over their life (or death) to their current or former partner. Sometimes they die only in spirit, becoming depressed and hopeless shadows of their former selves. When a woman metaphorically loses her life to domestic violence, she never gets to realize her true self-worth or the happiness she deserves to have. While physical death is the most tragic result of abuse, we lose far more women each year to the symbolic murder of the soul.

It is possible to be resurrected from the nightmare of abuse and live a fulfilling existence again. However, opportunities for deep transformation seldom offer us an easy course. If you are in an abusive intimate relationship, understand that once danger is recognized, it presents a fork in the road where difficult decisions must be made. One path can lead to certain death, either literally or figuratively. But the other represents freedom, and at the end, where the light shines in, a new dawn awaits. Break the chains of fear and follow your heart to embrace the safe, healthy, respected life you deserve.

You *can* escape. I did.

Chapter 2

Knowledge Is Power: Recognizing All Types and Patterns of Abuse

We fear violence less than our own feelings.
Personal, private, solitary pain is more terrifying
than what anyone else can inflict.
—Jim Morrison

One of the most common and dangerous misconceptions about intimate partner abuse is that women are not true victims of abuse unless they are physically assaulted to the point of being bruised, bloody, or broken. Unfortunately, this perception is so rooted in our culture that victims themselves believe this as well.

When I found myself in a dangerous relationship during my college years, I didn't see it as "abusive" either. And this despite the fact that I worked at a battered women's shelter as a resident assistant and counselor, where I encountered victims of domestic abuse who were in various states of turmoil. They came in for help and support, their lives shattered, children in tow, with only the clothes on their backs. Many had police involvement, divorce proceedings, medical, financial, and housing issues to navigate. Some were stitched and bruised from multiple severe beatings, injured on the inside and out. My relationship "problems" seemed innocuous by comparison. Even though my live-in boyfriend was verbally, psychologically, and somewhat physically abusive, I didn't identify as a victim because he hadn't beaten me bloody (yet). We didn't have children together, and I had never called the police to report his behaviors. In my mind, I wasn't a "battered woman." I simply had a boyfriend with a bad temper. I figured all couples fought like we did. And while I knew he had severe emotional problems, I thought it was my job to *fix* him, because a good woman wouldn't leave her partner when he clearly needed help, right?

When he put his hands on me forcefully, a slight grab or push at first, I brushed it off, because most of the time I felt able to adequately defend myself, and I had been in past relationships where aggression was not unusual. When he grabbed me around the throat one day and began strangling me because I told him to "shut up," I felt angry and hurt. But we were in public, in a restaurant parking lot, and I didn't want to make a scene. So I walked into the building and sat down in silence, fighting back tears while my throat ached and I coughed, breathless. When he grabbed the steering wheel while I was driving and tried to force us off the road into a tree, I blamed it on him being drunk and emotional. When he threatened or tried to kill himself (multiple times), I realized he had mental health issues but thought I could convince him to go into therapy, which he never did. I didn't tell anyone what was happening because I was embarrassed by the "drama" of it all and ashamed that I had chosen such an obviously flawed partner. It wasn't until I broke up with him and moved out of the home we shared that I began to see myself not only as a true victim of abuse, but one who was also still in danger.

While certain social beliefs, attitudes, and myths support domestic abuse worldwide, some of the most dangerous ones seek to invalidate women's experiences by minimizing and denying the perils they face: namely, that an abuser's actions must be physically violent in nature to be considered "abuse." This couldn't be further from the truth. While the general public often associates "domestic violence" with black eyes and split lips, abuse comes in a disconcerting array of damaging forms, including verbal, emotional, mental, sexual, economic, and spiritual.

Unfortunately, most women who are abused in this way believe they are simply in a "bad relationship," perhaps even one of their *own* making. Worse, they avoid using resources such as domestic abuse hotlines and women's shelters because they believe they are not *truly* battered women. This is a dangerous misconception. Just because a woman has never been physically or sexually assaulted by an otherwise abusive partner doesn't mean she is safe! Not only can nonphysical abuse evolve into violent assault, but hundreds of women each year are also killed by current or former partners who never laid a forceful finger on them before then.

Here are the straight facts: It's still abuse if you are assaulted but not physically injured. It's still abuse if it only happened once, or if it happened when he was drunk, or when he was high. It's still abuse if you were able to fight him off, or if he stopped when you agreed to do what he wanted. Abuse is not defined by the severity of your injuries or by the number of police reports you've made. Avoid comparing your experiences to those of other people and ask yourself if *you* feel okay about what is happening in your relationship. For example, do you feel right now that you can speak your mind, go wherever you want, and associate with whomever you please? Can you dress the way you want, express yourself openly, and pursue your dreams without fear of being hurt, either physically or emotionally? If the answer is no, then regardless of what anyone else thinks, you are in an abusive relationship, and you deserve a better life.

TYPES OF ABUSE

Practitioners typically categorize abuse into one of six types, with frequent overlap between them: physical, sexual, verbal, psychological, economic, and spiritual. Abuse often exists in more than one category simultaneously. For example, a client I worked closely with several years ago told me about how her husband would force her at gunpoint to walk around their yard searching for her imaginary lovers that he insisted

Case in Point

When Jessica met Isaac, he did everything right. An educated, wealthy banker, he seemed to be perfect, the kind of partner all her friends envied. They had been together eight months before they even had an argument, but that was when his true colors started to emerge. Isaac had became increasingly preoccupied with who Jessica talked to, how she spent her time, and what she wore. He became critical and overly concerned about how "she made him look" in front of his colleagues. One evening, he took hold of a new dress she was wearing and ripped it off her shoulders, calling her a "whore" and an embarrassment. When Jessica objected and tried to push him away from her, Isaac erupted, throwing her to the floor. He grabbed her by the hair and demanded that she apologize for her choice of clothing and her disrespect toward him. In that moment, Jessica realized that not only was Isaac not who she thought he was, but that he was also someone who had the capacity to hurt her both inside and out.

were hiding in the bushes. This is both physical and psychological abuse, likely with some verbal assault included as well. Another client once explained to me how her ex-boyfriend physically forced her to have sex with a dog while he took pictures that he later sold online. In a single incident he had inflicted physical, sexual, psychological, verbal, and financial abuse all at once (not to mention animal abuse and exploitation as well).

Sadly, throughout my career I have worked on cases of abuse that would shock a guard at Guantanamo Bay: a woman whose abuser held her head under water, another who was burned with chemicals and blowtorches, others slashed with meat cleavers or strangled with telephone cords. The variety and extent of abuse a victim endures is limited only by her perpetrator's imagination. And it's important to remember that most abuse starts with nonassaultive behaviors that often move forward on a continuum of ever-increasing aggression and control tactics.

Verbal Abuse

"You're so fat and disgusting I can barely stand to look at you. What other man is gonna want that?"

"Just shut your mouth. Everything you say reminds me of what a fucking idiot I married."

"You and your whole family are nothing but trailer trash. I'm ashamed to be seen with you."

"You're lucky you have me. No man could love a dumb ugly bitch like you . . ."

Brutal statements, to say the least, but they're just the tip of the iceberg of negative abusive language millions of women live with on a daily basis. Defined, "verbal abuse" is a pattern of offensive behavior primarily involving language that is used to attack, control, or mentally injure a victim. While it is one of the most common forms of abuse, it is also the most difficult to recognize because many people grow up thinking "sticks and stones will break my bones, but words will never hurt me." Unfortunately, they *do* hurt. Many abused women report that the verbal assaults, put downs, and attacks levied against them are the most damaging and lasting aspect of their experience.

"On my worst days, when I look in the mirror, it's like he's standing right beside me, calling me a 'fat piece of shit,'" admits Regan, a thirty-eight-year-old teacher. "Even though I know those words were more about his insecurities than mine, sometimes I can't help but wonder if other people see me the way he did, and if I'm ever going to be happy with myself. It takes a lot of focus to drown out his voice." Verbal abuse typically includes the following:

- Calling victim hurtful and degrading names
- Criticizing and/or ridiculing victim relentlessly
- Diminishing victim's achievements or questioning her decisions
- Insulting her gender, race, ethnicity, family background or religion
- Mocking victim's goals, accomplishments, physical appearance, etc.
- Threatening to commit suicide
- Threatening to harm the victim or a person or animal she loves
- Threatening to separate a victim from her children, either legally or illegally

Economic Abuse

This is a classic control method of batterers, particularly those who either believe that women should not have access to money or those who practice a parasitic "use and abuse" lifestyle. Sometimes couples make mutually consensual agreements about how money is divided or handled, but as with many of the other examples listed here, financial abuse is defined as such when accompanied by other types of mistreatment. Tactics include:

- Demanding that partner turn over her earnings
- Exploiting partner sexually for profit ("pimping out" partner, forcing her to strip or selling sexual images of her)—this is also sexual abuse
- Failing to contribute to finances in any way, while using resources freely
- Maintaining rigid control of family finances, making everyone account for every penny spent
- Preventing partner from working or attending school
- Refusing to include partner in major financial decisions
- Refusing to pay child support
- Running up or defaulting on debt in partner's name
- Sabotaging partner's employment by making a scene in person, harassing her by phone, or making her late or absent
- Stealing from partner
- Using partner's credit or bank accounts without permission
- Withholding access to money or credit cards, or giving partner a strict allowance
- Withholding food, clothes, medications, shelter, or other basic necessities

Spiritual Abuse

Mina had grown up attending church and always felt very strongly about her religious beliefs. She enjoyed the sense of community she got from weekly services and often used the comfort she found there to ease her worries about her increasingly controlling husband, Albert. His drinking had become much more frequent as their financial situation went downhill, and when he became angry, Mina felt afraid. Soon Albert began accusing her of "airing their dirty laundry" in church. He called her beliefs "stupid" and forbid her from attending worship or speaking to her fellow parishioners. He even threw her Bible in the trash. In order to control Mina, Albert had to break down her supports both spiritually and socially. He had to insure that she had no one to help her, either in or out of the relationship.

By making it dangerous for his victim to pray, worship with others, or do what she feels is necessary to fulfill her religious obligations, the abuser is taking away a powerful emotional reinforcement. In effect, it is a method of "soul destruction." The abuser is dismantling a victim's internal and external supports so that she will become more dependent on him and less able to consider ending the relationship. Most of all, she'll have no one to tell about his increasingly abusive behaviors and no one to help her with escape. Examples include:

- Forcing her children to be reared in a faith without her consent
- Preventing her from practicing her religious or spiritual beliefs
- Ridiculing her religious or spiritual beliefs
- Using religious or spiritual beliefs to manipulate partner or justify the abuse

Psychological Abuse

Although this type of victimization often employs verbal abuse, it's also in a category of its own because an abuser never has to say a word to intimidate, control, or punish his victim. For example, my abuser would sometimes leave nooses of rope hanging from the staircase in the home we shared. I also once worked with a client whose abuser made a wooden box and put it in a corner of their house. A sign on the front read "Janet's Body Parts Go Here." Without uttering a single word, these men were able to send powerful and disturbing messages. Tactics of psychological abuse include the following:

- Attempting to damage victim's social or business relationships
- Blaming victim for abuse
- Brandishing, displaying, or pointing of weapons (please see more about this behavior in Chapter 7)
- Checking victim's clothing, purse, bedding, and phone or computer messages/records for "proof" of suspected infidelity
- Demanding an accounting of expenditures, time schedules, and personal decisions
- Destroying victim's possessions, such as items that have sentimental value or cutting up pictures of male friends, or burning clothes he thinks are too revealing
- Filing frivolous lawsuits
- Humiliating victim in front of strangers, family, or friends
- Intimidating looks, postures, or signals such as shaping hands into a gun or drawing a finger across the neck to simulate cutting her throat
- Lying (please see more about this behavior in Chapter 6)
- Minimizing, justifying, or denying abuse
- Sabotaging victim's work or school commitments by failing to provide childcare or transportation as promised
- Subjecting victim to sleep deprivation by arguing with and abusing her throughout the night

While all these behaviors are unacceptable, there are more insidious forms of psychological abuse. These tactics may not be as overt but are still deeply damaging and often far more terrifying. Three common types are discussed below.

Crazy-Making

Also called "gas-lighting," this technique is designed to throw a victim's judgment off by making her question her own sanity. An abuser may hide a victim's car keys, change the time on her clocks, or deliberately withhold phone messages from her, and then suggest that she is going crazy. He may lie just to upset her, such as when my abuser told me he had killed my dog. The dog was in fact unharmed, but his sole purpose was to cause me mental anguish.

An abuser may also insist that he never said or did the things his victim *knows* she experienced, or act as though they had conversations that never occurred.

If a victim does have mental health issues, it becomes easier for the abuser to perpetrate this fraud by capitalizing on her vulnerable state and existing lack of confidence in reality.

Isolation

Initially, it may seem flattering that your partner wants you to spend all of your time with him, and in the beginning you may want that as well. But as time goes on, if he expects to be the only person in your life, his motives may be more sinister than loving. By shutting out your friends and family—people who are your primary support system—he is not only making you lonely and more dependent upon his company, but he is also eliminating them as *observers* in your life who may see things about him or your relationship that you may otherwise be blinded to because of love or manipulation.

An abusive partner may begin the process of isolation by criticizing your friends, referring to them as losers, addicts, sluts, or troublemakers. He may even project his own behavior onto them, making statements like "Tina is always telling you what to do, why don't you cut that bitch off?" He may accuse you of having sexual relationships with male friends, female friends, or even relatives that you spend a lot of time with.

An abusive partner will make it look as though he has your best interests in mind; that he's merely trying to protect you from "bad influences." If you choose to ignore his "advice," he may try to guilt you into complying by saying things such as, "If you loved me, you would stay here with me tonight." Or if you go out with friends or even travel to visit family, he may wait until you return to wage his guilt punishment, questioning your emotional priorities, acting hurt or betrayed—even threatening to leave you. Or he may accuse you of trying to hook up with other men. Ultimately, these confrontations are negative conditioning against interaction with others. You begin avoiding social situations with friends and family to avoid confrontation.

The ugly irony is that not only is he succeeding in isolating you, he's also making it seem like the decision to shrink or sever outside connections was your choice, not his demand.

Some isolation techniques are more literal, such as locking a victim in the house or making her live in a remote area with no neighbors to provide witness or assistance. A victim can also be living in the middle of a city but may be cut off from communication, with no access to a phone or computer. Often, isolation is some combination of both physical and mental tactics.

Stalking

A common misconception about "stalking" is that it only happens to celebrities, or it's a random act perpetrated by a masked stranger hiding in the bushes. In truth, stalking is much more common than most people believe; it's almost always perpetrated by somebody who knows you—in the case of this book, by a current or former partner—and it occurs in far more mundane and subtle settings than a dark alley. A young woman I once worked with named Stephanie told me that she had become afraid to leave her home because her ex-boyfriend was watching her. "Craig was a jealous partner when we were together and after the breakup it got even worse. He could never accept the fact that I didn't want to be with him anymore. He acts like I'm still his girlfriend, and I'm not allowed to have any friends or dates. He sits outside my apartment in his car, and calls my phone about thirty times a day. He's even threatened a male friend of mine from work. I feel like I'm always looking over my shoulder."

There are two types of stalking, "internal" and "external":

- *Internal Stalking*—This refers to acts carried out within a relationship that are meant to achieve control through harassment and intimidation. Examples include third-party information gathering (like asking others to spy on you), uninvited "pop-ins," following you, checking your phone log and messages, emails, social networking posts, car mileage, bank accounts, etc. This dangerous indicator is an extension of the abusers need for control, and is sometimes a test to determine how much domination he can exert over you and what your reaction to it will be. It is already a form of abuse, not just a warning sign, and a blatant disrespect of your rights as an individual. The internal stalker will often become an external one after the relationship ends and at that point will be exhibiting not just a sign of mistreatment but one of serious violent risk as well.

- *External Stalking*—This occurs outside the relationship, most frequently just after separation. It is motivated by the abuser's desire to regain control over or punish the victim, and it can be far more frightening and dangerous than internal stalking. Studies show that intimate partner stalking is highly correlated with femicide, particularly when combined with previous physical abuse.[1] While the tactics are much like that of internal stalking, the estranged-partner stalker has already lost control of the situation and is often desperate to reassert it through any means necessary. He may be contacting, surveilling, or tracking a victim for the purpose of terrorizing her, acquiring proof of imagined betrayals, or most concerning, as pre-attack behavior. In order to launch a successful attack, a predator must know where you are, what you are doing, and who will be with you. Following or spying on a victim is much more than "looking out for her" or "trying to win her back." This type of stalking lasts longer than nonintimate stalking and is more likely to end in violence than nonintimate stalking. In many cases, the abuser is setting up the necessary conditions to kidnap, rape, violently assault, or even kill his victim.

Endangering Behaviors

Often a precursor to physical abuse, endangering behaviors are actions that could potentially put a woman in harm's way, although legally they don't typically constitute domestic abuse. Abusers often fall back on these tactics because they can commit coercive and punishing offenses without crossing the line into physical violence, hence allowing them to intimidate and control a victim without leaving marks or breaking the law. As an additional tool for their self-justification, they can minimize the abuse by saying they "never laid a hand on her." As part of an overall pattern of mistreatment, endangering behaviors can have harmful consequences that an abuser may later describe as "an accident" or attribute entirely to the victim.

For example, when I was living with my abuser many years ago, I was driving us home from a formal event we'd attended in another town. It was late at night, on a desolate stretch of interstate highway, and we'd argued briefly over some minor issue that I can no longer recall. He'd stopped yelling, and I thought the worst was over. Then he turned to me calmly and said, "You must be tired of driving. Let's switch seats." I agreed, but as I got out and walked around to the passenger side, he locked the door, slid across into the driver's seat, and hit the gas, nearly running over my foot as he drove away. There I stood, alone in the middle of a cold night, wearing the same high heels and dress I had donned for what I thought would be a night of celebration. This was before the time when we all carried cell phones, so I had no choice but to begin walking into the darkness. Several times, cars full of creepy men pulled up alongside me and asked or *told* me to get in. Terrified, I began walking in the trees along the wooded roadside to hide from passing cars that contained a possibly worse fate. After walking for several miles, I finally reached a gas station and called a friend to come get me.

While my partner didn't commit an offense that I could report with confidence to authorities, he certainly put me at great risk and left me emotionally wounded just the same.

Other common types of endangering behavior include the following:

- Driving dangerously, which includes speeding, swerving, driving drunk, threatening to intentionally crash, tampering with the mechanics of a vehicle, grabbing the wheel, or attacking you while you're driving

- Forcing you to enter into dangerous situations, such as drug buys or prostitution
- Locking you out of your home or forcing you to leave, or taking your car keys or cell phone away
- Punching walls or windows, which is a sign that an individual has little self-control and a high potential for physical violence
- Throwing objects in a fit of anger

Noninjurious Physical Aggression

Stationed just at the border of physical abuse, noninjurious aggression is often a prelude to more dangerous contact. While in some states it may be considered "menacing," the lines are often blurry and you, the victim, may have a hard time defining what has happened to you. But make no mistake, regardless of legal boundaries, this is still abuse and has no place in a healthy relationship. Examples include:

- Aggressively grabbing phone or child from you
- Blocking you from leaving a room
- Chest-bumping
- Dumping food or beverages on you
- Spitting on you
- Standing nose to nose screaming in your face

Some types of noninjurious physical aggression are illegal, and may cause psychological but not direct physical injury to you. A few examples include the following:

- *Confinement*—Locking you in a room or closet, hand-cuffing or tying you up, or putting you into the trunk of a car, to name a few.

- *Pet abuse*—While you are not the one who is injured, this type of abuse is typically perpetrated on an animal that you care about, both to torture you and to send a threatening message. Studies indicate that at least 70 percent of victims who own pets report that their animals were threatened, injured, maimed, or killed by their abuser.[2] Some perpetrators also use pet abuse to manipulate and frighten children in the home to ensure compliance and silence around their actions.

Injurious Physical Abuse

Technically, physical abuse is defined as actions potentially or actually causing injuries, ranging from mild to life-threatening. Methods of physical assault are as varied as the sadistic creativity of the abuser conceiving them; therefore, this list is far from exhaustive. Consider twenty-three-year-old Olivia's experience: "When John first put his hands around my neck from behind as I walked down a crowded street, I didn't realize it was him. I thought I was being attacked by a stranger. He choked me and I fell to the ground where he pushed my face into the pavement, splitting my lip and breaking my front tooth. It wasn't until I heard his voice that I knew it was him. 'Why you out walking the street, bitch? You pickin' up men out here? My woman doesn't walk the boulevard alone.' Then he kicked me and I heard my rib crack. All those people just stood around and watched. No one moved to help me because I think they were scared of him too."

These are the most common methods of physical abuse:

- Burning
- Choking/strangling
- Denying access to medical treatment or medications
- Restraining or holding down

- Shaking, shoving, slapping, punching, kicking, biting
- Shooting
- Stabbing
- Tripping or pushing down stairs

While all physical violence is serious, and an indicator of heightened risk, there are some means of abuse that are of particular concern because their tactics and messages smack of lethality. Two such methods are choking, or strangulation, as it is more technically known, and use of weapons. Please read more about this and other types of injurious physical abuse in chapters 6 and 7.

Sexual Abuse

When I worked as a rape victim advocate, I was called to the local hospital one night to meet with Tricia, a dental technician in her thirties. Her partner, Victor, had attacked her because he thought she was cheating on him and he wanted to punish her in a way that she "wouldn't forget." The nurse had to explain what he had done because Tricia couldn't see the extent of her own injuries. "He raped her repeatedly over the course of a few hours," the nurse said somberly, "Then he took a razor blade and cut her from her vagina to her anus. She could easily have died from all the lost blood." When I asked Tricia if he had ever raped her before, she said simply, "Whenever Victor wants sex, he gets it, whether I willingly participate or not."

Being abused sexually by a current or former partner is a highly underreported crime that encompasses a wide variety of offenses. Often it is linked to physical abuse; they may occur together, or the sexual abuse may be backed up by the threat of bodily injury. A 2005 study published by The American College of Obstetricians and Gynecologists found that 68 percent of battered women surveyed also experienced sexual abuse in addition to physical violence.[3] Prior sexual abuse was

The Power and Control Wheel

The following chart, created by the Domestic Abuse Intervention Project in Duluth, Minnesota, offers a comprehensive view of the methods abusers use to gain and maintain dominance over their victims. It shows us that while tactics may vary, power and control lie at the center of all types of abuse. The diagram also conveys that even when abuse does not include bodily assault, it is always backed up by the implicit threat of physical or sexual violence.

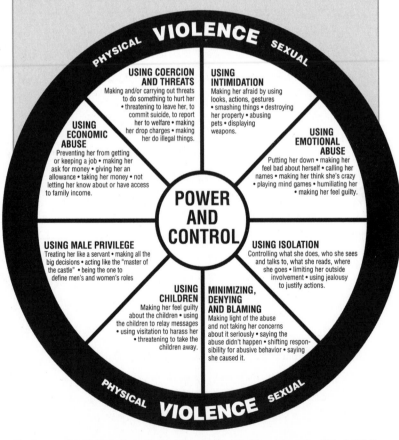

The Power and Control Wheel was Developed by the Domestic Abuse Intervention Project, Duluth, Minnesota, and is reprinted here by their generous permission.

also found to be a factor in 57 percent of cases where the woman was killed.[4] The threat of sexual assault continues and sometimes increases after separation, when batterers are determined to regain control over their estranged partners. Methods of sexual abuse include but are not limited to the following:

- Conditioning money for child support or necessities on sex
- Denying reproductive choice (coercing pregnancy or abortion)
- Engaging in unprotected sex with others
- Forcing or coercing a victim into sexual activity that she finds degrading, immoral, or painful
- Forcing victim to have sex when they are sick or injured
- Forcing victim into prostitution/sex with other people or animals
- Forcing victim to view pornography
- Knowingly passing sexually transmitted diseases
- Physically abusing victim before, during, or immediately after sex
- Raping victim
- Refusing to wear a condom
- Sexually abusing partner in the presence of children or implying sexual interest in children to control partner
- Threatening infidelity if victim doesn't comply with demands
- Torturing victim sexually
- Unfavorably comparing victim's appearance or sexual performance to others
- Using alcohol or drugs to facilitate rape

- Using sexually degrading names or insults to hurt or control a partner
- Withholding affection

PATTERNS OF ABUSE

While in the midst of an abusive relationship, it is often difficult enough to fully understand what is happening to your life, let alone see any discernable patterns. But in hindsight, many women agree that the events of their relationship did seem to repeat themselves over and over, eventually emerging as a recurring cycle of abuse. Forensic psychologist Dr. Lenore Walker first identified the sequence of the victim's experience in the 1970s with her Cycle of Violence model, based on theories of learned helplessness. Her hypothesis described the predictable rotation of abusive behavior by dividing it into the following three phases.

The (False) Honeymoon Phase

Abusive relationships often begin in this stage, which is typified by the appearance of the abuser's "good side." During this time, he will be kind, compassionate, and romantic, often showering you with gifts and praise. Throughout whatever may follow, this phase remains "the hook" on which he keeps you strung as you hope he is returning to that loving version of himself.

The Tension Building Phase

This period is represented by an overall air of increasing unrest within the relationship. While your abuser becomes more jealous, aggressive, and accusatory, you become more anxious and attempt to placate or step around his anger in response. Many women describe this feeling as "walking on eggshells."

The Explosion Phase

When the tension comes to a head, an abusive event (frequently an intense argument or assault) occurs. Afterward, your partner will often return to the Honeymoon Phase by offering apologies, gifts, excuses, and promises in order to "hook" you again. As the third segment completes, the cycle rolls over into the next succession, where the details may change but the pattern remains the same.

The time between phases of the cycle can be anywhere from minutes to years. In most relationships it rolls along in days or weeks. It is often noted that the sequence becomes shorter as time goes by and sometimes the honeymoon phase disappears all together because the abuser no longer finds it necessary to keep his victim in the relationship through intermittent affection and apology. Instead, he relies on fear, financial control, children, threats, and the complete destruction of his partner's self-esteem to keep her trapped in a seemingly hopeless situation.

As the victim is experiencing her cycle, the abuser also goes through a parallel but different sequence of stages. His cycle overlaps hers, and they experience the same events but from different perspectives. While the victim senses tension building, the abuser is in the **Fantasy and Planning** stage. At this point, he is not necessarily thinking in specific, concrete terms about the abuse he is about to perpetrate, but is cultivating angry energy and self-centered feelings of entitlement that he is willing to back up with physical violence. For example, an abuser might be driving down the road thinking to himself, "She has been really flirtatious around my friends lately. The next time she gives one of them the eye, I'm going to show her who's boss. No one treats me like that and gets away with it."

These thoughts often lead to **The Set-Up**, during which an abuser establishes unspoken and frequently shifting rules that his victim will inevitably break, therefore rendering her deserving of punishment in his mind. To use the previous example, if she so much as looks at another man in his presence, he feels justified in "showing her who's boss" through whatever means occur to him in the moment. Moving along the cycle, both victim and abuser will experience **The Explosion** (or abusive event) simultaneously.

As this phase concludes, often with the victim injured and/ or extremely upset, the abuser moves into a stage of **Guilt and Fear of Reprisal**, feeling anxious not necessarily over the harm he's done but rather over the possible consequences. After a verbal or physical attack, the perpetrator is primarily concerned with the possibility that his behavior may be discovered by others, that he may go to jail, lose his reputation or job, or that his partner (and possibly children) may leave him. These concerns lead him to scurry for cover under one of three **Rationalizations**: Minimizing—"I didn't hit you that hard"; Denying—"I didn't hit you at all"; or Blame—"Yeah, I hit you but it's your fault for pushing my buttons."

Often, the abuser will also couple these justifications with False Honeymoon Phase behaviors, such as inauthentic apologies, empty promises of change, and sentimental romantic gestures. While in this stage, many abusers will try to gain pardon through tactics such as enlisting outside parties on his behalf, talking about his "difficult childhood," feigning illness or emotional breakdown, or invoking sympathy for *his* distressful remorse. All of these methods are designed to establish him as the victim and reinforce his partner's feelings of guilt, pity, forgiveness, and hope for change. When the dust has settled, both victim and abuser move into a period of **Normalcy** in which they will remain, existing much like any non-abusive couple, until the next Tension Building/Fantasy and Planning Phase begins.

Displayed as a diagram, the abuse cycle looks like this:

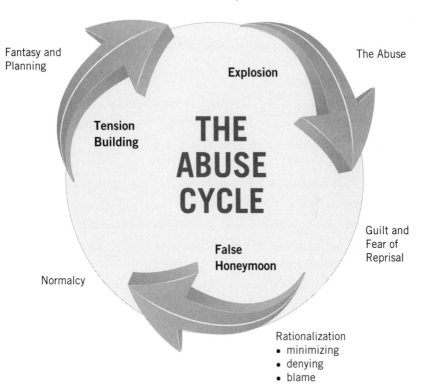

The Set-Up

Fantasy and
Planning

The Abuse

Explosion

Tension
Building

THE ABUSE CYCLE

Guilt and
Fear of
Reprisal

False
Honeymoon

Normalcy

Rationalization
- minimizing
- denying
- blame

Many women I have worked with have both recognized these cycles and been at a loss to articulate exactly why they remained in such an obvious pattern of continual harm. Perhaps one of the clearest explanations can be found in traumatic bonding theory, sometimes known as the Stockholm Syndrome. The term was coined by psychiatrist Nils Bejerot after a 1973 Swedish bank robbery, in which the hostages not only bonded with their captor but one of them also actually became engaged to him afterward. This psychological phenomenon, typified by support of and positive feelings toward a captor, has been seen in abused children, prisoners of war, cult members, and even concentration camp victims. It arises as a survival strategy and coping mechanism when faced with extreme fear and mistreatment. Researchers agree that four components must be present to result in the syndrome:

1. An apparent threat to the victim's safety
2. The presence of small acts of kindness from the abuser
3. Isolation from outside perspectives
4. The perceived impossibility of escape

While all these factors were involved in the famed Stockholm robbery, they are also seen in many abusive relationships, resulting in a similar traumatic bond between victim and perpetrator. Victims see their abuser's capacity for violence toward themselves and others in a multitude of ways. While a bank robber might allow his hostage a drink of water, an abuser will offer his a bouquet of flowers. Most abused women are socially isolated from friends and family who would normally notice the problem, and many victims doubt that their abuser would let them leave without reprisal, or even that they could make it on their own if he did.

Another theory that can help explain why some women appear to tolerate abusive behaviors is "cognitive dissonance." Psychologists use this term when a person's feelings about their reality become too conflicted and difficult to face, so they force themselves to believe and espouse an alternate truth. For example, if a woman cannot handle the fact that her wonderful new boyfriend just punched her in the face out of nowhere, she sometimes constructs a substitute explanation for what happened and why. She may try to explain it away by insisting that she provoked him, or that he couldn't control his behavior because of alcohol or stress. The more others try to convince her of the truth that he is a dangerous abuser, the more she defends him, becoming convinced of her false certainty that it is "him and her against the world." Their union becomes even tighter and can at times be more emotionally intimate (in a twisted way) than the bonds of a non-abusive relationship, due to the powerful secret shared between them.

The feelings a woman experiences within an abusive relationship are anything but simple and surface. Living with abuse can be much like existing inside a snow globe, where a violent, blinding blizzard swirls constantly around your head, rendering you confused and unable to find your way out. People on the outside may be able to see into your world and wonder why you can't get out, but to you, the storm is often too intense to see exactly what you are trapped in.

The good news is that every one of us can possess the wisdom to recognize dangerous situations and the power to extract ourselves before it's too late. But it takes education, emotional strength, and the knowledge to put together the right team for your defense and assistance, which you'll gain as you continue your journey through this book.

Safe and healthy relationships *are* possible, and with the right information, they're well within your grasp.

Chapter 3

Armor Up:
You Are Your Best Defense against Abuse

Nobody can make you feel inferior without your consent.
—Eleanor Roosevelt

From child abuse and neglect to poverty and volatile households, the lives of many women are rife with misfortune and trauma, yet why do some seem to emerge unscathed, even stronger for it, while others succumb to misery and helplessness?

Many social scientists and psychologists believe the answer lies in "risk and protective factors" and a character trait known as "resiliency." When viewed in light of partner abuse, risk factors are elements that may make a person more susceptible to abuse, while protective factors may help to insulate them. Risk and protective factors exist at every level of interaction in a person's life and can be divided into "life domains," including individual, family, community, and society. What this means for women is that our relationships are often based on our *early life experiences:* what was modeled for us and what we feel is normal or acceptable between partners.

Researchers at the Centers for Disease Control in Atlanta have identified several factors that contribute to a person's susceptibility to victimization, including low self-esteem, young age, childhood abuse, poverty, and weak community sanctions against violence, such as the unwillingness of neighbors to report situations where they witness abuse.[1]

Conversely, protective factors generally include high self-esteem, financial independence, strong family and community support, and education. What adds strength to protective factors and guards against elements of risk is *resiliency,* or the ability of the human spirit to "bounce back" from adversity. Resiliency means having the capacity to "land on your feet," embrace change, and reinvent yourself when needed. In scientific terms, it is defined as "the property of a material to absorb energy when it is deformed elastically and then, upon unloading, to have this energy recovered."

Clearly, if human beings can absorb their positive energy (e.g., optimism and self-esteem) and recover it when abuse ends, their healing will be faster and more complete than that of someone who retains negative energy forever. It's not that resilient women don't meet abusers or have problems, it's just that each time they face a challenge and get through it, they come out stronger on the other side. In effect, they're depositing strength into their "life bank," which they can withdraw whenever needed. Building that inner wealth means developing healthy coping skills, fostering optimism, knowing your own strengths and weaknesses, and cultivating a belief that you are unstoppable—that nothing is insurmountable, impossible, or unrecoverable.

So how do we nurture these assets in the event that we may someday be the one in three women who experiences intimate partner abuse? Because we cannot change the circumstances of our past, we must look to present and future feelings about our self-worth and social support systems, and learn to be assertive. These factors will strongly dictate how we deal with the emergence of an abusive partner in our lives. Let us begin with the importance of a positive self-regard.

THE SIGNIFICANCE OF SELF-ESTEEM

Does having good self-esteem prevent women from meeting or becoming involved with abusers? Simply put, no. In the beginning of an abusive relationship, a master of deceit can employ such a high level of trickery that even the most shrewd and self-assured woman may not sense the risk. However, having a positive overall appraisal of self can help women to start out with higher standards and be less tolerant of partners who do not meet them. Believing we are valuable, capable, and deserving of happiness may help give us the strength to escape if we do realize we are in danger. When we recognize ourselves as worthy of a healthy, respectful love we can see more clearly the relationships that do not reflect that right. But if your sense of self-worth is low to begin with, you may not only be more vulnerable to the initial compliments of an abuser but also more injured by his insults and degradation when the false charm falls away. This is especially true for women whose self-image has been tarnished through the shame and pain of physical or sexual abuse, particularly if it was inflicted in childhood.

Women from abusive backgrounds may have a higher tolerance for abuse because they don't always react as quickly to the pushing and breaking of their personal boundaries; it's something they are familiar with and some may not even know that relationships are supposed to be any different. Clever predators can perceive weakness like a dog smells fear and after pretending briefly to understand your pain they will often exploit it in the most vindictive ways possible. If you let him know there is something he can "save" you from, an abuser will oblige and then never let you forget about the debt he holds over your

⚠️ **Take Action**

If you are interested in assessing your self-esteem, check out the Rosenberg Self-Esteem Scale below. Developed by Dr. Morris Rosenberg, it is a series of ten questions designed to measure an individual's feelings of self-worth.

Instructions: Below is a list of statements dealing with your general feelings about yourself. If you strongly agree, circle **SA**. If you agree with the statement, circle **A**. If you disagree, circle **D**. If you strongly disagree, circle **SD**.

1. On the whole, I am satisfied with myself.
   SA   A   D   SD
2. At times, I think I am no good at all.
   SA   A   D   SD
3. I feel that I have a number of good qualities.
   SA   A   D   SD
4. I am able to do things as well as most other people.
   SA   A   D   SD

head, or the "mess" you were without him. Your past pain becomes yet another tactic through which a dangerous person can exert mental control and destruction.

But the good news is that being wounded doesn't have to be a permanent state. Help is available through empowering therapy with sensitive and experienced professionals who can help you to achieve a level of posttraumatic growth you may not have thought possible. Start the search by contacting your health insurance or employee assistance program (EAP) for referrals. If you don't have insurance or a job that offers EAP, try contacting your community mental health department

5. I feel I do not have much to be proud of.

    SA   **A**   **D**   **SD**

6. I certainly feel useless at times.

    SA   **A**   **D**   **SD**

7. I feel that I'm a person of worth, at least on an equal plane with others.

    SA   **A**   **D**   **SD**

8. I wish I could have more respect for myself.

    SA   **A**   **D**   **SD**

9. All in all, I am inclined to feel that I am a failure.

    SA   **A**   **D**   **SD**

10. I take a positive attitude toward myself.

    SA   **A**   **D**   **SD**

Scoring: SA = 3, A = 2, D = 1, SD = 0. Items with an asterisk are reverse scored, that is, SA = 0, A = 1, D = 2, SD = 3. Sum the scores for the ten items. The higher the score, the higher your self-esteem. Scores below fifteen suggest low self-esteem.[2]

or the local battered women's shelter. They may be able to suggest a sliding scale or pro bono (free) therapy resource.

Psychotherapist Nathaniel Branden defines self-esteem as "the experience of being competent to cope with the basic challenges of life and being worthy of happiness."[3] He refers to it as a basic human need, with recognizable value for survival. Specifically, Dr. Branden noted:

> *Positive self-esteem is the immune system of the spirit, helping an individual face life problems and bounce back from adversity.*[4]

A good deal of our self-regard develops in childhood, the time during which we are most vulnerable and least in control of what is happening in our lives. Our interaction with the world and the feedback we receive from family, peers, and even strangers influence how we perceive ourselves. They're our "mirror," and if what you saw in that reflection was negative, chances are your sense of self-esteem suffered for it. And as women, we carry the double burden of growing up pummeled by a culture that espouses unreal beauty and behavior standards that undermine our confidence in ourselves, especially if we fall outside the narrow parameters of those ideals. Thus, the path to becoming an adult can be a tumultuous one, magnifying our low self-regard.

A secure woman, on the other hand, is able to identify and take credit for her unique character and strengths. She doesn't believe she is perfect but rather recognizes her own weaknesses and consistently tries to improve herself as a person. Historically, social etiquette has discouraged female assuredness, but it is just this confidence that will help protect you against the intimate partner predators among us.

CULTIVATING SELF-ESTEEM

When we begin to ignore the hurtful words of others and understand that our opinion of ourselves must be the prevailing one, that's when we truly begin to cultivate self-esteem. Regardless of who comes in and out of your life, from birth to death, the only true constant is you. How can you expect anyone else to accept you for who you really are if you don't? Decide to put an end to negative internal dialogue, catching yourself each time that little voice in your head says something mean or discouraging. If there are others in your life who are sources of criticism, consider whether or not you have anything to learn from their perspective. Perhaps you'll discover instead that their judgment isn't credible. If so, discard the disparagement and move on, knowing

Case in Point

"When I was growing up, my family acted like I was nothing but a burden to them. My mother and sisters were constantly calling me fat and "retarded," like I was the scapegoat for all their problems. I got the feeling that no one cared if I lived or died, you know? That's why I felt so good around Jacob. He was the first person to ever tell me I was beautiful, right before he started beating me. It wasn't until I got rid of that bastard that I started to see that my family was just as mean. That's when I started to find my own life. I stopped taking calls from my mom and my sisters, and I don't go to the family gatherings that caused me so much pain before. I have a lot of friends now and I know I'm a strong person. There's no room for someone else to tell me I'm not."

—Maureen, age thirty-three

that you don't deserve to have another person's foul mood or insecurities projected onto you.

Sometimes, it's difficult to ignore put-downs and insults when they come from people we are forced to maintain a relationship with, such as relatives. If so, limit your contact with them and try to establish boundaries that will protect you from their vitriol. For example, if your mother constantly criticizes you, vow to only talk with her once a week or once a month, or tell her that you have to hang up the phone whenever she says something that undermines you. Try to shield your daily interactions and conversations with others from as much negativity as you can. You deserve to have your positive attributes acknowledged and recognized by yourself and others, not dwell in real or imagined shortcomings. As author Barbara De Angelis once said:

We need to find the courage to say No to the things and people that are not serving us if we want to rediscover ourselves and live our lives with authenticity.[4]

Once you have established that you honestly forgive and like the person you are inside, you can begin to grow self-assurance through confidence in your decision-making skills. Even if it's something as small as picking out a pair of cute, comfortable flats instead of this season's fashionable but painful stilettos, experience what it feels like to trust your own opinion. Don't worry about what others might approve of, simply sit in comfort with the choices you have made and the reasons you have made them.

The next step in building self-confidence is the setting and achieving of small but meaningful goals. These should be designed to improve your life and bring you further success and happiness. Small personal achievements cultivate an overall sense of positive self-regard. Examples include:

- Reconnecting with an old friend
- Learning a new computer skill
- Joining a local gym or yoga studio
- Doing something adventurous (from going to a movie alone to skydiving, depending on your threshold)
- Volunteering for a local nonprofit (from animal shelters to food banks, opportunities abound)
- Enrolling in a community college course or program (financial aid is often available)
- Eating healthier (studies show eating well improves mental and physical health)
- Starting a small garden, even on your windowsill
- Finishing a book you've been meaning to read

⚠ Take Action

Go ahead and take the daunting step of assessing and tackling your current problems: Do you have leftover issues from childhood? Get to a therapist and work on them. Do you have concerns about your weight? Begin a fitness program. Are you failing financially or professionally? Get a career plan, visit a financial advisor, or go back to school. Whatever their origins, deal with your demons first before searching out a partner. The reason it is important to battle your dark side now is because whatever negative things you think about yourself, an abuser will sense, seize onto, and use against you to further chip away at your self esteem.

Once you begin to feel more self-reliant and confident, consider your motivations and objectives in finding a partner. What is your *purpose?* Some women, often when they reach a particular age, become anxious to pair up with someone (anyone!) who will bring them to the place society expects them to inhabit—be it the role of wife, mother, or girlfriend to a successful man.

When you're frantically looking for love, you tend to lower your standards and may be willing to consider men that are beneath you because you hope kissing a few toads will bring the prince. Ask yourself this: Is your level of desperation (for a father figure, male acceptance, or to cover low self-esteem) clouding your perception? Do you want so badly to find the perfect man that you see him in everyone you meet? A romantic optimist's threshold for deception can be dangerously high. Don't take Prince Charming at face value, make him prove his worth and earn your high regard over a reasonable period of time.

The options are endless; just keep in mind that it's not about perfection. Mistakes and failure are a part of life. We eat chocolate, forget to water plants, lose interest in books, skip classes, and who among us really makes it to the gym every day? Not only is perfection an impossible achievement, but it discounts the valuable education that disappointment can provide us. I'm not saying it's okay to be irresponsible, but if you do stumble, forgive yourself and try to learn as much as you can from the experience. Maybe computers aren't your thing, or you're so busy trying to earn a living as a single mother that you really can't take on more than a once-a-week workout regimen. It is not failure that measures our strength or intelligence but rather the ability to take from it lessons in grace and progress.

Case in Point

When your bottom line is finding love, you often don't see the red flags of an abusive relationship. Take Regina, for example: "Talking about it now, I feel foolish. If a friend of mine described a boyfriend like Cliff I would be appalled and tell her to get away from him immediately. But I didn't see him like that when we first got together. I guess I was lonely and tired of being the only one in my circle who didn't have a serious partner. My biological clock was ticking and I reasoned that if I couldn't make it work with him, I couldn't make it work with anyone. I thought I could mold Cliff into someone worth having, but instead he just dragged me down. Now I feel like I wasted six years of my life, when I could have just stayed true to myself and waited for the right man. Being alone is always better than being with an abuser."

—Regina, age forty-two

EVALUATING YOUR SUPPORT SYSTEM

Although independence is a vital quality for women to cultivate, we should never underestimate the importance of a strong and healthy support network in our lives. While a tight and trusted inner circle is valuable to all people, it becomes especially important when we are faced with crisis and danger. In fact, protection (safety in numbers) is one of the very reasons human beings have been living in groups since the beginning of their existence. Sadly, however, many women who experience partner abuse go through this challenge alone, never telling anyone about their situation out of shame, fear, or guilt. But speaking the truth about his actions and opening the doors to a painful secret might just lend you the strength you need to break free from the bonds of abuse.

Case in Point

"I had always believed it was a sign of weakness to depend on others, and that adults should be able to take care of themselves. Asking for help was not my style. But when I found myself alone in an abusive relationship I had no choice but to reach out. Some people thought I had made bad decisions and they wanted to punish me for it by denying their support. But the people that mattered to me, my family and a few close friends, were really there when I needed them. Thank God they didn't abandon me—I should have never cut them off for that son-of-a-bitch to begin with."

—Malia, age twenty-seven

A good support system should consist of the following elements:

- A mix of family, friends, neighbors, and coworkers.
- People with whom you have common interests, such as attending church, working out, writing poetry, or going hiking, to name a few.

- People who make you feel good when you are around them, practice an even "give and take" of energy, and encourage you to live a healthy and fulfilling life.
- At least three people to whom you can tell anything, ask anything of, and turn to in an emergency.

Does this sound like your life right now? If the answer is no, then you may be unprepared to look for a significant other because if something goes wrong in that most primary of adult relationships, you will lack allies to turn to for guidance and help (more on the importance of support systems in Chapter 10). Strengthening your support system with nourishing connections ensures that your time will be taken up with positive and stimulating interactions. This is important because feeling alone and bored can make women vulnerable to the influence of "intriguing" men who offer excitement from dangerous sources. Instead of intimate dinners or a day of hiking, abusive men will show you the thrill of high-speed police chases and alcohol-fueled bar fights. This is the kind of exhilaration most women can live without.

MAP YOUR ALLIES

A helpful way to assess your support system is by drawing an "eco-map" of the people in your life. Developed by social worker Dr. Ann Hartman in 1975, the eco-map is a graphic representation of the various "systems" in an individual's life—family, friends, work, school, neighborhood, clubs, religious organizations, volunteer groups, or your community as a whole—and how they affect us, either positively or negatively. Create your own eco-map by doing the following:

1. On the center of a blank sheet of paper, draw a circle with your name in it.

2. In the space around it, add a smaller circle for each system that you are a part of.

3. Draw lines connecting these smaller circles to your own, like the spokes of a wheel connect to its center. Straight and thick lines represent strong, solid relationships, and wavy lines represent weaker ones.

4. Next, if there is a relationship that you feel is one-sided, make the connecting line an arrow that points away from the source of energy. For example, if you feel like you are always giving to your friends but never receiving support in return, the energy arrow would go away from you, and toward them.

Now sit back and examine your eco-map, getting a broader picture of who is in your life and the benefits you derive from your relationships with them. These are the people surrounding you who could serve as important sources of support if you should face a future challenge—such as an abusive relationship.

The map is also helpful in distinguishing unhealthy personal connections in your life or areas that could be improved. Now is the time to work on those bonds, setting your social house in order *before* you need to make requests for help or advice. Locate the individuals and communities around you that you think might be valuable allies in a time of need—such as neighbors or coworkers—and seek to strengthen those links in advance of crisis.

If your eco-map reveals that you have a limited support system, throw yourself into the world and go create a better safety net. Sign up for a class at a local art or cooking studio, volunteer at a retirement home or youth mentoring program, or take up a sport in an adult intramural

> ⚠️ **Take Action**
>
> As you flesh out your eco-map with the allies in your life, consider ending any toxic relationships you have with people who aren't respectful of your needs or boundaries. Perhaps it's a childhood friend who sucks you into their drinking or drug addictions, or a family member who constantly berates and criticizes you under the guise of "trying to be helpful." Although it may cause you temporary pain to release harmful people from your life, you will be happier and healthier for it in the long run.
>
> Give yourself permission to "look out for number one," making social selections that are best for *your* conscience and future. "Trimming the fat" so to speak, will strengthen your base and give you practice for the road of dating that lies ahead, one in which you should be able to end a relationship with someone if you know it isn't good for you.

league. Use social networking to seek out old friends online, and call up the college roommate whose company you so much enjoyed. Go out on a limb and ask a coworker to have lunch with you, or join a jogging club where you'll see the same people week after week.

Friendly energy is strongly attractive and others will soon pick up on your confidence, desiring your presence and companionship. If you are willing to extend yourself and be a support to those around you, your own circle will grow exponentially.

LEARN TO ASSERT YOURSELF

Much like animals, human predators select prey based on subtle signals given off by their potential victims, such as a slow or nervous stride, lack of coordinated movement, or submissive posture and gaze.

Whether they are conscious of it or not, they will make a decision within seconds about whether or not you are a suitable target. They intuitively form opinions about how easy or difficult you will be to control (see Chapter 4 for more on "targeting"). Clear indications of strength or defiance can often cause a predator to abort his quest and look elsewhere.

While this information may seem better suited to stranger attackers, it rings true for abusers as well because they are looking for someone to dominate long term, rather than just in the moment. Most psychologists and violence experts agree that men with an abusive mindset may be less likely to try their game on a woman who, from the beginning, shows that she is assertive, self-assured, and confident in her personal boundaries. From learning how to say no, to strategies for leveling the playing field during dates, there are several ways you can practice assertiveness, which ultimately nourishes your self-esteem.

Just Say No

Many abusers gage a target's amenability to control through their continued persistence, disguised as intense attraction. A commonly used tactic is to make a woman feel irresistible by repeatedly asking for personal information, dates, and tokens of physical affection, even though his object has clearly indicated her lack of interest (or so she thinks).

As previously mentioned, when an abuser identifies a victim, he simply doesn't take "no" for an answer. Many women who are victims of domestic violence have shared a common theme with me when describing their initial interactions with their partner. They recall that he asked them out repeatedly after they told him no, or that he accused them of being "stuck up" when they refused to give him their phone number.

> ### Case in Point
>
> "Louis was always after me to hook up, even when I had a boyfriend. I heard bad stories about him from other girls and didn't want to get involved. Next thing I knew, he was going around school calling me a whore, and telling people he had sex with me. He said he would stop if I agreed to one date. I was scared so I did it, and things moved quickly into a very abusive situation. I felt like I was blackmailed into that relationship. Saying yes to him was the worst mistake of my life."
>
> —Gabrielle, age twenty-three

Stories like these turn into recollections of later being pressured for sex after they had said no, and being coerced into cohabitation, marriage, or pregnancy. This is known as a "push for quick involvement" and it is often a red flag of impending abuse.

When my abuser first asked me to be his girlfriend (I was nineteen), I said no several times, but in very vague and tactful ways, trying not to offend him or lose his friendship. Eventually I got tired of coming up with excuses, so I told him we could try dating for a little while and "see how things went." I reassured myself that I'd tell him that I just wanted to be friends after a week or so. But abusers are crafty trappers, and once they have their foot in the door of a relationship, they will employ ever-increasing methods of manipulation to control the scenario. He offered to let me live in his house for free when I could no longer make rent on my apartment, and he also began to systematically drive a wedge between myself and the one nearby friend that I could turn to for support.

Little did I know that I had just stepped into a spider's web and wouldn't be out for several years to come. In hindsight, I know that what I *should* have done was say no with conviction and then dump *him* as a friend, because he wasn't respecting my boundaries.

Does your version of "no" come across as definite and consistent? Does it leave any possibility for a reversal of opinion with continued harassment? Consider how you say "no" because meek or ambiguous use of this word can signal a willingness to compromise or relent. If we tell someone we aren't interested in a timid or conditional way, we are opening the door to further negotiations. By practicing the skill of refusal, we cultivate an inner strength that we can call upon when needed, even if it's not front and center all the time.

⚠ Take Action

Take time out this week to practice being assertive in a simple scenario. For example, if someone at your child's school asks you to make three dozen cookies for the bake sale and you just don't have the time, politely say "I would love to help, but this week just won't work for me. Could you put me on the list to chaperone the museum trip next month instead?" This may seem like a far cry from telling an abuser you don't want to be involved with him, but small exercises like this can help you feel more comfortable expressing your feelings and not doing what others expect of you.

Holistic Self-Defense

How do we display confident and decisive behavior that shows others that our personal boundaries will not be violated easily? Sara Johnson, coordinator of WomenStrength (the nation's longest-running free self-defense program for women), says a powerful strategy is to embrace the concept of "holistic self-defense," which encompasses physical, mental, and verbal protection tools.

The basic principles of the program assert that confidence, self-respect, and trust in your own intuition are the internal foundations that allow us to show assertiveness—or the ability to advocate for ourselves in any situation—to the external world. Assertiveness, explains Johnson, is apparent in movement, language, and eye contact, but for many people it is a learned skill and must be built upon by standing up for oneself in increasingly challenging circumstances. She suggests that if we practice assertiveness in our daily lives (with store clerks, fellow bus passengers, and friends) it will be more accessible to us when we need it in a dangerous situation.

⚠️ Take Action

The WomenStrength program tells us that developing a sense and appearance of physical assertiveness also includes adopting an upright posture and exhibiting relaxed movements that make you look comfortable in your body, not easily intimidated. The organization recommends taking up extra space when sitting and standing to present strong physical boundaries that you will protect. Even your face can reflect confidence: practice making brief eye contact with a neutral facial expression that says, "I see you and I'm not afraid." Try breaking eye contact by looking to the side. It appears more self-assured than dropping your gaze toward the ground. Small adjustments such as these can help to prevent you from being targeted by an abuser, or any other human predator looking for an easy mark.

Develop Healthy Mistrust

Another step toward defensive assertiveness, suggests Johnson, is maintaining a degree of "healthy mistrust." When I first heard her say this I was reminded of the original Grimm Brothers version of Little Red Riding Hood, in which the innocent main character is warned by her mother not to talk to strangers. But once she ventures out into the woods, the wolf approaches her. At first she ignores his greeting, but then relents when he says, "Can't you even wish me a good day?" Not wanting to be rude, she engages him in conversation, and we all know how the story goes from there. This culturally ingrained fairy tale begs the question, "Why is Little Red Riding Hood, or any female for that matter, perceived as rude for not speaking to a stranger?"

When a man approaches a woman uninvited, she owes him nothing—not her name, not her phone number, not even a glance. If this makes her rude in society's eyes, it is a poor reflection on the society, not the women for wanting to stay safe.

Certainly, giving people the benefit of the doubt is commonly accepted as a standard of social politeness. If we are good people who have a generally positive outlook on society and human nature—what social psychologists call a "just world" perspective—we often assume that individuals get what they put out. Therefore, if we treat others with respect, honesty and fairness, we will get the same in return. However, expecting that people should *earn* our trust is a safer standard. Ask yourself first, "Do I have good reason to trust this person?"

If you get a funny feeling about a guy and don't want to see him again, don't. You are not required to give him or anyone else a "valid reason." You have the right to change your mind if you've decided to go out with a man and then cancel at the last minute, or if you've decided to make out with him but then want the physical intimacy to end there. You have the right to listen to your instinct and are not required to offer explanations or excuses to justify your behavior.

As Charles Darwin said: "The very essence of instinct is that it's followed independently of reason."

Know What You Want

Before embarking on the search for a mate, it's important for you to know your core likes and dislikes, morals, beliefs, and ambitions. Start by creating a mock profile of your future dream partner. This sketch could include a list of characteristics you would want him to have, a list of what you definitely don't want in a partner, negotiable points, and a section about your life goals. Do you want a family? A career? Where do you see yourself in five, ten, or twenty years, and how will your ideal partner fit into that picture?

Once you have decided what you want in a man, leave room for revision and personal growth. Keep in mind that while some details may be flexible, don't settle for anyone less than you deserve. Also, remember that this knowledge is yours alone. If you share it with a potential mate, you are drawing him a map of how he should behave to win your trust, possibly duping you into believing he is the man you've been looking for instead of the man you've been looking to avoid.

With a list of solid preferences at your disposal, you are asserting your own desires about what you want in a partner, giving you more control in how you define dating and relationships, which ultimately feeds your positive self-regard. Keep in mind, however, that a few seconds (or even a few dates) isn't usually enough to spot a potential abuser. Many have made themselves deception experts through years of "impression management" and will look just like every other man in the room, only often more charming.

Flip The Script

Another way that women can maintain independence from the outset of a new relationship is by taking charge of the direction and speed in which it travels. Men are typically used to asserting control early on in social situations, so he may be pleasantly surprised to find out that you are independent and self-confident. But if he is an abuser, being assertive will let him know that you are not an ideal target. The following are a few ways in which women can "flip the script" on potential partners to give themselves a better position for making crucial decisions.

- When you first meet a potential partner, get his phone number instead of giving him yours. Not only is it safer, but the power is in your hands and you decide if and when you want to call.
- Take your own vehicle or public transportation to the first few dates so that you aren't dependent on him to drive you home.
- Consider making the first few meetings double or group dates, bringing friends along for safety and opinions.
- Always let someone know where you are, who you'll be with, and when you're expected back during the initial dating phase.
- Be aware that your guard is down both mentally and physically when using drugs or alcohol.
- Consider "going Dutch" or splitting the bill, so you keep a level playing field and there's no insinuation of you owing him anything.
- For your first few dates, meet in a museum, coffee shop, or public park so that there are others around and the temptations of nightlife (such as alcohol) won't cloud your judgment, make you more vulnerable, or encourage early sexual involvement.

Practice Zero Tolerance

As a young woman, I asked my father's advice on buying a car—my first. I was afraid that a shrewd salesman would dupe me into paying too much, given my inexperience. My father's advice was simple but to the point: "Don't walk in unless you're willing to walk out." In other words, when searching for an ideal match, you must make up your mind *beforehand* that you are comfortable ending the negotiation if your needs are not met. You have to decide early in the process that you will never become so attached to an outcome that you sacrifice your principles or your safety.

Thus, women looking for a partner should know in advance what they want, what they are willing to bend on, and what they will have a "zero tolerance" policy for. If you know where your standards and limits lay, you will be able to quickly and easily spot a partner who doesn't measure up. More importantly, if you withhold your feelings of intense attachment until you know someone is a safe person, then you will be more able to walk away if he isn't.

The very beginnings of physical violence may not be obvious to everyone, particularly someone who was brought up in an environment of conflict and chaos. Early stage abusive actions can include punching walls, smashing objects, raising fists, and verbal threats. Even if no bodily assault occurs, he has let you in on an important clue about his persona and how he will conduct himself throughout your time together. It is at this point that you must begin a serious evaluation of and possible extraction from your situation. It doesn't matter if you've made a commitment to someone or share children with him. It doesn't matter if he has "anger control issues" but there are a hundred other things about him that are great. It doesn't matter that he was drunk when he did it, or that he promised to "get help." If you decide before you even meet him that you will walk on the first sign of abuse, then you become the controller of your own destiny.

Understanding yourself and your own boundaries puts you on firm ground, presenting you to potential partners as a strong and decisive woman who cannot be easily swayed or shaped. While your female nature may encourage you to forgive and forget, try looking at romantic partnerships as if you were a businesswoman. If a sharp entrepreneur just saw the company she invested in fail miserably, would she keep hanging on, waiting for rock bottom, or would she cut her losses and pull out? Knowing when to let go is a powerful trait that can serve you well in relationships. Don't stay with an abuser to repair him, teach him a lesson, prove a point, or get revenge. None of these stubborn ego-driven reasons is worth risking your safety or even your life. Instead, assert your right to a safe and happy existence. Walk away, and as author Julia Cameron said, "Let the pain turn into something much more useful: wisdom."

The purpose here is not to discourage you from connecting with new people but to create a strong core that is guided by self-respect instead of a desire to please others. Wonderful men do exist in the world and when you find one who has proven his worth, it's okay to let down your guard and enjoy the experience of love. If you eventually do choose to shed your armor and let someone inside your heart, just be sure that your central vision is clear enough to see them for whatever and whoever they truly are. Then your happiness will be all the more rich, lasting, and real.

Chapter 4

Forewarned Is Forearmed:
How Abusers Test, Prime, and
Ensnare Their Victims

We are never deceived, we deceive ourselves.
—Johann Wolfgang von Goethe

One of the great fallacies about abusive relationships is that somehow the *woman* is flawed, that she is drawn to abusers. I refer to this as the "Myth of the Broken Picker." In this self-fable, women believe that their ability to choose a good man is faulted and hopeless, like an apple picker with a damaged handle that can't reach the healthier fruit higher up in the tree. They believe that they are somehow attracted to "bad apples," that their judgment is defective. They're tired of being "fooled" and wish that they could see potentially dangerous men more clearly before becoming so deeply entrenched with them. But the fact is, abused women aren't actually doing the picking, abusers are. And any woman, regardless of where she falls on the spectrum of psychological well-being, can fall prey to an abuser. This, of course, raises the question: Do abusers really have a "type"? Do they look for a particular profile in women that adheres to their desires or assumptions?

The truth is, most abusers do not consciously hunt for new victims the way a burglar might case houses for an easy break-in. Instead, it's a manifestation of their intrinsic nature. An abuser simply has a predatory instinct for certain traits in a woman that make his job of deceiving and dominating her easier. And while many abusers often seek out victims with damaged self-esteem and previous abuse experiences, others look for healthy, educated, professional women who are simply too free with their trust, demonstrating a propensity toward emotional overexposure. The abuser may be subliminally looking for targets who show an optimistic and forgiving heart (a "just world" woman), one whose desire to see the best in everyone may blind her to malicious intent. Believing these women will be susceptible to his lies, and unguarded against tactics of coercive control, the abuser moves quickly to reel in his catch. Unfortunately, due to a combination of our experiences, our personalities, and the historical oppression of our gender, some of us are the perfect prey.

But regardless of background or character, all victims share one thing in common: the misfortune of stumbling into an abuser's path.

Like any man out on the prowl, once an abuser has zeroed in on his potential conquest, he's looking for *access*. You can be assured that a woman who immediately responds to his uninvited advances, or one who freely provides her personal information when he asks for it, becomes an easier mark. A woman with an "open book" personality works well for him, and if she happens to have a life story of woe, all the better. He can listen with manufactured empathy, ingratiating himself into her life. But his prospect becomes an even better potential victim if she's willing to listen to *his* tale of woe and offer him sympathy and encouragement, because then he's hit the jackpot: He's found a "saver," a nurturing woman who compulsively takes in troubled souls, blind to the inherent risks to her own well-being.

In her book *Women Who Love Psychopaths*, psychologist Sandra L. Brown, founder of The Institute for Relational Harm Reduction and Public Psychopathy Education, writes about "super traits" in women who become involved with dangerous men. Most of the characteristics are seemingly positive, but when presented to an abusive mind, they become weaknesses ripe for exploitation. While all abusers are not psychopaths, their characteristics often match up, as does the mental and physical damage they inflict on intimate partners. Sandra's discoveries are important because they warn about traits we may unconsciously possess that enhance our vulnerability to a batterer's victim-tuned radar. The super-traits include:

- Hyper-empathy
- Extreme altruism
- High relationship investment and high attachment
- Hyper-focus on the sentimental aspects of the relationship
- Low impulsiveness
- High resourcefulness

In my extensive work with abused women, I have found that women who become involved with pathological and nonpathological abusers alike share similar traits. Women who are "savers"—those scoring high in empathy, altruism, tolerance, and sentimentality—will almost always be drawn to a relationship where they think they can help or reform a "diamond in the rough" partner. Highly invested, nonimpulsive, and attached women will often try to stick it out and fix a bad situation. Those who are highly resourceful frequently try to

Case in Point

Because Giselle had dealt with mental illness in her family, she wasn't scared off when she found out that her new boyfriend, Oliver, had been diagnosed with schizophrenia several years before they met. Oliver promised to keep taking his medications and she believed she could help him by being a grounding presence when the disease reared its ugly head. But when Oliver decided that the side effects of his medication were too much, he stopped taking it, and things soon began spinning out of control. Oliver became paranoid and started accusing Giselle of being a mafia spy. He struck her from behind with a frying pan one day because he believed she was trying to poison him. Still, Giselle attempted to calm Oliver and talk him down.

"I felt like I'd been through a lot of things in my life, and I was strong enough to handle the challenge. I loved him and I knew his illness wasn't his fault, but I thought if we took him to the hospital he would get committed and lose his job."

It wasn't until Oliver ambushed her with a gun that Giselle realized she couldn't handle the problem anymore. Only the watchful eye of her neighbor saved her, as he spied Giselle standing at her living room window while Oliver held the gun to her temple.

"I was in over my head," said Giselle later, "I just didn't think he would go that far."

handle risky scenarios all on their own without seeking the necessary assistance of others.

In the nonabusive world, the characteristics listed above are admirable features, but when exposed to the malicious traits of a predator they can become poisonous to our self-preservation. This is not to say that we as women should repress or withhold these commendable virtues, but rather that we should be careful that we are spending them on worthy individuals who won't use them against us in pursuit of ulterior motives.

Conscious of his actions or not, the abuser nonetheless has a pattern of behaviors he employs early on to both test and lure a woman into his life—and ultimately, his control.

EARLY STAGE ASSESSMENT

To ascertain whether or not a woman makes a suitable target, an abuser often subtly employs the following experiments. He may begin his "assessment" by requesting personal information from her, or even a date, for which "no" (as you learned in the previous chapter) is usually not an admissible answer. It may be a play for physical contact, such as an arm around the shoulders, which she's made to feel guilty for not accepting; or he might lob a "playful" insult her way that she does not refute, such as, "You look good, but I don't really go for older women." This is known as a "negative hit" or simply a "neg": an insult intended to lower a woman's self-esteem so she will seek the approval of the man who is coming on to her. Unfortunately, there are men in this country profiting off of books and training courses that teach other males how to "pick up" women through the use of offensive wit, including books with titles like *The Game* and *Bang*. Even though these men may not be abusers, their techniques support the fact that while many women view the singles scene as a search for potential love, some men see it as a ruthless sport where scoring is based on sexual conquest through deception.

An abuser's inquiry may be small, like a sexist or racist joke to test her response, or it may be more significant, such as a petition for the woman to do something illegal—like take drugs or sneak into a secured building. The point, however, is not the method of his pushiness, it is the desired outcome: He is dipping his toes in the water to see if his target shows any sign of weakness or vulnerability. If chinks in a woman's armor are to be discovered and penetrated, it will be very early on in the relationship, so the abuser knows whether or not he is wasting his energy.

TESTING YOUR VULNERABILITY

Once an abusive man has identified a potential target, he'll begin testing her boundaries to see just how susceptible she is to his desires, sometimes by using a method called "Intrusion, Desensitization, and Isolation." Some men employ the tactic during a single social interaction, say at a bar, where he's zeroed in on a particular woman; while other abusers stretch the boundary-pushing phase over a period of months. Recognizing this test can help you to understand the true nature of your new acquaintance, allowing you to withdraw from the relationship before the cement of commitment dries around your feet.

In the **intrusion** phase of the test, a breach of propriety occurs. Say you're on a casual date with a potential abuser. He may place his hand on your leg, or caress you in some uninvited way. If you reject him, either verbally or physically (by shifting your body away from him, or politely telling him you're not comfortable with his advances), observe closely how he responds to your reaction. Does he apologize and remove his hand (as he should), or does he become offended and mildly accuse you of being too sensitive, prudish, or uptight? If so, he may be trying to move into the **desensitization** stage, aiming to imply that you are stuck up or frigid for reacting disapprovingly to what he thought you wanted based on signals you *supposedly* gave off. This is a way of pushing you into the third phase of **isolation**. Here, he psychologically segregates you from "normal women" by making you feel that you are odd or wrong for not accepting his advances like other females would.

Just as a rapist might try to get his victim in a room alone so he can violate her, an abuser will work at emotionally infringing on you in order to gauge your malleability. Each time he crosses a boundary and gets away with it, he is taking a mental note, consciously or not, that he can continue. When combined, these notes confirm to a dangerous person that you are both pliable and vulnerable, giving him the green light to further twist your limits.

INSTANT DEBT

In an attempt to shackle their partners quickly, some abusers may employ the "instant debt" trick. The following story reveals how a seemingly innocent gift or favor can be used to entrap and manipulate its recipient.

When Ellen first met Michael shortly after moving to town, they hit it off right away. On their first date, they talked for hours at an enthusiastic pace. She liked him. But when he showed up on her doorstep the next day with an expensive new stereo, instinct told her it was a bit over the top, even though she'd mentioned the night before that she didn't have a sound system. Ellen insisted that she couldn't accept it, but Michael was adamant, saying, "It's just a loan, you can give it back to me later when you get your own." The next thing she knew, he was in her living room hooking it up. A voice inside echoed a warning, but she was flattered by his generosity. For the next few weeks, Michael brought over CDs to play and left them there in ostensibly giving gestures. He pushed for a relationship, and before long, they were a couple. But after some time, Ellen began to see traits in her new boyfriend that were concerning to her. When things didn't go his way, he would snap, departing from his normally relaxed and friendly self into a belligerent, intimidating person. He became increasingly jealous and suspicious and wanted to dictate what she wore, who she spoke to, and how she spent her time. During a particularly explosive argument, Michael shouted, "You selfish, ungrateful bitch—I do so much for you, like when I gave you the stereo!" Fed up, she told him to come and take it back the next day, but he never showed.

The "loan" had quickly become her debt, but with a bonus for Michael. When Ellen broke up with him, he used it again by arriving unannounced and drunk "to retrieve the stereo." He then used that opportunity to get in the house and assault her as punishment for behavior he referred to as "using him" and "playing with his heart."

Michael's use of a material hook was exactly what he needed to reel Ellen in, attack her verbally, and finally employ the item as an excuse for contact and abuse after the couple's split.

⚠ Take Action

When we allow someone to "take care of" us before we know their true intentions, we are providing abusers both ammunition to fire at us and a rug to pull out from under us whenever they so choose.

Until you have made sure beyond a reasonable doubt that your new partner is safe, neither a borrower nor a lender be. Keep your money and possessions separate, accepting only honest expressions of affection and commitment through *behavior* instead of judgment-clouding, over-the-top gifts.

FROM MR. RIGHT TO MR. CONTROLLING

Once inside a relationship, a dangerous individual will continue to test you by pushing your boundaries in subtle and crafty ways. Even gestures that seem adoring or spontaneous in the beginning can show a lack of concern for your opinions, desires, or schedule, reflecting only the abuser's need to use you for his own fulfillment. For example, when Becca met Nathan he seemed like he was always thinking about her, making weekend plans for them, ordering her meals at restaurants, or buying her new clothes. She thought he was an "old-fashioned" romantic, so Becca accepted Nathan's somewhat patronizing gestures. After a while he began to criticize her choices and embarrass her in public by insulting whatever outfit, food, or activity he hadn't hand selected. Becca began to feel like she couldn't do anything right, and Nathan was more than happy to take over making all her decisions. Eventually, formerly independent Becca couldn't make a move without Nathan's approval, and he berated her fiercely, calling her stupid and naïve whenever she dared to think for herself. What had at first felt like doting had now evolved into oppression.

No woman should allow pushy behavior just because it makes her feel special or adored. Closer examination of such overbearing action by a partner reveals a failure to ask about your preferences or honor your opinions. It shows that he believes himself to "know what's best for you," much as one might treat a child.

If he doesn't change these behaviors when you point out his condescension and lack of consideration, it may indicate that he is moving from what threat assessment expert Gavin de Becker refers to as a "benevolent controller" to a "malevolent controller." Having a partner who takes on an early role as "relationship manager" may be initially charming, but that same power imbalance can feel suffocating when you decide to start making your own decisions and find that you are not allowed to.

When the relationship is underway, cues about conflict may give an abuser information about how to proceed. During your very first argument, regardless of what it is about, he will watch closely for compliance, fear, and a willingness to forgive. Is it the end of the relationship or will you pardon him, rationalize it, and blame yourself? If you do, then he gets the green light to continue, and you may have identified yourself as a further candidate for victimhood.

If a new or potential partner does something once that you are uncomfortable with or hurt by, his transgression could be seen as a genuine mistake or joke. But if he does it again, after you have made your dismay apparent, then it becomes a separate issue. Forget about the source and words of the disagreement, as specifics no longer matter when evident boundaries are being intentionally crossed. At that point, it is no longer about whether he is kidding or you are too sensitive, it is about the fact that *you told him to stop and he didn't*. He ignored your sincerely expressed wishes, resulting in a clear message from him that your boundaries do not matter, and he will continue to break them in that same way and others.

He is telling you what he is. Your future depends upon your willingness to listen.

INSTANT COMMITMENT

While Hollywood films would have us believe that a whirlwind romance is the highest form of destined love, in reality, being "swept off your feet" can quickly turn into just that: a situation where you have no grounded stance and no way to support yourself or escape your captor's grasp.

According to domestic violence researcher David Adams, half of all intimate partner homicides he studied had a courtship of three months or less (from meeting to living together).[1] This is certainly not to say that a whirlwind romance makes people commit murder—or any other type of violence, for that matter. What it does tell us, however, is that short courtships are highly correlated with violence, even fatality. Part of the reason may be that the victim simply didn't have the time to get to know who she was becoming entangled with before doing so. Even abusers will put their best face forward when beginning a relationship, and he may stay "perfect" for the first six months to a year—even longer—before revealing his true self. Consider this: If you suggest slowing things down with a normal man, he will respect your wishes and allow you whatever space and time you need, but an abuser will react differently. He may pick up the pace and intensity to keep you from catching your breath. With this sudden acceleration, you are less able to think through his actions and respond to any warning signs. For instance, if you think, *What he said to me on the phone today was pretty belittling and inconsiderate,* and then two dozen roses show up on your doorstep, you're more apt to forget that slight and feel grateful instead of resentful.

Normal healthy relationships develop over a reasonable amount of time, with both partners deciding to move forward together. If your new partner pressures you to connect with him before you are ready—through sex, exclusive commitment, cohabitation, marriage, or pregnancy—you may be walking into a dangerous trap.

In the context of prevention, it may be just as important to avoid early sex as it is to eschew premature talk of love and loyalty. Through a combination of chemical and cultural forces, sexual intimacy can increase both an abuser's sense of ownership over his victim, and her sense of connection and obligation to him. Abusers are often overly intense and hypersensitive individuals who can become enraged when experiencing what they perceive as an emotional betrayal. His delusional sense of ownership may not run as deep with someone who has clearly established a casual relationship with well-defined boundaries, thus reducing the level of danger when you decide to back out. Therefore, we exercise wisdom and prudence by waiting to get to know someone's true self before consummating the relationship.

Although the road to romance for women can seem fraught with dangers, proceeding cautiously doesn't have to translate to a boring and lonely existence. Think of a fresh love affair as an exciting trip down the highway in a brand new car. Sure it's exhilarating, but if you'd never driven that car before, you'd want to adjust the mirrors and seat before taking off, get a feel for the engine. You wouldn't accelerate on the curves if you couldn't clearly see the road ahead of you. If something doesn't feel right with your new partner, hit the brakes and put it in park before the journey becomes unsafe. Speed limits, on roads and relationships, are there for a reason.

Case in Point

Rayleen was only seventeen years old when she met Vince. He was twenty-eight and she was a virgin. "My whole world was wrapped up in him," she admits. "That man could have convinced me to walk through fire for him."

When he asked her to elope just six weeks after they met, she felt mature and glamorous but had no idea what was to come. While Rayleen pictured a private wedding on the beach, Vince had planned a quick courthouse union with only the clerks as witnesses. They moved directly into a trailer park four hundred miles away, where Rayleen was cut off from her family and friends. That's when Vince began hitting her and refused to let her use the phone or talk to neighbors.

"I had this romantic idea that we would be a family," she said, "but he took me into a world I wasn't ready for. By the time I got pregnant with our son at nineteen, I felt like a prisoner."

> ⚠ **Take Action**
>
> Beware of the partner who tosses out ultimatums around commitment, particularly early in the relationship. For example, if he tells you that he wants you to move in (a month after you met) or he will break up with you, that isn't a sign of love, it's a sign of a desperate need for control. Regardless of the exact phrasing, if he asks you to do anything you are uncomfortable with under the threat of leaving you, hurting you, sleeping with someone else, or telling secrets about you, that is a major red flag—one that should stop you right in your tracks. Get out now, before you find that you can't.

PRESSURE TO SHARE A ROOF

Another common and effective way that abusers ensnare a woman is by gaining control over her living situation. If your new partner pressures you to move in together, particularly in a home he owns or an apartment he holds the lease on, remember that you will be left with few legal rights, little ground to stand on in arguments, and he will have absolute control of his domain—and thus, you. If you're financially strapped, out of work, or a single mother, be warned that an abuser will exploit that, and he'll make moving in together sound like a smart and reasonable decision. This gives him a powerful hand to play, because for many women, especially those with children, living with an abuser may seem preferable to living in poverty, a homeless shelter, or worse, ending up on the street. But this can be a dangerous, if not deadly, choice. Numerous studies show that women who live with their abusers are more likely to be killed by them (during and after the relationship) than women who do not. This is likely because

Case in Point

"The night I met Grant, I was blown away by how funny and handsome he was, but mostly by the fact that he seemed totally focused on me, like I was the only girl in the world. He followed it up by asking to see me the very next day, and we were together all the time from then on. He kept telling me how he felt we were "soul mates," and said he'd waited his whole life to meet me. No one had ever said those things to me before, so when he asked me to move in with him eight weeks later it seemed like destiny. Shortly after I moved in, he got pretty possessive and didn't want me to go out with my friends. He kept accusing me of picking up guys and cheating on him whenever I did, so I just stopped hanging out with anyone else to avoid making him mad. Once I got a phone call from a male classmate at my college and he flipped out, throwing stuff at me and chest-bumping me. I got scared and screamed that we were done, that I didn't want to be with someone like him. He pushed me up against a wall and put his hands around my throat. 'I'll see you dead before I let you ruin this relationship!' he said. I cried myself to sleep that night because I felt totally trapped and terrified. How did something that started out so good suddenly turn so bad after just a few months?"

—Lauren, age twenty-four

a controlling perpetrator doesn't feel the same sense of ownership with a woman he is dating but not living with, so he won't experience the same level of perceived abandonment if she tries to leave.

Sometimes the situation is reversed, and a new intimate may want to ensnare you for financial gain, by moving in with you, getting on your lease, cell phone account, car insurance, etc. As you learned in

Chapter 2, this is a form of economic abuse, and this type of abuser is an adept scam artist who moves from partner to partner, draining each one financially and emotionally until she can no longer offer what he needs. Such a man might feign wealth to make you think he wouldn't need your money, or manufacture a story about paying you back through some off-shore accounts, a pending lawsuit, insurance settlement, or inheritance that will never materialize. Until you are certain about who your partner is, insist that he take care of himself

Case in Point

"My sons' biological father didn't want anything to do with us. That's why Sean was so appealing to me at first. He said he loved kids, and mine really seemed to enjoy his company. I saw him roughhouse with them but never thought he was hurting them. When we got an apartment together, Sean insisted that the boys call him daddy, even though they weren't ready for it. He started saying that I overindulged them and it was his job to provide some discipline. Whenever they wanted hugs from me, he would say I was raising them to be 'sissies.' One time he even said that they couldn't touch me because my body 'belonged to daddy.' It was like he was jealous of a couple of little boys! After a while they started showing up with bruises on their arms and welts on their bottoms. When one of the kids told me 'daddy' was hitting them with his belt, I confronted Sean and he accused me of siding with them. It got to the point where I was afraid to say anything because I felt like he would take his anger out on them when I wasn't around. To this day, I feel horrible about letting him into their lives, and I know they resent me for not protecting them."

—Wendy, age thirty-four

> ## ⚠ Take Action
>
> If at all possible, be the owner of your own home or the holder of your own lease before entering the relationship, and do not relinquish it until you feel sure (two years or more into the relationship) that he is not an abusive person. If you do move in together, insist that your name be on the lease so he cannot legally kick you out at his every whim. If for some reason, your credit or rental history is not good enough to be on the lease or deed, please reconsider the decision to cohabitate. You may be entering what you think will be the perfect place to "play house" with your new boyfriend but actually be giving up the last bastion of freedom you possess.

and you take care of yourself. Love should be all he asks of you in the beginning of a new relationship, not financial favors.

While partner abuse is a primary reason to avoid a fast courtship and early cohabitation, it is not the only one. Sometimes, a woman's children are targets. Studies have found that the person most likely to sexually abuse a child is not a parent, teacher, neighbor, or stranger. It is their mother's live-in boyfriend or their stepfather.

According to a 2005 study in the *Journal of the American Academy of Pediatrics,* children living in households with unrelated adults are nearly fifty times as likely to die of inflicted injuries as children living with two biological parents.[2] Additionally, research by Dr. Jacqueline Campbell revealed that the presence of a child that is not the abuser's biological offspring increases your level of risk for intimate partner homicide.[3] A child not of an abuser's blood serves as a daily reminder that his partner has been with another man, deeply impacting his fragile masculine ego. He also often lacks parental attachment to the child(ren) and may resent the time and attention they require from his mate.

Blending families is a delicate matter, and the children's safety should always trump a new boyfriend's desire for quick cohabitation, even if it provides an economic advantage to you.

While I have rarely met an abuser who will admit to actively hunting for, testing, and ultimately ensnaring new victims, they are simply denying the manifestations of their intrinsic nature. It's not necessarily a choice they consciously make with awareness and foresight. Rather than deliberately seeking targets, many abusers simply set unrealistically high expectations for their partners and then demand that they live up to them under penalty of abuse and assault. When you inevitably fail to be a perfect servant and fulfiller, the abuser becomes angry, takes on a victim role, and then uses it to justify the emotional and physical violence. Often, he sees it as self-defense or a force that he claims is beyond his command, so that he never has to face up to his own terminal need for power and control.

One benefit of studying his methods is learning that testing a new partner doesn't just go one way. We have a responsibility to ourselves to examine our prospective mates as well. The following chapter will give you some concrete ideas on how to spot a potential abuser *before* you get caught in his web.

Chapter 5

Turning the Tables:
Time to Test Your New Partner

Do not bite at the bait of pleasure till you
know there is no hook beneath it.
—Thomas Jefferson

When I began telling women in personal and professional circles that I was writing this book, many seemed to divide themselves into one of two camps. The first group consisted of women who were in, or had survived, abusive relationships and wanted desperately to share their stories in an effort to warn other females about what they'd missed in hindsight, clues that could have foreshadowed what they were about to experience. Some of their accounts provided examples for the risk factors that appear in upcoming chapters, and I am grateful for their candor and courage. The second group consisted of mostly single women who had never lived through violence themselves but didn't want to fall victim to an abusive relationship. They were interested in learning about "tests," ways they could spot abusers early on and get out before becoming trapped in potentially life-threatening situations.

This chapter is a toolkit for identifying abusive personalities in the early stages of connection. While using these strategies is not a guarantee that an abuser will never enter your life, the awareness that they promote can afford some protection against "relationship predators" through knowledge and increased trust of yourself.

THE 3-STEP MODEL OF ASSERTIVENESS

One of the best ways to gauge a potential partner's demeanor and personality is by the way he communicates, particularly during confrontational discussions. WomenStrength's Sara Johnson recommends using a technique called the 3-Step Model of Assertiveness to test a potential partner before you invest yourself in a relationship. The very first time your prospective mate does something that upsets you, offends you, or makes you feel uncomfortable, follow the three steps below for soliciting and evaluating his responses.

1. *Name the Behavior:* Verbalize his offending actions immediately, so that he realizes you understand what he is doing. Example: "You are raising your voice with me."

2. *Criticize It (the behavior, not the person):* Example: "Yelling makes me uncomfortable and makes it hard for me to communicate with you." The emphasis here is on "I" statements, ones that talk only about your own feelings and how you are affected by the behavior.

3. *Tell Him What to Do:* This step is designed to let him know how you expect to be treated. Example: "Talk to

me in a calm voice, and we can discuss this issue like
adults."

The key here is to note his *reaction* to the three-step method, since
it is a reliable barometer of how he will behave in the future. A worthy
partner will respond by acknowledging his actions, apologizing for
the inappropriate behavior, and changing it immediately. Ideally, the
same behavior will not occur again. However, an abuser will respond
differently, often by denying any wrongdoing, handing the criticism
back to you, and acting upset that you dared to confront him. Do not
back down—you have just stumbled upon a clue to his true personality
and how he handles conflict. Do not ignore this revelation or second-
guess yourself. Remember that while you are testing him, he is testing
you. By retreating, you have shown him just what he wants to see—that
you can be cowed and manipulated, despite your own instincts.

DETECTING DECEPTION

When screening a potential new partner, be prepared for the fact that
if he is an abuser, much of what he tells you during your first few
interactions may not be true. Abuse is often built and perpetuated
on lies, since the abuser conceals his true self and hides his behavior
from the outside world. Therefore, when meeting a new acquaintance,
take little at face value. Of course, recognizing dishonesty and danger
would be easier if iPhone made a polygraph application for dating.
But because we are typically on our own, the following information
is designed to help you become a human threat-detector of sorts, with
the ability to uncover hidden signals in words and body language that
may indicate risk. The advice comes from deception expert Donna
Brown of Analies Enterprises in Toronto, Canada, who honed her skills
catching smugglers with the Canadian Border Patrol. She has a few

tips for women on the behavioral clues of potentially dangerous men, which you can apply on your next date:

1. People's speech patterns can often reveal how they truly feel, regardless of the words they use. When you first meet someone you are interested in, observe the pace of their words. Is it laid back and comfortable, or is it manic, as though they are adamantly trying to convince you of their point or sell you an idea? If so, this rapid-fire language could indicate a critical and judgmental man who may discount your opinions and wishes in favor of his own.

2. If his views are challenged by others does he engage in lively debate with a sense of fairness and respect or does he tense up, turn red in the face, and speak more quickly? Arrogant and self-centered individuals cannot typically tolerate affronts to their power, and as much as they try to hide their anger it will seep out in small ways.

3. Aggressive people often use telltale hand movements, such as chopping one hand against the other or punching their closed fist into their palm. While this may not mean they are a violent individual, it does suggest that their frustrations and anger are channeled in physical ways, which could mean trouble for whoever they are angry at.

4. Many abusive people push boundaries. Even in early interactions, they may come in too close to talk, or put their arm around your shoulders or waist. While this is clearly inappropriate for a casual conversation between people who are not yet romantically involved, someone who doesn't

respect limitations will appear blithe about breaking them and act innocent or even offended if called out.

5. Technology can block your ability to read people, since you can't see a man's face over the phone and are denied even verbal clues to his demeanor in a text or email. While online dating is popular and can result in great connections, an abuser can misrepresent himself in many ways through his virtual smokescreen. Insist on *at least* one in-person meeting before bestowing or accepting words and gestures of affection.

6. Consider what his body language is saying. For example, when you hold hands, is his hand always on top of yours? If you stand up and try to walk away, leading him by the hand, does he pull back or let go? If so, he may be uncomfortable with you taking a position of power. Many abusers have rigid ideas about the roles of men and women, believing males to be dominant. Even if his words say otherwise, he may be resistant to having his power usurped.

7. Is he flexible? If you were supposed to go to dinner and you suggest a movie instead, can he roll with the change or is he clearly bothered that things aren't going his way? It could be that he had a special night planned and feels disappointed, but on the other hand you might be dealing with an unyielding control freak.

8. Be wary of men who frequently encourage you to spend your money (especially on things that benefit him), ask

to stay at your home, or borrow your car. Ask yourself why an adult male hasn't learned to take care of himself, applying healthy skepticism to tales about a temporary "rough patch." While there is nothing shameful about being poor, a man shouldn't ask his girlfriend to cover all his expenses and cater to him as though he were a child. That attitude shows an alarming lack of responsibility, maturity, and trustworthiness.

9. Even experienced liars cannot always remember their lies well. If you think his story doesn't quite add up, reword the question later and see if the old answer matches the new.

10. A lot of people think that lack of eye contact is a sign of deception, and it is . . . in bad liars. A seasoned fibber or true pathological liar will have no problem looking you right in the face as he lies, and may in fact do it more often than a truth teller. However, almost all liars will momentarily avert their gaze to the side, floor, or ceiling when confronted—even if they resteady it a second later. This is an involuntary reflex known as neuro-linguistic programming, or NLP. Please note that cultural differences may be a factor in duration or appropriateness of eye contact.

11. Liars also have a tendency to give away their deception through body language, such as shifting their feet and fidgeting when answering questions. They also may touch, contort, and cover their mouths when lying. The hands of a fraud often face downward, and they

frequently turn their bodies away, angling their center slightly from the person they are deceiving.

12. Language is also key in determining truth. For example, many liars almost whisper their response, lowering their vocals significantly. Their pitch, however, may go up, indicating discomfort with what is coming out of their mouths. They also use contractionless phrases like "I was *not* there" as opposed to "I wasn't there." If he tries to change the subject, or throw questions and blame back on you, it is likely he has been caught linguistically unarmed. Does he clear his throat before launching into an explanation? This may be a way to buy a second's worth of extra time to craft a lie, or an involuntary gesture that indicates a lack of truth behind the words that follow. Some deception experts call this "the growl."

13. Lips aren't just for kissing. They may be dead giveaways as well, because many people purse their lips if they are holding a secret, or bite and move them if they are about to tell a lie.

14. Is he sweating, even though the room temperature is perfectly comfortable? Something you said or asked about may have put him on the spot. If he tightens his jaw and literally puts his foot down, chances are he is sticking with his story and plans to defend it even in the face of clear evidence to the contrary.

While tips like these are not foolproof, they will give you an advantage the next time you are doing a "Q&A" with your new or even current partner. Knowledge is power, and the more you understand about the person you are dating, the safer you will be.

After reading about both the negative qualities of abusers and their uncanny ability to mask them, you may be wondering how women are supposed to tell the difference between nice guys and the ones who are faking it. The answer is usually in your calendar. While many dangerous people are skilled at hiding their true persona for extended periods of time, few can keep it up for more than a year and a half to two years, particularly if you live together. Time is on your side, and if a partner can repeatedly pass test after test, never revealing a violent or controlling facet over several years, then he is likely safe and genuinely worthy. Does this mean you have to hold off a good man forever, risking that he might get tired of waiting? Absolutely not—enjoy the positive aspects of your relationship, but do so while maintaining your self-confidence and financial independence, armed heavily with risk-reducing knowledge that guides safe decision making. Try not to step into the bonds of co-habitation, marriage, and parenting until you are absolutely certain your partner is stop-sign free. A solid, healthy, honest relationship is always worth the wait.

TEN SIMPLE QUESTIONS

When you first meet a new relationship candidate, asking him a series of innocuous questions can tell you a bit about his depth of character and allow you the opportunity to observe his level of comfort with personal inquiry. Think of it as a secret interview, designed to see how open he is with sharing private opinions. Created by journalist Bernard Pivot, the following queries are intended to reveal information about a person's thoughts, feelings, and beliefs. I suggest you make up your own slightly reworded versions and sprinkle the questions throughout an evening to avoid sounding like James Lipton on *The Actor's Studio*.

1. What is your favorite word?
2. What is your least favorite word?
3. What turns you on creatively, spiritually, or emotionally?
4. What turns you off?
5. What is your favorite curse word?
6. What sound or noise do you love?
7. What sound or noise do you hate?
8. What profession other than your own would you like to attempt?
9. What profession would you not like to do?
10. If Heaven exists, what would you like to hear God say when you arrive at the Pearly Gates?

When you are listening for answers, consider the following: How do his statements make you feel? Do the words he says match the expressions he makes? Was there anything he said that intrigued or frightened you? Perhaps he couldn't or wouldn't come up with responses at all, and that in itself would tell you a lot about his personality (or lack thereof).

This simple list will not reveal if someone is an abuser, but it will allow you to learn more about them and take note of how they handle a woman trying to poke around in their brain. It will also give you an opportunity to see how compatible you are on several different levels. An experienced abuser may lie to match whatever he thinks you want him to be, but a less clever one may reveal his darker sides before you meet them in a more dangerous situation.

TEN SERIOUS QUESTIONS

The following more important questions are for *you* to answer about your prospective partner. Replies should be obtained through natural and casual conversation with him and with others who know him, not through pointed queries. The answers he or others give, and the way in which they are given, will offer you clues about the nature of this person and whether he may turn out to be an abusive individual.

1. How does he feel about the people who raised him and the way in which they did it?

Find out about your prospective mate's childhood and his relationship with his parents, grandparents, or guardians. Are his family ties on solid ground and does he speak of relatives (particularly females) respectfully? Did his parents do any of the following:

- Abuse him?
- Abuse each other?
- Abandon or neglect him?
- Fail to protect him from the abuse of others?
- Always let him get his way?
- Always bail him out of trouble?

Often, a potential batterer's relationships reflect an abusive upbringing with little equality or reciprocity. They may describe themselves as having been self-reliant their whole lives, not receiving support or help from loved ones. They may also talk about witnessing or experiencing violence in their own household as a child, either toward a parent, themselves, a sibling, or a pet. However, just because a person grew up the victim of an abusive household doesn't mean that, by default, he's destined to be an abuser. Many wonderful men (and women) escape the cycle of abuse. Others don't. Particularly alarming would be if they justified past abuse. For example, if they talk about how their father "kept family members in line" through violence, they too might consider abuse an acceptable form of punishment or a suitable method of maintaining control over others.

Conversely, someone whose family put them on a pedestal, allowing them to shirk responsibility and treat others poorly without consequence, will likely continue that sense of entitlement into adulthood. A man who was his parent's "prince" may expect you to treat him the same way, and he will probably not feel guilty about living a self-centered existence.

2. How many significant romantic relationships has he had and how does he describe his past partners?

Multiple failed past relationships may indicate a track record of problematic behavior, particularly if the story is always the same: he was the perfect partner and she was a bitch/slut/psycho/addict, etc. If he describes every one of his ex-girlfriends/wives as "crazy" or a "whore," look out. Either he has a misogynistic view free of self-blame or has very low standards in women. Men who talk about their exes in extremely critical and denigrating terms may in fact be abusers, blaming their previous partners for their own inability to maintain healthy relationships. A consistent series of relationships and/or marriages that ended badly (especially if he takes little to no responsibility for the failures) may be a good predictor of unsuccessful future couplings. In fact, studies show that the success rate of marriages decreases exponentially with each consecutive nuptial.

(Note: If he broke up with the most recent "Jezebel" over six months ago and he's still seething about her, you may be dealing with a revenge-focused ruminator and possibly a currently practicing stalker. You could be next.)

3. What does your inner circle think of him?

Introduce him to your friends and family over several occasions. After a few meetings, ask their honest opinions and be ready for what you might not want to hear. Consider their motives: As people who love you, they probably want to protect you and see you happy. Don't be afraid to tell them what your honest thoughts are as well; often, we feel embarrassed revealing our doubts about our new partner after we've talked him up to people we're close to. Just because you thought he was wonderful at first doesn't mean you should feel any shame at discovering otherwise. Even the most intelligent among us can be misled—it is what we choose to do upon discovering the deception that seperates the foolish from the wise. Many people close to victims of domestic violence and intimate partner homicide admit to having had an uneasy or ominous feeling about their loved one's significant other, even if they couldn't quite identify why. Trust not only the instinct of yourself but of those around you, particularly your mother, sister, or best friend. They share the women's intuition that can save your life, both literally and figuratively.

4. How does he relate to the people in his life, and what do they think of him?

How many authentic, egalitarian relationships does your new partner have? Make small talk with his buddies, such as, "So, how long have you known Jason?" or "What is Jason's best quality as a friend?" Someone who grew up with him will undoubtedly know him better, but they'll also be more loyal to him. However, angry abusive people seldom have many strong and lasting friendships, unless the friend either somehow knows nothing of their true character or shares the same behaviors himself. Does he talk behind other people's backs but is then nice to

Case in Point

Candace, a former client, was smitten over her new boyfriend, but the few times she ran into his mother and sister, who were not on speaking terms with him, they outright cautioned her against becoming involved in the relationship, referring to him as a "psychopath." She brushed them off, choosing instead to believe her partner's explanation that they were just bitter over old family quarrels. A few months later, in a horrible example of "I told you so," the boyfriend violently assaulted Candace and sexually abused her young daughter.

If a potential new partner's family or friends are raising red flags in your direction, and you're unsure of their motives, ask yourself what they have to gain from making up blatant lies about him. Consider that you may simply be blinded by what you want your partner to be, rather than seeing what he truly is.

their faces? That may indicate that he has a need to put others down, and is duplicitous, or fake.

If you have mutual acquaintances, ask around about him. Sometimes, the best sources are his ex-girlfriends/wives. If you think these women are biased, you're right, but it may be for a very good reason. Women who have been abused by a man often feel the need to warn his future partners. You may assume (with his insistence) that the other woman is lying, that she's jealous and wants to interfere with your relationship, but pay attention to specific details in what she says. Don't let your excitement about a new significant other prevent you from hearing potentially life-saving admonitions. Realize that he has a good reason to lie about abuse, but she very rarely does.

Even though abusers sometimes have friends and family who are just as bad as they are, his close pals or relatives may try to alert you to concerning behaviors, more often subtly than openly. Is he jokingly described as "difficult," "crazy," or someone who has "problems"? Do people in his inner circle say that he is misunderstood and you just have to get to know him to see his finer sides? These may be subtle attempts to warn you about what you are getting into without compromising their relationship with him.

5. How does he treat women in positions of service or authority? How does he feel toward women in general?

Observe how he treats women in positions of service—such as waitresses—and women in positions of authority, such as female police officers. Ask him what he thinks of the idea of a female judge, football coach, or president. Abusers are often deeply threatened by the idea of women in charge. If a man objectifies women or holds a disrespectful attitude toward them, he'll quickly reveal it through his language, media choices, sense of humor, and the company he keeps. If he makes misogynistic comments or jokes and then claims to be "only kidding" when confronted, he is either obtuse or truly feels that way about females. A man who commonly uses words like "bitch" and "whore" to refer to women perceives them as objects of disdain, deserving of mistreatment. Don't fall for the man who says he would never use those words to describe *you*, or that "You're different from them, honey." You simply haven't fallen out of his favor yet.

6. How does he feel about the subject of domestic violence?

Test his attitudes toward abuse by bringing up news stories about partner abuse (like the Mel Gibson or Chris Brown cases) or personal stories (even hypothetical ones) about things that happened to nameless acquaintances. Does he side with or defend the actions of the abusers in question? Does he blame the victims? Explore his true persona by asking him neutral questions in response to his stated worldviews such as, "How did you decide that?" or "Have you always thought that way?" An abuser will either respond aghast, "I would never hit a woman!" and then do it down the road anyway, or he will say, "If a woman hits a man/cheats on a man/disrespects a man, etc., she gets what she deserves." This indicates a very dangerous mindset, one that should be a deal breaker in anyone's book.

7. How does he react to challenges and frustrations?

When he's stuck in traffic or gets cut off on the highway, does he get irritated and hostile? How does he respond to long lines at the store, or disappointment over something he'd been looking forward to? Does he get huffy and annoyed, cursing under his breath, even yelling at the cashier? Does he rant, rave, and sulk for hours because tickets to a game were sold out? Does he spend the next month cursing the friend who promised to get him the tickets, plotting his revenge? Is everything always someone else's fault? These are important character traits to note, ones that provide valuable insight into his levels of self-control, empathy, sensitivity, and morality—or lack thereof.

8. Has he been violent toward anyone in his past?

Listen for clues not only of past violence against intimate partners (a glaring stop sign) but also against family, childhood classmates, pets, police, enemies, and strangers. If he does admit to such occurrences, note his tone—does he regret his use of force or does he feel justified? Does he brag about his aggression or strength, hoping to impress others with his warped version of masculinity? Such an individual clearly views himself as tougher than everyone else, and he will use your reactions to his "fight tales" to see if you understand and respect his self-perceived superiority as well.

9. What else is in his past?

Has he been expelled, dismissed, fired, or dishonorably discharged from anything? Why? Having such an experience doesn't necessarily make him more likely to be an abuser, but the way he explains it might. What you're looking for here is accountability and a willingness to learn from his mistakes. Does his explanation indicate that he took responsibility and fixed his errors, or is an external source always to blame? Lack of accountability is a common trait shared by many abusers.

Case in Point

Abusers with a history of arrest or incarceration will often tell a different story about their track record, either lying about the offense or spinning a self-acquitting version of how it occurred. I once worked with a teenage client who felt defensive about her older boyfriend's status as a sex offender. She stated emphatically that he had "explained the whole thing" to her and she knew that he was on the state's registry because he had a consensual sexual relationship with a seventeen-year-old when he was nineteen. Imagine her shock and horror when I revealed to her that his so-called "girlfriend" involved in the crime was only four years old.

> ⚠️ **Take Action**
>
> If you're dating a man with an admitted criminal record, check it out. Most police reports are public knowledge and can be reviewed upon request. The main exceptions are reports marked "confidential," which usually involve serious crimes such as child abuse, rape, and murder. If you cannot view his reports because of confidential designation, that should be cause for serious alarm.
>
> If you are not sure whether he has a record, or don't think he's being honest about its source, do some investigation. Many websites offer background checks for a nominal fee, including data such as divorce records, civil lawsuits, and bankruptcy claims. You can also run his name through the database at www.domesticviolencedatabase.org, a free site where women can look up a potential partner to see if other women have reported him as an abuser. He doesn't ever need to know that you checked him out and doing so isn't "snooping"; it's proactive risk reduction.

Even nonviolent crimes are cause for concern. Whether he was caught or not, offenses like shoplifting, cheating, and embezzling can be indicators of impulsive, low-conscience, and deceitful behavior. Look out, because these traits can manifest in far darker ways.

10. Does he seem absolutely perfect for you?

Beware of perfection. During the first few interactions with a new partner, discuss your interests and hobbies. Does he respond with contrasting replies of his own or does everything he says match up in an eerily ideal way? For example, let's say you mention that you like jazz, the New York Yankees, and fresh vegetables. If he tells you over the next few minutes, days, or weeks that he has an extensive collection of Charlie Parker albums, knows Derek Jeter personally, and is a maestro of backyard gardening skills, look out. Particularly if he is also gorgeous, rich, and sensitive. In other words, if he's too good to be true, he probably is.

When feeling out a potential victim, abusers will throw a bunch of stuff at the wall and see what sticks. If you tell him what you are looking for in a man up front, that makes it easier for a con artist to verbally conform to your prerequisites. During conversation, he will look for enthusiastic reactions to statements and then key in on those responses by amplifying his involvement or interest to match yours. It is a way of getting in your head, making you think that he is wonderful and can see into you like a "soul mate."

The more you want to hear that a new acquaintance is flawless, the easier time he will have convincing you that he is. As self-defense expert Marc MacYoung states,

> *If you can remove your emotional involvement from the equation, you will clearly see how people attempt to hide (negative) behaviors. But before you can remove your emotional investment you must critically review your motives. What are you getting out of the situation? What do you expect to get out of the situation? What are you afraid of losing if you were to allow yourself to see this behavior and recognize its significance?* [1]

If a new partner seems like Mr. Right, don't just take him at face value. Demand long-term and sustainable proof of his excellence and trustworthiness before you invite him to share the most sacred aspects of your life, such as your body, your home, or your children.

Answering the questions above can help you to see through the fog of an exciting new relationship and recognize traits that may indicate future risk. But to benefit from them, you must be prepared to accept and act upon any stop signs that spring up. There is no point in finding out more about a new partner unless we are willing to draw limits and abide by them. It is always better to ask the important questions early on, before emotional attachment blurs our judgment. Once you know what you need to know about him, you can begin to ask yourself whether or not he meets your standards, and if he truly deserves to be with you. Even though it takes strength to reject a potential mate, it doesn't mean you won't find someone better, it means that *you're* better for recognizing your self-worth. Remember feminist icon Gloria Steinem's quote: "God may be in the details, but the goddess is in the questions. Once we begin to ask them there's no turning back."

INSTINCTUAL ARMAMENTS

Finally, the last test a prospective new partner should pass is the "gut check." Many women who have survived abuse talk about "a little voice inside" that tried to tell them something was wrong with their partner. In hindsight, they can often describe why they ignored it: They didn't want to be rude or make him feel bad, they brushed it off as first date jitters, they didn't trust themselves enough to believe it, or they simply didn't want to.

In the primal design of human beings, instinct plays a powerful and necessary role, protecting us from lurking predators through subtle sensory stimulation. But as humans evolved, the need to avoid saber tooth tigers lessened, and those vital senses became dulled. We still have them, women particularly, and they are available for use if we allow ourselves to heed them. If we are open to messages from our intrinsic "guide," she will tell us which direction to move in, and when to pull the plug on a relationship, even in the absence of obvious signs. Learning all you can about a new partner, and beginning to understand the language of your "inner voice," can provide protection against the "tigers" that seek to overpower us today.

Chapter 6

The Devil You Know:
Risk Factors by Characteristic

If someone shows you who they are, believe them.
The first time.
—Maya Angelou

As you learned in previous chapters, when evaluating a partner, if we only look for obvious signs, like a violent temper, we may be missing the more subtle but equally dangerous red flags. Since abuse may not at first (or ever) be as palpable as a punch to the face, women need to develop "peripheral sensitivity" to detect more insidious behaviors and traits.

Most of the personal attributes provided in the following pages do not by themselves indicate a propensity toward violence, but when assembled together, they reveal a picture often associated with abusive situations. All abusers have the potential to commit violent or even lethal acts, and while each abuser's personality, upbringing, and intrinsic disposition makes him distinct from other abusers, they generally share common character traits that foreshadow an abusive nature even *before* they become perpetrators. Certainly, if your current or former partner exhibits one or more qualities listed below, it does not automatically mean that he will harm you or anyone else. But when observed in *concert,* these traits do increase the likelihood that an individual is a risk to the safety of others, especially if the markers are seen in combination with the behaviors and situational factors you will read about in Chapter 7.

ARTIFICIAL CHARISMA

An often baffling aspect of domestic violence, in the eyes of both victims and outside observers, is how charming and affable the abuser can seem in public. Perpetrators of abuse put great effort into cultivating a likeable facade because it allows them to court victims and remain above suspicion to others when the inevitable mistreatment occurs. It is a technique used to disarm and gain trust quickly, one that is also seen in rapists, con men, and other predatory criminals. Researcher David Adams found that eighteen of the twenty victims of attempted partner homicide he interviewed rated their abuser as "charming to others."[1]

As mentioned in Chapter 5, if someone is "too good to be true" at first blush, or he appears to be trying too hard to make people like him, there may be cause for concern. This trait can be particularly seductive when combined with other appealing features, such as good looks or wealth. If a man is trying to fool and manipulate you, it won't be long before you see it, but it may take outside observers (family, friends, colleagues, neighbors) more time to catch on, depending on how close they are to the individual. Be wary of the person who seems wonderful but has few genuine or lasting relationships with others.

You may be witnessing a trap designed to lure and ensnare naively optimistic victims.

Case in Point

Manufactured charisma ultimately falls apart, but it's often difficult from the outset to know just how authentic it is. The story of Dina, thirty-nine, is all too common:

"From the outside, a lot of people thought Billy was a winner, a charmer who did everything right and had lots of friends. But that's only because he spent a lot of time making it seem that way. He always acted like he was busy socializing and working, all with an outgoing confidence that made him seem very attractive to me when we first met. But after dating him for a while I realized he was actually quite a failure professionally, and all these supposed friends he had never really materialized. He would go as far as to pretend he was at a party when someone called him, even though he was sitting on the couch alone. It seemed like those who did know him really didn't want to spend any time with him. In hindsight I should have realized there was probably a very good reason for that."

COMPARTMENTALIZATION, LYING, AND SECRET-KEEPING

The act of separating one's life into different boxes that do not intersect is called "compartmentalization." The danger of this trait is that it allows an individual to develop schisms in his personality and lose touch with his true self. This trait is often seen in men who cheat, because a partner who is unfaithful over and over again is likely putting a lot of work into creating alibis and cover ups. While deceptive acts such as repeated infidelity alone may not increase the danger in a relationship, the chronic lies and alienation from reality that often accompany it do. Not only does it show that he is insensitive to your feelings (and sometimes health), but it requires that he lie to you as well. Someone who repeatedly cheats lacks a sense of guilt and morality, and believes the rules don't apply to them. These types, ironically, also hold to extreme double standards. Woe to the partner of this man who is caught doing the same. Additionally, the deeper he sinks into his web of lies to cover for his actions, the less empathy and respect he has for you as well, because deceiving you on a continual basis shows that he doesn't see you as deserving of the truth. These are the same traits violent people must cultivate in order to bring themselves to a mind-place where they can carry out their deeds. Sometimes cheating can be a sign of far more harmful capabilities.

When asked what he believed to be the number one common trait of the many domestic killers he had worked with, renowned forensic psychologist Dr. Frank Colistro said simply, "Lies, lies, lies."[2] He noted that these men lie about everything: the important and the mundane, some for the purpose of personal gain, but others just for "fun."

For a particularly dangerous class of abusers, their pretense goes far beyond the average white lie. Some set up entire alternate realities for themselves and the people around them, signaling that they are more concerned with creating a facade than living in reality. Often they are hiding issues of financial insolvency and professional or educational failures. The real danger comes when the liar fears they are about to be discovered and regards desperate action as their only solution. Consider the cases of domestic killers Mark Hacking and Neil Entwhistle.

To those who knew Mark Hacking, he was a dedicated medical student preparing to study at the University of North Carolina, Chapel Hill. His wife, Lori, was newly pregnant and looking forward to starting a family. Although friends and family knew of no abuse between the couple, Mark was hiding a deep secret. The medical equipment and textbooks he laid around the house were real, but his enrollment in college was not. He had never even applied to UNC but enjoyed the prestige of claiming that he was a doctor-to-be. Mark went to such an extent to perpetrate his fraud that he even spent time "studying" and writing fake term papers. He also lied about drinking, smoking, and at least one extramarital affair. Even close friends and family in law enforcement bought into Mark's facade. Lori's colleagues stated that three days before her disappearance she received a phone call at work that reduced her to tears—this was likely the moment she learned about her husband's deceptions, a discovery that along with the argument that followed, may have triggered her July 19, 2004, murder. Mark, after days of assisting in the search for Lori and pleading for help through the media, admitted that he had killed her and dumped her body in a Utah landfill.

According to British internet entrepreneur Neil Entwhistle, his computer-spamming activities were paying off. His wife, Rachael, believed he was making good money, as evidenced by their beautifully furnished new home, but did not realize that everything was being charged onto credit cards, amassing huge debt for the family. He also told her he was hiding money in offshore accounts when what he was really hiding were his sexual relationships with other women, both online and in person. When the bills came due and the lies began to crumble, Neil killed Rachael and their nine-month-old daughter, then fled the country. He was eventually captured and convicted on the basis of physical evidence, despite his tale of finding them already murdered by an unknown assailant.

The only way to avoid such situations is to be fully aware of the truths in your partner's life. Do not be afraid to seek out evidence of their claims. An honest and open individual should have no problem showing you his diploma or his paystub because a real relationship is based on transparency. This type of information gathering can be presented as genuine interest in someone's past or present affairs, in the spirit of full disclosure and trust. Be wary of the person who refuses to show you such proofs or displays anger at your inquiries. If you suspect fraud, contact the school they claim to be enrolled in, or the employer they claim to work for. It's not snooping if they have given you reason for suspicion, it is merely exercising your right to protect yourself.

DEPRESSION

Many abusers suffer from the inner malady of depression, which can contribute to (although it does not directly cause) outward actions, such as addiction and violence. In many cases, it is what researcher Terence Real refers to as "covert depression," a condition that men may feel less able to reveal to themselves or others because they are fearful of appearing weak or "unmanly."[3] While some scientists believe that depressive states connected with violence and aggression arise as a result of biological factors, such as low serotonin levels, others point out that no form of mental illness should be used to excuse abuse.

Personality disorders and other mental health problems may aggravate domestic violence, but with the exception of serious illnesses like schizophrenia, they typically do not cause it. Most men who are mentally ill *can* have functional lives and relationships, providing that they are attentive to their issues and address them properly. If you find out that a new man in your life has been diagnosed with a mental illness, determine how he is handling it. Is he responsibly dealing with the condition or allowing it to wreak havoc with his life and those of the people in it? For example, if he sees a therapist or psychiatrist regularly, takes prescribed medications, monitors himself, and practices preventative maintenance—such as taking care of his body and stress levels—then he may still make a suitable partner. If not, you may be looking at a genuine violence risk factor. A scale created by Barbara J. Hart of the Minnesota Center Against Violence and Abuse lists depression as the seventh indicator on a scale designed to predict lethality in domestic situations. She states:

> *Where a batterer has been acutely depressed and sees little hope for moving beyond the depression, he may be a candidate for homicide and/or suicide. Research shows that many men who are hospitalized for depression have homicidal fantasies directed at family members.*[4]

Again, this does not mean that depressed people are dangerous, but merely points out the potential problems with individuals who display this trait in conjunction with others on the list.

EXTREME CONTROL ISSUES

Control is the abuser's art form, and some have elevated it to conditions of unfathomable cruelty and rage. I once worked with a young wife named Aliyah whose Muslim husband exerted stifling command over her every move. I had to meet her in secret while he was at work, as her two young children played at our feet. A Caucasian woman who was raised Christian, Aliyah told me she had converted to Islam in part because she enjoyed the sense of calm at her husband's mosque, and the kindness of the people she met there. But her husband was a man who understood the teachings of his faith differently than others, and when extreme interpretations of a religious dogma are combined with an already abusive mentality, it can be used to justify violence. Aliyah's husband wouldn't allow her to leave the home or receive visitors. She wasn't permitted to use a phone, a television, or a computer. She was punished brutally for speaking to others, particularly men, and had received her most recent beating for coming to the door when a delivery driver knocked. The jealousy and need for control that Aliyah's husband demonstrated went so far that he routinely checked the contents of the toilet after she used it because he said he could tell if she had been unfaithful by examining her feces. She also told me that when she "misbehaved" her husband would often withhold the medication Aliyah required for a life-threatening illness, forcing her to beg for her treatments.

A controlling abuser may want decision-making power over everything from your clothing, to your eating habits, friends, and your job. Even if he doesn't physically abuse you, he may still demand that housework, cooking, and child-rearing be done in a particular way. He may force you to account for all of your time and expenditures. In many cases, the need to have his thumb over every aspect of your life will extend into conversations, social and financial affairs, family activities, and even into the bedroom. His extreme control may make you feel too inept or afraid to have a say in anything. And what happens if you do exert your will or opinions, especially if they don't align with his? Will he yell at you? Embarrass you in front of friends or family? Threaten you? Might he push or slap you? This is particularly anxiety producing when you cannot predict his explosive reactions. If the ground is laid with emotional landmines, even a simple stroll can compromise your safety.

While issues of power and control are at the core of all abuse, highly dangerous cases show a more intense and insidious variety of domination. Some abusers may run their home like a prison, using tactics of coercion and intimidation to ensure the compliance of their partners and/or children. Simply put, in the mind of an extremely controlling abuser, it's his way or the highway, 24/7, no discussions allowed. All of these demands are backed up by the overarching threat of abandonment or physical and sexual violence, even if such words are never spoken aloud. In abusive situations, control issues are of particular concern because of the lengths some abusers will go in an effort to preserve control or punish a partner for defying it. These desperate attempts to regain command over the victim by recapturing, stalking, hurting, or even killing her are typically visible when she leaves the relationship or states the intention to do so.

Remember Aliyah? She didn't want to leave her husband right away for a variety of reasons and as her advocate I respected her autonomy, so we worked together to create a plan for an escape in the close future. Unfortunately, she never saw that plan to fruition. Aliyah passed away, at twenty-six years old, mother to an eight-month-old boy and a two-year-old girl. Her husband immediately returned to his home country with their two children. The coroner's report stated that she died from "complications" of her life-threatening illness.

EXTREME JEALOUSY

When jealousy first appears, it is one of the "Trojan Horse" aspects of a dangerous relationship. At first glance, it feels like a welcome gift, to see evidence of a lover's strong feelings, his fear of losing you to another. But when it opens up, great danger springs from within, and "the gift" is seen for what it truly is: a destroyer of love, and sometimes life. For abusive individuals, their feelings are not about real love but rather ownership and betrayal. An abuser would have you believe that your actions create his jealousy, that if you weren't talking to that man at the party then he wouldn't have to feel that way. But jealousy lives inside him, and it will appear whenever his fragile ego isn't being constantly stroked and fed. Jealous people are exhausting to keep up with because one never knows what will set off their insecurities. Those invisible tripwires present a particular danger because victims cannot anticipate the ever-shifting parameters or even know when or if they're unwittingly breaching them.

To determine if you're dealing with a man whose jealousy is abnormal, ask yourself the following questions:

1. Does he check your voicemail or telephone call history?
2. Does he insist on access to your diary or journal?
3. Has he eavesdropped on private conversations?
4. Does he read your emails or check your contacts on social networking sites?
5. Does he demand that you account for your time and the company that you keep?
6. Does he constantly accuse you of being unfaithful?
7. Has he ever checked your clothing or linens for "signs" of infidelity?
8. Has he ever demanded that you change clothes into something he deems more appropriate?
9. Has he ever hidden, disposed of, or damaged clothing or makeup of yours that he considers provocative?
10. Have you ever caught him following you, spying on you, or enlisting someone else to do so?
11. Does he accuse you of "flirting" with people you are merely speaking to, working alongside, or obtaining services from (such as a waiter or supermarket clerk)?
12. Does he accuse your male friends of trying to seduce you, or "steal you away"?
13. Has he discouraged you from going to school or getting a job because he is afraid you will "meet someone else"?

If you answered yes to any of these questions, then you are at increased risk for abuse, particularly if your partner is also controlling and/or physically aggressive.

EXTREME SHIFTS IN PERSONALITY/MOOD

Professionals in the field of domestic violence, along with abuse victims themselves, often refer to individuals who change personality without warning or provocation as "Dr. Jekyll and Mr. Hyde," the famous murderous literary character who went from good to bad in a split second. A subject who experiences rapid and extreme shifts in mood, going

Case in Point

One of the things Lucy initially liked about Tom was his sunny, humorous disposition. But it wasn't until they'd been together for several months that she saw a different side. One night they were watching a movie together on the couch, laughing and commenting on the scenes. Tom got up to get a beer and realized there wasn't one in the refrigerator. The next thing Lucy knew, an empty glass bottle from the recycling container flew across the room and smashed on the wall. It had been thrown by Tom, who had suddenly changed into an angry, red-faced monster. Lucy reported that he screamed, "Didn't I tell you to buy me beer for tonight?! What are you, a fucking *idiot?* I should kick the shit out of you for ignoring me!" Lucy froze in shock. At first she thought it was some kind of joke, but with awful clarity soon realized Tom meant business. In a split second, the man she adored and admired had shifted into a raving lunatic, and it was only the first of many times thereafter in which Lucy witnessed this dark and inexplicable transformation.

from happy to angry in the blink of an eye, can be highly unpredictable and hazardous. They may appear to have a "split personality" and seem unable to control the swings in their duality. Such behavior demonstrates an unstable impulsivity that may endanger anyone around them. Many survivors of severe abuse and even homicide attempts report that their abuser's face changed when he was attacking them, recalling a "possessed" or "deranged" look about his expression that differed from anything previously seen. If the man you are assessing exhibits such extreme and quick changes in disposition, he is highly predisposed to being violent. However, it will be difficult to determine *when* he may erupt, so caution should be exercised at all times, not just in moments of confrontation.

LACK OF EMPATHY

Empathy is defined as our ability to identify with and respond appropriately to the feelings of others. While the absence of it is not a psychological syndrome in itself, it is a trait of many diagnoses, such as Narcissistic and Antisocial Personality Disorders. Few abusers understand what their victims are experiencing, simply because they are defined by the pursuit of their own needs and desires. Often, any remorse an abuser shows is related to the consequences he must endure for his actions, not the actions themselves. Beware the individual who laughs at the pain of others and fails to see how his behavior frightens or upsets them. Lack of empathy is a known characteristic of violent individuals and is best seen by those with the opportunity to closely and frequently observe the subject.

LACK OF IMPULSE CONTROL

A person lacking impulse control often exhibits "knee-jerk" reactions to stimuli without any thought or concern for the consequences.

Sometimes impulsivity is connected to other issues, such as Attention Deficit Disorder, substance abuse, low serotonin levels, and brain damage. Psychologists categorize disorders such as pyromania (fire setting), kleptomania (compulsive stealing), and habitual gambling as Impulse Control Disorders, or "ICDs," meaning that the person committing the actions is unable to control their behavior. Some mental health professionals recognize a form of ICD known as Intermittent Explosive Disorder, characterized by outbursts of rage and violence directed toward others. In domestic violence, nearly all offenders could be eligible for this diagnosis but it fails to thoroughly explain why they typically only abuse their partners. After all, most perpetrators that claim to "lose control" do not do so in the presence of police officers, bosses, or judges, only with their partners. However, whether the lack of control is genuine or not, it is an important warning sign if your abuser claims he can't "control his actions." If you are involved with a man who states that he can't stop himself from committing violence, he is only one step away from claiming that he would kill independent of his intentions. By sidestepping responsibility for his violence, an individual is admitting to being a loose cannon, and someone you don't want to be around when he goes off.

LACK OF PERSONAL ACCOUNTABILITY

Abusive individuals want to have their cake and eat it too: They want to be in control of everything, except when it better suits them to give that control over and blame others for their feelings or actions. For example, abusers will often state that someone has "made" them angry, sad, or violent, suggesting that they are led around on puppet strings, allowing others to force them into a particular behavior, through no fault of their own. This convenient method of avoiding responsibility also serves to project guilt onto others, most often the individual's partner. Abusers may even see themselves as the long-suffering victim in the relationship, an innocent and good man whose partner uses and takes advantage of him, relentlessly "pushing his buttons" until he snaps in a justified violent response.

Case in Point

Alana, twenty-five, dated a man who blamed everyone but himself for problems in his life. Accountability was not his strong suit, and it served him well when he became angry and abusive.

"When Dennis got mad, it was always because of me. He blamed me," she said. "When he got fired, it was because his boss was a jerk or a coworker had sabotaged him. When he got a DUI, it was because the bartender had overserved him. Dennis had an excuse for everything . . ."

Acclaimed author and psychologist Lundy Bancroft has this to say about accountability:

> Because of the distorted perceptions that the abuser has of rights and responsibilities in relationships, he considers himself to be the victim. Acts of self-defense on the part of the battered woman or the children, or efforts they make to stand up for their rights, he defines as aggression against him. He is often highly skilled at twisting his descriptions of events to create the convincing impression that he has been victimized. He thus accumulates grievances over the course of the relationship to the same extent that the victim does, which can lead professionals to decide that the members of

*the couple "abuse each other" and that the relationship has
been "mutually hurtful."* [5]

This trait is often visible in other arenas of a partner's life as
well, seen most clearly in places where he is required to demonstrate
responsibility, such as work or school. If your love interest has had
ten jobs in three years, it's likely that the economy is not to blame.
While he may string together a list of excuses about bad bosses,
conniving coworkers, and missed opportunities, it is essential to look
at specifically why he was fired or quit. Perhaps he was always late
and just angry that his supervisor noticed, or he failed to complete
assignments and then became indignant when confronted about it. It's
possible that he intimidates coworkers, using the same bully behavior
he shows at home. Abusers have a hard time taking direction from
anyone and cooperation for the good of the team is not in their self-
absorbed nature.

Constantly adopting the "injured party" stance enables an abuser
to assert that any negative situation such as abuse, unemployment, or
general failure in life is not his fault. Regardless of what he would like
you to believe, as adults we are all ultimately responsible for ourselves.
The differences in people's responses to various situations prove that
sane individuals are capable of controlling ourselves, some just choose
not to because it's the easy way out of culpability and shame.

LOW CAPACITY FOR FORGIVENESS/FOCUSED RAGE

People who obsess over vengeance against those they feel have
wronged them can be dangerous individuals because victimizing
their partner is key to their own satisfaction and resolution. Abusers
focused on revenge will never let a grudge go, but instead plot
actively to seek their reprisal. If you notice that your current or

former intimate partner constantly talks about retribution toward others, how long do you think it will be before he sets his sights on you? A ruminating lack of amnesty for even the smallest offenses combined with the tendency to act out physically creates the perfect recipe for violent conspiracy and preparation.

One particularly frightening aspect of some abusers' personalities is the ability to sustain rage over a long period of time, for hours or even days. Some women have experienced weeklong beatings, during which their perpetrator's anger never seemed to waive or subside. Some of these cases may be attributable to the artificial energy and aggression of certain drugs, but others have been perpetrated by entirely sober individuals. The tendency to preserve steady levels of fury and brutality is a highly lethal trait and may eventually result in what homicide detectives refer to as "overkill," signs of excessive ferocity such as sixty-five stab wounds on a body.

Another disturbing facet of some abusive anger is "cold rage," quiet and especially cruel expressions of wrath that seems almost enjoyable or stimulating to the abuser. When University of Washington researchers Dr. Neil Jacobson and Dr. John Gottman set out to explore abusive male partners, they hooked them up to machines that measured physiology indicators, such as blood pressure and heart rate, while they argued nonviolently with their wives in a clinical counseling session. What they found was astonishing: Some of the men actually grew calmer, inside and out, as they spouted icy, sadistic threats and verbal attacks. Instead of ramping up, they coiled and became calmer while their aggression increased; hence, the name the researchers gave them: "cobras."[6] These men were found to be more likely to use weapons against their partners and employ violence against strangers, children, and even pets. They are considered highly dangerous perpetrators and such a trait can be even riskier than the explosive, "hot" variety of rage.

MALEVOLENCE TOWARD/DISDAIN FOR WOMEN

Despite the obvious changes society has made in the past fifty years, many abusive men maintain rigid beliefs about gender roles. They may view men as intellectually and physically superior and think that husbands should control money and make major decisions alone. Many international cultures support this patriarchal worldview that, while backward, is not necessarily always violent. But beyond just being old-fashioned, an abuser's outlook becomes dangerous when combined with a genuine contempt and malice toward females. His objectification of them may be evident in degrading language, humor, or pornography. He may also show his disrespect by discounting the opinions or authority of women, frequently interrupting and talking over them, or refusing to show common courtesies to females in public. Even a man who doesn't openly admit to misogyny may exhibit subtle disapproval or condescension toward women based on their gender alone. If your current or former partner considers women to be inferior and even malevolent, he probably sees them as deserving of punishment and expendable as well.

NARCISSISTIC TRAITS

The true center of an abuser's world is most often himself. What he wants, needs, fears, and believes come first, and he is often annoyed at anyone else's request for attention. Getting his way is more important to him than anything and he will go to great lengths to achieve it. He does not believe that he must share with others, wait in line, or take no for an answer, so suggesting that he should can result in an angry reaction. Abusers are certain that the world owes them and will use this sense of entitlement to justify pushing everyone else out of their way. From the perspective of the abusive mind, you should drop everything when he calls on the phone, hang up on your sister when he wants to talk, stop talking when he wants to speak, and speak for him when he is too lazy to pick up the phone. It doesn't matter if you are busy, tired, sick, or sad. He may in fact escalate abuse at the very times when you need help, understanding, and support.

Take the case of a woman named Eileen I worked with in a support group for victims of domestic violence. Over several sessions, she shared stories about her husband, Tyler, who thought so much of himself that he often spoke of himself in third person, or referred to himself by nicknames such as "The King." But it wasn't simply insecurity at play; there was a sinister theme to his narcissism. Not only would he insist that Eileen wait on him hand and foot, but he sometimes forced her to kiss his shoes. If she refused, he shoved her face into the floor. Another time, Eileen had a sudden asthma attack and begged Tyler to take her to the hospital, but he refused to get off the telephone to help her. He later said he had been having a quarrel with his brother and wondered why Eileen didn't have more respect for his sibling relationships. According to Eileen, Tyler asked, "It's like you want me to drop everything to help you, even though I'm going through a difficult emotional moment. Why can't you think about my feelings once in a while?"

Like in Eileen's case, the abuser expects to be the center of *your* world as well as his own, and your failure to constantly confirm this position constitutes rejection to him. Anything other than complete and unquestioning support of such a person's every action and word can be seen as a betrayal. Perceived slights are magnified, ruminated on, and disproportionately responded to by insecure personalities with a maltreated mentality. The unpredictability of these individual's judgment can cause partners to "walk on eggshells," ever fearful of eliciting an emotionally or physically abusive response. When you consider that a breakup, divorce, or restraining order would probably feel like rejection to a hypersensitive egoist, you will see how this mentality can quickly turn dangerous.

Another related feature of abusers is an attitude of superiority and ascendancy. This is not to be confused with a healthy sense of self-confidence, which is a positive trait, but is rather an over-the-top feeling of arrogance and authority over others. An abuser may put down everyone around him because by doing so he feels that he is confirming his own dominance, while in truth he is masking his internal sense of inferiority. He may make comments typical of a racist, sexist, or classist, but when confronted, he'll insist that he is only "joking" and then attack the accuser for being humorless and sensitive.

Opinions that don't align with the abuser's are "stupid" or invalid, so social friction is common for him. Therefore, he surrounds himself with people who agree with him, or are too afraid to admit that they don't. While the classic narcissist spends a great deal of time promoting his hollow grandiosity, he often changes like a chameleon to suit his environment. He may treat you well in public because he is trying to cultivate a certain impression, but if things do not go his way, he will accuse others (particularly you) of making him look bad. In his mind, he is always right, always smarter, and always without blame in any situation. This trait can easily become part of a dangerous mindset when it manifests as a lack of empathy or conscience.

OBSESSION WITH VIOLENCE

Just because your partner likes boxing doesn't mean he is obsessed with violence. An individual may enjoy action movies, martial arts, true crime books, or war history without being abnormal or dangerous. However, someone who collects Nazi memorabilia, watches "snuff" films on the Internet, and forces his girlfriend to play "Russian roulette" should not be considered typical.

Does your significant other identify with violent characters, admiring acts of vengeance as bold and justified? These individuals can be very good at convincing you that their knowledge and interest in violence is innocent or even a source of protection (which they assure will never be used against you). The reality is that an abusive person who loves fighting and hurting will always eventually turn toward the target of their true control obsession, their partner. There is simply no reason to give a violence-focused man the benefit of the doubt when the world is full of peaceful, egalitarian partners.

Case in Point

Trina and her children were residents in a transitional housing program for domestic violence victims. As her caseworker, I made weekly home visits to her apartment as we labored through a yearlong self-sufficiency plan designed to enable Trina to get back on her feet. With four young children, an eighth-grade education, and no job skills, her challenges were many. Trina had fled her husband, Hugh, who was a brutally abusive man. He was a former Marine and current hunter/survivalist. She reported that he ran their home like a military unit, and that everyone from her children to their pets were terrified of his wrath. "Hugh has lots of guns and knives, but he also collects strange stuff like these black leather masks, and electric tasers," she told me. "He watches all these shows on TV about murder and searches the Internet on how to kill someone and get away with it. I would probably be dead right now if I didn't run. I also know that Hugh won't be happy until he finds me, and he's a good tracker so I don't know how long we can stay here . . ."

To this day, Trina is still looking over her shoulder.

OVERDEPENDENCE ON PARTNER

Another "Trojan Horse" emotion is overdependence upon and idolization of one's partner. Sure, it seems wonderful at first to have a man who "puts you on a pedestal," or seems to hang on your every word, making statements like, "You are my life" or "I couldn't live without you." He may have few genuine supports and claim that you are the only person who cares about him. But when this emotional "gift" opens up, an immature and insecure dependency spills out, showing itself to be dangerous when the idol no longer wants to participate in the relationship. Suddenly, the man who seemed to love you above even himself decides that he must keep you at all costs, regardless of your wishes. He may feel that your steps to separate from him constitute a betrayal after he has, in his eyes, given you everything.

Take Bonnie's example. At the beginning of their relationship, her boyfriend, Roman, presented well, and Bonnie was flattered by the way he doted on her, calling her constantly, and surprising her with flowers at work. He treated her like a goddess and told her that he had never been in such a close relationship before. But after a while, Bonnie got tired of his insistence on being together every second of the day. "Roman said we were star-crossed. He said that I made him whole and he would die if I ever broke up with him. After a while, that kind of talk made me feel icky, like he was weak and pathetic. I told him I didn't feel the same way about him, and I thought we needed some space. That's when he really went off the deep end. He actually showed up at my office and threatened to cut his wrists in the lobby. When I tried to get him to leave he started screaming at me in front of all my coworkers, yelling that I was a heartless bitch and a slut that just wanted to be with someone else. I felt so embarrassed, but even more so I was scared of what he would do next."

A person who expects you to be "together forever" will not tolerate rejection well. He may decide that if he can't have you, no one will, and therefore begins to rationalize and justify the contemplation of violent action. Even if his thoughts don't result in abuse, who wants to be with a man who has no life beyond his relationship? The ideal partner has varied interests and contact points to the outside world; he is devoted but independent and respectful of his partner's space as well. Look for greatness in lovers, and you will find it—just be sure you've defined greatness the right way and that what you are seeing is actually what you will get.

PARANOID TENDENCIES

Subjects who carry this trait are not necessarily diagnosable as paranoid in the clinical sense, but may exhibit delusions of persecution or betrayal that influence their abuse. For example, a former client told me how her boyfriend held a knife to her throat, believing he had heard her having sex with his best friend in a bedroom during a party they attended. In reality, what he had heard was the audio from a pornographic film playing inside the room, a room she wasn't even in. Unable to convince him of his error, she was terrorized and assaulted for six hours before escaping to get help.

In other cases I have worked on, abusers have accused their partners of sleeping with the district attorney, bribing the police, and conspiring to have them fired. These men believe that the world is "out to get them" and if they ever give up their position of control, everything will come crashing down around them. They constantly struggle to gain power over others in order to escape the feeling of being powerless. This relentless sense of victimhood and defensiveness can combine, causing a subject to move rapidly across the continuum from paranoid thoughts to violent actions.

SENSE OF OWNERSHIP/POSSESSIVENESS OVER VICTIM

According to English and early American Common Law, once married, all of a woman's land, possessions, body parts, and rights belonged to her husband. She and their children became viewed legally and socially as his property. Some abusers probably wish they could return to a time when women were chattel and could be beaten, abandoned, or

Case in Point

To an abuser, sometimes the sense of ownership is not nearly enough. There must be a clear reminder of it, and in many cases, it comes in the form of permanent tattoos.

Take Nikki, a memorable young woman I once counseled who told me that she felt like people "got the wrong impression" of her because of the poorly drawn letters adorning her arms. Her ex-boyfriend Carlos had demanded that she get his name and some gang symbols permanently inked into her skin within the first few months of dating. She said that he frequently assaulted her in public and even seemed proud of the bruises he left on her body. "Everyone was afraid of Carlos," she explained. "In the beginning, I was kind of attracted to that because dating him gave me status in the neighborhood and I felt like he could protect me. I had seen my father and uncles abuse their partners that way and I thought it was normal." Pulling up her sleeves to show me the tattoos, she said, "But now I realize that he was the one I needed protection from. He treated me like I was his dog or something. I couldn't even speak to other people without his permission. I was able to get away from Carlos but I'll never forget him, because all I have to do is look at my arms. This ink is so ugly, and I know strangers look at me like I'm some kind of thug or a piece of trash. I feel marked."

slaughtered like livestock. In this dangerous perpetrator's mind, you belong to him both in and out of the relationship, and his likelihood of violence increases with sexual intimacy. In other words, if you have had intercourse with him, he probably feels even more bound to you and the outdated masculine tradition of men owning their partners.

In some street gangs, a woman in a relationship with a member is expected to have his name tattooed either on her neck or on her wrists (like handcuffs). This is the abuser's way of "marking his territory" and serves as a message to other males that sleeping with "his" woman is punishable by death, even if he is no longer dating her. I have met many remorseful women with a man's full name or street moniker inked into their skin, unable to get jobs due to the obvious gang-affiliated mark, and unable to escape their abuser's tag no matter how much they change their lives. Other women don't have the tattoos but the message is implicit: *If I can't have you no one will!* These are some of the most dangerous words in the English language. The person who says this is asserting his entrenched conviction that you have no right to a life that doesn't revolve around him, and he may be willing to enforce that belief with extreme violent actions.

As you will discover in the following chapter, the characteristics listed here can manifest in some very dangerous behaviors. The bottom line when assessing a new partner's tendencies is to ask yourself, "Does this trait stand alone or is it coupled up with other features and actions that indicate an abusive or potentially abusive man?" Either way, consider carefully if this person is worthy of the best you've got to give. Time is impossible to get back, particularly if you've wasted it trying to please or reform an abusive partner. Don't lose another minute of your life on someone who doesn't deserve it.

Chapter 7

Clear and Present Danger:
Risk Factors by Behavior/Method of Abuse

*Evil is unspectacular and always human, and
shares our bed and eats at our own table.*
—W. H. Auden

The idea that somebody who purports to love you could end up killing
you is inconceivable to most, let alone the awareness that you may
be in a potentially lethal relationship to begin with. To be sure, not
all abusive relationships accelerate to murder, nor are all abusive men
potential killers, but one fact is indisputable: All intimate partner
murders are committed by perpetrators who were abusive in one form
or another—from the subtle to the extreme.

Today in the United States, intimate partner homicide takes up
to four female lives each day—mothers, sisters, daughters, and best
friends.[1] Murder is the leading cause of death among African American
women aged fifteen to forty-five years, and the seventh leading cause of

premature death among women overall. Approximately 1,500–1,700 women per year are known to have been murdered by a current or former intimate partner.[2] I stress the word *known,* because this figure is derived from Supplemental Homicide Reports collected from law enforcement agencies by the Federal Bureau of Investigation as part of their Uniform Crime Reporting System. It does not include the missing women, those whose bodies have never been found, and those whose killer was never identified or proven guilty.

Most sources tell us that about one-third of femicides are committed by a spouse, boyfriend, or ex-spouse.[3] However, deeper statistical analysis shows us a more disturbing picture. Because these figures don't include a category for *ex*-boyfriends, we are missing a large chunk of intimate partner murders. If we include the previous partner (nonmarried) group, we find that up to 60 percent of women murdered are killed by a current or former intimate partner.[4]

Sadly, in cases where abuse has become deadly, it's often not just the woman who is killed. Children, family members, friends, and even neighbors or innocent bystanders may fall victim to an abuser's murderous acts.

One tragic example of this took place in Oregon during February of 2010. Charlotte Grahn, forty-seven, was socializing with two female friends in a local restaurant when her husband Jeffrey, a sheriff's deputy, came through the door. The couple had filed for divorce the previous August but were still living together with their children on that fateful night. Charlotte's relatives report that she was frightened of Jeffrey but concerned that if she reported his behaviors, he might lose his job as a law enforcement officer. Witnesses at the restaurant that night say that Jeffrey demanded to talk to Charlotte outside, and then soon after shot and killed her on the sidewalk. He then went inside and murdered her friends Kathleen Hoffmeister and Victoria Schulmerich before committing his final act of cowardice in turning the gun on himself. Most of us wouldn't think twice about offering support to a friend in danger, but it's important to keep in mind that an abuser will often target those who he sees as helping the victim or encouraging her to leave, so use caution.

How does abuse escalate to this deadly point? In abusive relationships, what risk factors might be seen *before* the lethal event occurs? As you read above, there are as many paths to murder as there are potentially murderous abusers. This chapter will help you identify behaviors in your partner that may be signs of imminent, perhaps even mortal, danger.

ACCESS TO AND/OR USE OF FIREARMS

When discussing this topic, it is important to differentiate those with a healthy interest in weapons from those with a dangerous fixation. For example, a legitimate sportsman may collect firearms, but a "gun freak" talks about and carries them constantly, fondling and playing with them, threatening or bragging about using them against people. He may perceive himself as a kind of "Rambo" avenger, talking about weapons as instruments of power or equalizers. If an attraction to guns stands alone, it might be considered a hobby, but when combined with other abusive traits, a perilous picture emerges. While having a gun doesn't cause someone to murder, it certainly makes the act a lot easier and more likely to be successful if one is predisposed to violence.

If an otherwise abusive man has a gun, even if he has never threatened his partner with it, her risk is increased simply because it's accessible. Most intimate partner homicides in America are committed using firearms, and according to researchers, the mere presence of a firearm in the home leaves abused women at five times greater risk of murder than other abused women. If the victim is threatened with a weapon, her risk increases to twenty times.[5] Contrary to popular belief, most guns used to kill intimate partners were not stolen, borrowed, or acquired on the black market, but legally owned by the abuser.[6] If your abusive partner totes a weapon, Chapter 12 offers several possible strategies to reduce your risk.

THREATS TO KILL

Receiving a threat can be a frightening experience, particularly if you are unsure about the aggressor's intent or capacity to follow through with it. Some threats are just that—they don't automatically mean you're in danger. The question that professional threat assessors ask when faced with verbal, written, or symbolic evidence of threats is the following: "Is this subject *making* a threat or *posing* a threat?" Is he all talk and no action, or more concerning, all action and no talk? Because the absence of an outward threat doesn't mean you are safe.

If the dead could talk, we would probably learn that most domestic killers had threatened their partner before committing homicide. According to police records and the friends and family of murdered women, 73 percent of them did.[7] This leads us to ask: Were the remaining 27 percent threatened and no one knew about it, or were their killers actually silent before striking? When domestic violence researcher and therapist David Adams interviewed victims of attempted murder, he found that 90 percent of them had received death threats from their abuser before separating from him, and a full 100 percent received threats afterward.[8] This information tells us that women who are threatened in relationships and those who are not may both be at risk.

Understanding the following four key factors (Context, Content, Direction, and Purpose) can help you make better decisions around which threats portend harm and which ones are actually designed to do something different, such as intimidate or manipulate.

• *Context*—Consider how and under what circumstances the threat is delivered. For example, if an otherwise healthy, nonabusive couple is arguing and one of them says "Ugh! You make me so mad, I could just kill you sometimes!" this statement may be seen as inappropriate but wouldn't necessarily be considered a serious threat. However, if a victim of domestic violence who has just left her abuser finds a note on her car describing what he will do with her severed body parts, she is likely in very grave danger.

• *Content*—As a general rule, the more detailed the threat, the more likely it is to be played out. Even a minimally identifiable plot shows that an abuser has put genuine consideration into how he will commit murder, and often, how he will get away with it. According to forensic psychologist and threat assessment expert Dr. Reid Meloy, there are three levels of threat:

1. A **Low Risk** threat is one that is vague, with no precise plan and/or little plausibility. For example, if your abuser says, "You're going to pay for sending me divorce papers," it is hard to know exactly what he means. Is he saying that you'll pay a lawyer or pay with your life? Even though it seems ambiguous, that does not mean the statement should be ignored. It depends on the circumstances. Likewise, if a man serving a life sentence in prison threatens to personally show up on your doorstep with a gun, his plan contains little credibility and is therefore highly unlikely. (But contact the parole board just in case!)

2. A **Medium Risk** threat is more concrete, with at least some general indications on the time and place it will be carried out. For instance, if an abuser were to say, "When these divorce proceedings are over, I'm going to kill you," that would be more concerning because he has designated a timeline, a trigger point, and he has a definite violent action in mind. This type of threat should definitely be reported, and in many cases, it may constitute a crime on its own.

3. A **High Risk** threat is one that is direct, specific, plausible, timed, and includes a plan of action. For example, if your estranged abuser says, "When you show up to get the kids tomorrow at noon, I'm going to blow your head off with my hunting rifle!" such a statement should be considered extremely dangerous and possibly indicative of close-range planning, meaning that attack may be imminent. Inform law enforcement immediately and follow your safety plan, if you have one in place. At a minimum, make other arrangements for a safe custody exchange and have the safety of the children evaluated. In many states, such words are grounds for the charge of "terroristic threats" or "menacing," and in most cases, offenders should be held accountable for uttering them, regardless of their intent to follow through.

- *Direction*—Ask yourself to whom the threat was communicated. Did he say it directly to you or did it come through another pipeline? If it was said to another person, did he intend for you to hear about it?

When an abuser threatens you, he may be doing it just to maintain or regain control of the relationship. Similarly, if he mentions his thoughts to someone whom he knows you're close to, he might be using that person as a conduit for fear, to scare and embarrass you. This doesn't mean the threat should be ignored, but it should be examined in light of other factors. However, if the abuser tells a third party (particularly one who has no communication with you) that he *intends* to hurt you, there may be more cause for concern. He may not have threatened you directly because he doesn't want you to see it coming and therefore get help or escape. Also, just the act of speaking his intentions may trigger the next phase. Said aloud, an idea becomes more comfortable

Case in Point

When an abuser's threats extend beyond the relationship, it is not only terrifying to hear but may be a sign of greater risk for follow through. Corinne, age thirty, is an example. After her ex-boyfriend's threats accelerated, she sought out help. "When I first left my abuser, Caleb, he made all sorts of subtle threats toward me, ones that were hard to distinguish, like, 'What comes around goes around, bitch.' But I wasn't really scared until I ran into a mutual friend who told me some concerning news. He said that Caleb had shown him a revolver and stated he was going to 'use it on me.' It was far more frightening to hear it from someone else's mouth, because I knew Caleb felt really strongly about being respected, and he wouldn't want his friends to see him as a bull-shitter or a coward."

and plausible, and gains traction as a potential action. He may even feel that telling others about the plan forces him to *save face* by following through, so everyone will see him as a *man of his word,* even if the word is deadly.

- *Purpose*—Many abusers do not use threats to foretell of future violence, but rather simply as a tool to manipulate and terrorize their partners. They can become a powerful instrument of control, especially if the recipient believes that her actions will influence the likelihood of follow-through. A crafty abuser will tailor his threat to exactly what is most precious or frightening to his partner. This can range from threatening physical harm to her or

Case in Point

The first time I heard Margaret's voice was on a domestic violence hotline I was covering. She whispered and kept putting the phone down to listen for footsteps. "I can't talk long," she said. "He'll be coming back soon." Margaret explained that she was terrified of her violent husband, Jack. He was a gun dealer and hunter who ran their home like a prison, forcing his wife and children to live as virtual slaves who suffered regular beatings. "Jack said if I leave him, he'll slaughter me like a deer and then sell my daughters to a child porn ring. I'd be okay with sacrificing my life for theirs, but what's the point of running if their fate will be worse than mine?" Fortunately for Margaret and her children, Jack's violent ways became his own demise. He was shot and killed by another man in a bar fight several months after Margaret and I first made contact. She and her daughters are now living free.

someone she loves, to public embarrassment, financial ruin, or abandonment. Playing on her guilt, abusers also commonly threaten suicide. In keeping with their goal, most of these threats are conditional, requiring his victim to act on his demands. These include resuming the relationship from which she was trying to escape, or changing legal actions she's taken, such as recanting testimony or dropping a protection order.

Many people think that by definition, a threat is a promise of specific fate, and that unless they actually hear the words "I'm going to kill you/her" the subject has not really demonstrated danger, or at least they don't see enough imminent probability of follow-through to warrant action. In reality, the threats of a domestic abuser can often be far more vague and mysterious. In one recent intimate partner homicide, the abuser used spray paint to draw a big black "X" in the driveway of his victim several days before killing her. Just because a message is indecipherable doesn't mean it should be ignored.

Threats may even come in the form of silence. What if you knew your partner to be a vengeful and violent abuser, yet during your contentious divorce he was quiet and composed, never once showing his anger? It is possible that he underwent a miraculous change or decided to take the high road for the children's sake, but he also might be what I refer to as a "seether," someone who keeps all his fury under the surface and then detonates under pressure. Instead of outwardly threatening his victim, a seether may exhibit what domestic violence researcher David Adams refers to as a "slow burn," longstanding grudges that progress as a contemptuous detachment as opposed to the intermittent bursts of a "short fuse." Particularly beware the subject who typically rages loudly and publicly but then suddenly falls silent without obvious reason. This period of stillness may signal a "calm before the storm" in which the subject is lying low, plotting and anticipating an impending attack.

SUBSTANCE ABUSE

The ancient and wise Latin saying *In Vino Veritas* reminds us that "in wine there is truth," something that abusers would have us forget. Simply put, whatever is deep within the core of a person often rises when they are under the influence of alcohol or other intoxicants. Alcohol doesn't change people into someone they are not, it just lowers the walls of inhibition that normally hide our true selves. For example, a generally pleasant person will usually become a happy and animated drunk. An individual who is depressed inside will sometimes cry or become withdrawn when drinking. But someone who carries deep-seated anger and insecurity may become belligerent and violent to those around them, instigating fights without provocation. The next day, these people will either minimize or deny their actions, stating that they don't remember what they did or said (how convenient!). They may also blame the alcohol, stating that they never would have behaved that way if they were sober. While this may be true, those capabilities exist regardless of his state, and remaining sober will probably not change that.

Also, some abusers may intentionally get drunk before confrontations so they have an excuse to act without inhibition. Domestic abuse researchers agree that men who have a history of substance abuse show higher risk for violence and murder. Dr. Jacqueline Campbell found that regardless of an abuser's past patterns, intoxication at the time of the assault (particularly in the case of illicit street drugs) shows significant risk to partners.[9] Similarly, David Adams reports that substance abuse preceded half of the domestic murders he studied (meaning that an intoxicant was used on the same day as the killing), although this was not a departure from the abuser's normal pattern of use.[10]

You may want desperately to believe that your partner abused you because he was drunk, and he may try emphatically to convince you of such, thus absolving himself of fault. But at some point you must question his view of common adult responsibility. If someone truly is "out of control" when drinking, and others have repeatedly told them as much, isn't it their duty to keep their consumption and behavior in check? No one should be allowed to retain the attitude of "I'm just a loose cannon when I drink, and everyone around me has no choice but to deal with whatever I dish out." The truth is that we do have a choice, so ask yourself now, what comes to the surface when your partner becomes intoxicated?

HISTORY OF BURGLARY

Burglary is not merely a property crime. It is the act of entering a premises with the intention of committing theft or another offense. When someone does this they are telling the world "I don't care about the rights or the security of this person, I will violate whenever I please." This is a dangerous attitude, and its bearer will use it to justify his actions in burglary or other more physical crimes. Abusers enter their current or former partner's dwelling or vehicle by breaking in, coming through an open window or door, or using a key that she may not realize he has. They may even convince a third party to let them in under false pretenses. Many do so to steal, spy, or vandalize, but some enter just to send a specific message: "You are not safe. I can get to you whenever I want." Sometimes they will snoop around the victim's home, leaving notes or small clues that only she will notice such as shifted furniture or belongings—whatever they think will achieve the spooky, violated feeling they want their victim to experience.

Other abusers burglarize with the intent of physically or sexually assaulting their current or former intimate partner. When David Adams looked into domestic killings, he found that over half of the perpetrators either broke in or entered uninvited to murder their victim.[11] For this reason, you should exercise caution when dealing with someone who has a past history of burglary attempts or convictions, whether they have been arrested or have simply told you about their secret talent. They are not only willing to commit the crime but likely have knowledge on how to pop locks and evade security systems. If this is a concern in your situation, please pay extra attention to the home-based target hardening section in Chapter 12.

Case in Point

I once worked for several years on a case that went to court multiple times for issues ranging from protective orders to child custody battles. The abuser would break into his victim's home time after time, solely for the purpose of upsetting and frightening her. He was very adept at picking locks, removing screens, and other tricks of the burglary trade, so that no matter how often the locksmith visited her home, he still always got in. Once inside, he would do things like steal medications, remove sentimental belongings, and leave notes that read "BOOM!" This word was particularly scary because the victim knew he had been a military explosives expert before they met.

KIDNAPPING/FALSE IMPRISONMENT/RESTRAINT

Once upon a time, a woman told her best friend how her husband had locked her in a closet over a period of several hours, beating her and leaving only to return every twenty minutes or so to repeat the assaults. In between the segments of violence, he watched football in an adjacent room. Within a year of that report, the woman was dead, her throat slit at her own home. That woman was Nicole Brown Simpson, and despite her husband's legal acquittal, strong evidence remains that he was most likely her killer.

When an abuser ties up his victim, handcuffs her, or locks her in a room or a small space, such as a car's trunk, he is sending a powerful message, indicating that he feels a sense of ownership over the victim and will go to great lengths to torture and abuse her. Kidnapping can be part of a homicide plan and is frequently the first step to containing a victim, whether the outcome ends in injury or not.

In one case I served on, a successful professional woman named Kaylee had been kidnapped and assaulted by her long-term partner, Aaron. They had broken up several months before and Kaylee had remained in the home they shared while Aaron moved to a new apartment across town. One day, Aaron showed up on Kaylee's doorstep demanding to come in so they could "talk." When Kaylee refused and tried to shut the door, Aaron produced a handgun. "Get in the car!" he told Kaylee. "We're going for a ride." They drove to Aaron's new apartment, where he tied Kaylee to a chair and gagged her mouth with a cloth. Aaron sat on the bed with the gun pointed at Kaylee and said, "We're going to stay here together until we work this thing out." Fortunately, after more than twelve hours, Aaron finally fell asleep and Kaylee was able to untie her hands and flee the apartment.

At its core, kidnapping is a symbol of the possessiveness an abuser feels over his partner and restricting her movement is how he tells her that she is not a free person. In his deluded mind, she belongs to him.

THREATS OF (OR ATTEMPTS AT) SUICIDE

Imagine what went through Alisha's mind as she entered the bedroom of her apartment and saw her boyfriend Robert face down on the floor. Empty pill bottles surrounded him, and a few stray caplets were scattered around his mouth. For all the world, it appeared like he had killed himself, just as he said he would, because Alisha had decided to go to work instead of stay home with him while he battled an apparent bout of depression. She was hysterically crying, consumed with guilt and grief, when Robert sat up and laughed at her. "Self-centered bitch," he spat. "Do you really think I'd kill myself over you?" It had all been a sick joke, a control tactic that would repeat itself several months later as he stood on the roof of their building, threatening to jump to his death. Robert's power over Alisha finally ended when she mustered the courage to tell him that she wasn't responsible for his actions or his safety. She withdrew herself from the blame game and asserted to Robert that control of his life (and death) was completely in his own hands and she would never again be made to feel guilty for not bowing to his manipulative demands.

While some abusers may be sincere about suicide and some may not, there is another reason that you will want to exercise caution when dealing with their threats. The consensus among many prominent researchers is that when combined with other risk factors, suicidal equals homicidal. In fact, time and time again I've heard law enforcement officers say: "The only difference between homicide and suicide is 90 degrees and half a second," meaning that the decision to take someone out with you (or instead of you) can be instantaneous for a suicidal individual. One fatality review team found that 41 percent of intimate partner homicides studied included prior threat of suicide by the perpetrator.[12] In contrast, only about a third of domestic killings include suicide of the murderer, which means some of these guys didn't have the guts to do to themselves what they did to their partner.[13] In some cases, we see killers who give themselves superficial or non-life-threatening wounds after murdering their partner, for the purpose of eliciting pity and appearing as suicidal individuals, when in reality they are calculating slayers.

> ## ⚠ Take Action
>
> If your partner, or anyone you know, is threatening suicide, it is likely beyond your ability to assess the seriousness of the threat. Call the police or put him in touch with a counselor or hospital immediately. Many towns have suicide hotlines where you can talk to a clinician right away. If your partner is serious about suicide, he might be more willing to accept help than the abuser who is simply looking to manipulate. However, a person who is truly and irreversibly bent on killing himself will often tell no one, and simply act on their own. Remember, it's not your job to fix a broken man. The best you can do is guide them toward a professional and let them take it from there. Start by contacting the National Suicide Prevention Lifeline at 1-800-273-TALK.

Some abusers who walk the line between killing themselves and killing another may use less specific language around their threats. They may engage in "end game" talk, speech that may indicate they are coming to a lethal resolution of the violent thoughts they have struggled over. For example, an abusive partner who talks vaguely about an "ending" to the current situation or an impending "solution" to the couple's problems may have an ominous plan up his sleeve.

Certain abusers may even try to trigger an event in which they hurt you, themselves, or someone else. For instance, I have been told by many women that their abuser asked to be struck or even killed—"Go ahead, hit me, shoot me!" they would say, "Put me out of my misery!" These abusers may have been trying to evoke pity in their victims or instigate an assault that would turn around, moving from a masochistic request to an attack on their partner—one that could be construed by others as self-defense. Some may even be hoping to create a barricade situation that could turn into a suicide-by-cop, or lay out a trap for unsuspecting officers or relatives to enter.

Do not underestimate a suicidal abuser, and do not let your guard down just because he is asking you for sympathy or support. An unstable individual can turn on you at the drop of a hat, so be sure to get immediate outside help if your partner has threatened to take his own life.

STRANGULATION

Of all the violent behaviors that abusers engage in, strangulation stands out as particularly dangerous. Its presence in an abusive relationship is indicative of extremely heightened risk for the victim. Many women call this act "choking" because that is the feeling they experience when it happens to them. But by definition, choking refers to an object, such as a piece of food, being caught in the throat, not someone else preventing you from breathing.

Although strangulation often goes unreported, it is fairly common in abusive relationships. One study of battered women found that 68 percent of abused women interviewed had been strangled by their partner.[14] Going one step further, Dr. Jacqueline Campbell discovered that more than half of intimate partner homicide victims had been strangled (not necessarily in moment of death, but previously in that relationship).[15] Strangulation remains an obvious signal of lethal potential and can be more deadly than other types of assault, for several key reasons:

- Only 8 pounds of pressure is needed to strangle a human being, even less if that person has a small or fragile neck. This means that it is a relatively quick and easy way for an abuser to kill his victim during an assault.

- Some batterers use repeated strangulation as a punishment or torture to control their partners. They may do it dozens of times throughout the relationship, increasing her risk of permanent brain damage. The reflex system in our bodies that allows us to "bounce back" from a lack of oxygen occurring during asphyxiation becomes inoperable after fifty seconds of sustained pressure. Therefore, even if a perpetrator is not intending to kill his victim, he may do so by not releasing his grip in time.

- Strangulation can kill a victim hours, days, or even weeks after it occurs due to medical issues such as a preexisting blood clot that is released during strangulation, a collapse of internal structures in the throat, or a septic shock reaction that can be caused by the undetected death of a fetus in a pregnant woman who is strangled.

Case in Point

One of the most tragic cases I've worked with was that of Melissa, a soft-spoken woman in her early forties who at first appeared to have a mental disability. She had trouble finishing sentences, couldn't remember facts, and had a very short attention span. After meeting with her several times, I encouraged her to get a medical evaluation, and we realized Melissa's communication difficulties were actually from hypoxic brain damage incurred during one or more of the hundreds of times her abusive husband had strangled her. "He robbed her," said Melissa's sister angrily. "He stole my sister's mind, and almost cost her her life."

The act of strangulation sends a powerful message to a victim: "I can kill you anytime, anywhere I want using nothing but my own body—I literally have your life in my hands." It is a death threat in itself and should be treated as such, even if it is not accompanied by a verbal warning.

PHYSICAL ASSAULT

Violence in the home causes more injuries to women than car accidents, muggings, and rapes combined, and while the insult and injury of domestic assault is traumatic in itself, it also represents a greater risk of homicide than relationships that include only psychological abuse. Researchers concur that the majority of intimate-partner homicides involve previous incidents of physical abuse in the relationship. Some of these findings have come from interviews with loved ones of deceased victims as opposed to police reports, due to issues with the underreporting and misclassification of crimes.

It is important to remember when we discuss violence that it comes in many forms, some of which are as unique and bizarre as abusers themselves (see Chapter 2). I would avoid structuring levels of violence as it would be unfair to compare the experiences of victims, but it is fair to make a separate category for types of physical abuse that do not result in injury because they can easily be overlooked and dismissed when they do not cause lasting pain or effect. In some of the cases I've worked on, women who've landed in the hospital from a severe beating or attempted homicide reported that until that episode, physical abuse had been limited to a shove now and again, which they didn't believe was abuse. This is indicative of the many women who believe that being "hit" consists of a full strike to the face, and do not consider themselves abused if their partner perpetrates lighter, non-injurious assaults, such as the ones discussed in Chapter 2.

Physical abuse may also be directed toward someone other than the victim, such as a child, pet, or other family member. This serves the dual purpose of punishing the victim, and simultaneously showing her what the abuser is capable of. Although these deeds are not necessarily directed at the primary victim, they should be considered dangerous and an indicator of future, often escalating abuse.

The "ramping up" of violence is also in itself a cause for concern. Many domestic homicide researchers have noted an uptick in the severity and frequency of physical abuse in the months and weeks before a killing.

VIOLENT/DEVIANT PORNOGRAPHY

As common sense might dictate, the average *Playboy* reader does not qualify for this category and someone who casually views mainstream pornography does not either. It is the viewers of rape images, child pornography, and "snuff films" who cause concern. In an interview with the group Morality in Media, retired NYPD Detective Raymond Pierce stated that in his professional opinion as a criminal-profiling consultant, about 80 percent of rapists and serial killers are heavy pornography users.[16]

And some reports show that increasing numbers of women who request help for domestic abuse are reporting that their abuser viewed pornography.[17]

Researcher David Adams found that while the killers he interviewed didn't differ much from nonlethal abusers in their viewing habits of traditional pornography, they were six times more likely to use child pornography, perhaps suggesting that interest in deviant sexual subjects can be linked to a propensity toward lethal violence.[18]

HOSTAGE TAKING

I had only been working with Brandy for three days when the hostage call came in. She and her boyfriend Doug had been holed up in a hotel room using meth for two days straight, and sometime during the binge he began beating her. Doug, a mentally ill addict, had done this before, often calling 911 himself to instigate a response. Brandy said it was almost a game to him, to see how many officers with guns he could bring to the location—he even liked to watch his stand-offs live on television from inside the hotel while they were occurring. This time, however, was a bit different. Doug didn't seem to want the attention as much as he wanted to hurt Brandy. He pulled her outside onto the balcony of the hotel facing a dozen cops and held her in front of him, a knife to her throat. Brandy was already covered in blood, making the police unsure about whether or not she had been stabbed. "I didn't think I was going to get out of that one alive," said Brandy. "I could feel his heart pounding through his chest and into my back as we stood outside. There was something about his face that day, his voice, that made me think my number was up." Eventually, hostage negotiators talked Doug down and took him into custody.

Luck was on Brandy's side that afternoon, but women have to rely on more than good providence to stay safe from partners like Doug.

An abuser who takes his victim hostage, deliberately drawing police attention in an effort to create a stand-off or suicide-by-cop situation is a very dangerous individual. The FBI estimates that between 75 and 90 percent of all hostage takings in the United States are related to domestic violence situations.[19] High-risk factors in a hostage situation include a perpetrator's use of weapons, direct threats against the victim with no demands, threats of suicide, a history of violence and similar behaviors, and an abuser with multiple life stressors and few supports.

USE OF WEAPONS IN ASSAULTS

Use of weapons during assaults can take on many forms. For example, aside from being used to shoot someone, a gun can be brandished, pointed at them, placed to their head or inside their mouth, fired next to them, or used to pistol whip. Many women report that their partners have verbally threatened them with a gun in the home, either by plainly stating that they will shoot them or simply making comments or gestures that are mutually understood. One woman I worked with named Rebecca talked about how her husband kept several guns in the basement of their home. Whenever they argued, he would start toward the cellar door and say, "Do I have to go downstairs now or are you going to shut up?" Another woman named Ann told me that her partner, a law enforcement officer, kept his firearm under his side of the bed, near the pillow. He would sit over it, on the edge of the mattress during conflicts, as if to indicate that death was only a reach away. These men never actually brandished their guns but their intentions were clear just the same.

Other weapons can be used to threaten and terrorize as well. For example, I will never forget Maggie, a developmentally disabled woman whose case I handled for more than two years. She told me that her partner often held a screwdriver to her neck during arguments. While this would be petrifying to anyone, it was even more so for Maggie because she knew he had spent ten years in jail on a murder charge for stabbing a man in the neck. Even when not combined with abusive maneuvers, his history alone was enough to prevent Maggie from escaping, out of complete and constant fear.

Even common household items can become weapons in the hands of an abuser. Everyday articles such as belts, plates, shoes, chairs, telephones, pens, and lamps can be transformed into tools of terror. However, most weapons used to kill are designed for such, and many have been preacquired by abusive individuals with the intention of using them for the purpose of violence.

ANIMAL CRUELTY

In many abusive homes, the perpetrator is like an advanced version of the schoolyard bully, someone who wants to perpetuate an environment of control and omniscient power. Generally, bullies avoid conflict with someone who can hurt them and will instead choose to intimidate a victim they consider weaker and less likely to fight back or report their behavior. In many cases, this means the family pet. Aside from the typical beatings or torture that one might expect from a perpetrator of animal cruelty, domestic abusers often use pets as leverage to threaten, manipulate, or distress their primary victim. On the occasion in which I had my wisdom teeth removed, I experienced just such a tactic. My abuser stood over me while I laid in bed after the operation, drugged on pain medications, with a mouth full of bloody gauze. "I got rid of your fucking dog while you were gone," he said with a dark smile. I couldn't speak, so I wrote on a nearby pad of paper, "What did you do to her?" "I took her out to the woods and left her there," he replied. "Please go get her!" I begged in pencil, tears rolling down my face. "I can't," he said, "I lied. She's already dead." Several hours later he left and returned with the dog, unharmed. The whole story had been a ploy of psychological torture, conjured up to confuse and upset me while I lay in a vulnerable state. It was his way of getting back at me for the crime of, as he said, "Loving the dog more than I loved him."

According to the ASPCA, there is a significant connection between animal cruelty and domestic violence. They cite a Wisconsin study in which four out of five battered women indicated that their partners had also been violent toward pets or livestock at their home.[20] Similarly, a survey by the National Coalition Against Domestic Violence discovered that 71 percent of women at domestic violence shelters reported incidents of pet abuse.[21] In an effort to curb these numbers, some states have begun to include protection for pets within restraining orders. In other places, battered women's shelters are partnering with animal

> ⚠ **Take Action**
>
> If fear for the safety of a pet is causing you to stay in a dangerous situation, please visit the following link for a Humane Society list of Safe Haven Programs: www.humanesociety.org/issues/abuse_neglect/tips/safe_havens_directory.html

assistance organizations to provide temporary "Safe Havens" for pets, while their owners are fleeing domestic abuse.

MURDER PRACTICE

Although no major study has been conducted on this theory, many cases seem to indicate that if an abuser has made a failed attempt to kill his victim, or he has committed an assault that could easily have resulted in her death—regardless of his stated intentions—her chances of actually being killed by him in the future may skyrocket. Through these actions, he has shown himself to be both mentally and physically capable of homicide and may have actually been rehearsing to see if he was. As researcher David Adams discovered, the only difference between the killers and would-be killers that he studied was the ineptitude of the latter. These were not men who changed their minds partway through a homicide attempt, backing off because they felt guilty or scared. Their victims lived only because the abusers failed to use guns (the most effective and guaranteed lethal tool), they failed to plan properly, and their targets received medical attention quickly enough to save their lives.[22]

If you have ever been the victim of a near-lethal assault, consider the actions of the perpetrator during and after the event. Many survivors of attempted murders report that their abuser's face looked different than they had ever previously seen it, that he looked "evil" or "possessed." They also mention postattack behaviors that indicate the subject's perceived success. For example, one woman told me that she was stabbed by her boyfriend and collapsed, only to hear him call his brother on the phone and say, "Come pick me up, I finally killed her." Another recounted a severe strangulation ending in unconsciousness. She awoke to see her husband entering the room with black plastic garbage bags and a shovel.

As demonstrated in the previous examples, the methods of abuse that a perpetrator uses can be as varied as the individuals themselves. Some are extreme, but just because your partner has never put a gun to your head or strangled you, doesn't mean you aren't at risk. Nearly 30 percent of intimate partner homicides included no previously reported physical abuse. Don't underestimate an abuser based on a lack of egregious violence. Any of the above listed behaviors are important stop signs to observe, and all indicate a need to take immediate steps toward safety. Even after committing some of the more concerning actions, your abuser may try to convince you that he has the ability and intent to change. Please don't believe him without reading the following chapter.

Chapter 8

But He Can Change, Right?
Knowing When and How to
Make Self-Protective Decisions

The best protection any woman
can have . . . is courage.
—Elizabeth Cady Stanton

If the partner you are with has shown any of the behaviors identified as already abusive, I'm going to be painfully honest with you about the likely prognosis for your union. The most difficult thing you'll have to face won't be recognizing that the man in your life—whether it's a new boyfriend or long-time husband—possesses abusive traits, perhaps even six, ten, or fifteen red flags. The difficult, often heart-wrenching part, will be choosing how to act on that knowledge. Your reflexive heart core may resist the idea of letting him go, because all the sweet, endearing memories of your lover will come rushing in to defend his actions. Altruism and sentimentality will combine to create an idealized image of the man you wished or thought he was, and the person you think he has the potential to someday be.

As women, we tell ourselves that we can shape our partners, buffing out the rough spots and accentuating the good qualities. While some of these rationalizations can be harmless, ignoring potentially dangerous signals can put us at risk by suppressing the very survival

Case in Point

"I've always been a fixer," explained Krista, age thirty-one. "Every friend or boyfriend that entered my life became like a project to me, and I was convinced that with the right amount of love and support, anyone can become a better person. When I met Doug, I knew I had my work cut out for me. He was a brilliant musician but couldn't stay sober long enough to keep a gig. Doug had a rough life and a lot of emotional issues, but I was studying psychology at the time and thought I could 'counsel' him into becoming the star he had the potential to be. I tried to get him involved with a band, but he ditched all the practices. I got him a job at my uncle's restaurant, but he got fired after getting in a fistfight with a customer. When he came home drunk, I tried to be somewhere else because it felt like everything I said was the start of a fight. He swung at me once but was so drunk that he fell over before his fist made contact. I felt sorry for Doug, but by the time I realized he wasn't going to change, it was too late. He started threatening to kill himself if I ended the relationship and said things like, 'You're all I have.' He reminded me of those stories where someone tries to save a drowning person and ends up getting pulled underwater by them. Doug's problems became my problems and there didn't seem to be any end to the misery he brought."

instincts that have kept our female ancestors alive for millennia. Allow your center of higher thinking, the "North Star brain," to guide you, and be proactive in how you discern whether or not your lover truly has the capacity to change. It may tell you that in the long run the situation won't improve, the good won't outweigh the bad, and someday the abuse may become downright awful, even deadly. And if children are involved, the risk—to you and them—is all the greater. Learn to follow your instinct, despite the lies, distortions, and fallacies inherent in your relationship. Allow your true, deepest inner voice to ring louder than that of anyone else. It seeks only to protect you, opening a path to both physical and emotional survival.

THE LIES WE TELL OURSELVES

An abuser's job is made far easier when his victim believes she can control or stop the downward spiral of abuse, or even render herself immune to it, by telling herself lies that explain away his actions. We want to believe that if we just understood why he's the way he is, we can change him or live with it, knowing he "can't help himself." But the abuser's mind is a labyrinthine place; an intractable web of deep-seated influences and experiences that comprise his psyche and behaviors. And often, it's a mindset savvy enough in its darkness to avoid detection and fault, whether the abuser is aware of his subterfuge or not. Unfortunately, there is very little you can do to change him.

While the origins of an abusive mindset are complex, contributing factors can include mental illness, substance abuse, childhood maltreatment or overindulgence, extreme stress, societal patriarchy, and even traumatic brain injury. Usually, the cause is not any single one of these things but a combination, resulting in an individual unable or unwilling to control their actions. Blaming and addressing any one piece of the puzzle and thinking it will shift the entire picture is faulty reasoning. This is why prescribing treatment for just one facet, such as anger management, doesn't change the core power and control tactics of the individual.

Many abusers, having felt powerless at some vulnerable point in their lives (usually childhood), believe that they must control anyone who is important to them in order to avoid the rejection and abandonment they fear. They may profess their deep love and attachment to you, elevating you almost to the point of worship. This may feel good to you in the moment, and in fact may be entirely true inside his mind. But when accompanied by abusive traits and behaviors, such feelings are neither genuine nor safe. Faulty attachment is at the root of loving someone "to death," and recognizing your partner's need for possessive connection is key to your assessment. And with this desperate need for power and control comes a sense of entitlement to use force in obtaining it. It doesn't stem from one specific source but rather from an overall mindset that needs to be completely addressed, dismantled, and replaced before a healthy adult relationship can occur.

I realize that love doesn't turn on and off like a faucet. It is natural to feel attachment and responsibility toward someone who you initially thought was "the one," regardless of what he's done to make you realize he wasn't. But the key is in caring more about yourself, and realizing that it's okay to love someone and still know that you can't be together. The following are seven lies we tell ourselves to maintain the illusion that we *can*.

1. He's been violent with others (bar fights, gang activity, admitted previous battering), but he would never hurt me.

If your potential new partner has a violent criminal history or has admitted to previous physical assaults, you are dealing with someone who probably believes that "might makes right," and he will gladly show you that attitude when he feels it's necessary. Some women who are attracted to physically assertive men may be subconsciously looking for the status and protection that mating with an "alpha male" can offer. Historically, this was a valid point, but in the modern world you may be more likely to become a victim of his anger than be shielded by it. Be particularly wary if he has admitted to past assaults on a woman while justifying it with a story about how "she started it," or somehow asked for or deserved the abuse. According to this bully logic, anyone who fails to demonstrate submission to his complete authority is a target for violence, ensuring that you too will somehow warrant his aggression in the future.

2. He'll change when we . . . get married/have kids/move in together.

Yes, he might change—by becoming even *more* abusive. The stresses of cohabitation, marriage, and childrearing are a challenge for average nonviolent people to handle. It is hard to imagine an abusive partner becoming better under such pressure instead of worse. Basing the future success of a relationship on your ability to change your partner is a futile and sometimes dangerous mistake. Too many women have noted disturbing features about their future boyfriends and husbands but thought, *If I can just get him to settle down and stop drinking (cheating, lying, etc.), then his good qualities will take over and he'll become the man I want him to be.* It is a wishful thought but one that rarely happens. It's not that abusers are incapable of true change, but to achieve real transformation takes hard work and many people are not willing to commit to the effort and sacrifice. Threat assessment expert Gavin de Becker states the following:

One of the most common errors in selecting a boyfriend or spouse is basing the prediction on potential. This is actually predicting what certain elements might add up to in some different context . . . What a person is doing now is the context for successful predictions, and marrying a man on the basis of potential, or for that matter hiring an employee solely on the basis of potential, is a sure way to interfere with intuition. That's because the focus on potential carries our imagination to how things might be or could be and away from how they are now.[1]

If I had a dollar for every time I heard a woman say, "I thought he would change," I could fund a shelter large enough to house them all when he doesn't. Trust your sincere judgment of the partner who has shown a controlling and violent personality; it is the problem at the core of all his others, and it will not alter easily.

3. Love hurts: It's not real if it doesn't.

Sometime at the start of second grade, a cruel, hostile boy stole my lunchbox and shoved me to the ground, resulting in copious tears and a school year full of anxiety around future attacks. When I complained to the teacher, her only response was, "He's just teasing you because he has a crush on you." And so begins for many girls the social conditioning that leads them to believe that conflict and passionate aggression are to be associated with romantic relationships. While love can inspire powerful emotions in people, nowhere is it written that mental, physical, or sexual abuse is in any way excusable or tolerable. Poetry and roses are expressions of love; jealousy and threats are not. Sure, lovers argue, but healthy relationships don't include prolonged patterns of psychological torture, and they certainly don't include violence. The moment that a man or a woman intentionally causes physical harm to an intimate partner, they have crossed a line into the entirely unacceptable. They have not only committed an act of abuse but also demonstrated their willingness to "up the game," embarking on a ladder of aggression and risk. In true love, it may hurt to be away from someone, but it should never hurt to be with them.

4. If it doesn't work out, I can just . . . get a divorce/break up/ move out.

I can picture her in the limousine, dressed in white, a mile away from the church. Her palms are sweating, her jaw is clenched, and she tries desperately to brush the feelings away as "cold feet." But she can't forget the taste of blood in her mouth or the humiliation of having him scream at her in front of all their friends last month. As the car comes to a stop, she tells herself that things will be better after the wedding. She feels like she can't possibly back out now, after all the money spent, guests invited, and dreams sent up like balloons to the sky. But secretly, she's already researched her state's divorce laws and hopes they'll work to protect her if and when she needs them.

Despite the relative ease with which people can split up these days, getting out of an abusive relationship will always be harder than you think. Intimate partner abuse is like a spider's web, where unsuspecting women tread hoping to find love but instead becoming wrapped tightly in a cocoon of control and fear. The further you step in, the more difficult it will be to extricate yourself. Commitments, emotions, entangled finances, shared property and children, all make the act of leaving exponentially more challenging. If you are attentive enough to hear the voice inside your head that presages danger, then heed the warning. Know that the situation will not improve on its own or through increased investment, and may not be as easy to exit as a legal website makes it look.

5. He loves me, so he wouldn't really hurt me.

When you say you love someone or ask if they love you, keep in mind that we all have different definitions of that word. To you it might mean commitment, openness, and trust. To an abusive person, love often means ownership and control over their partner, a fluid definition of monogamy, and violent displays of jealousy to prove the extent of their passion. Although most abusers do not truly understand what love is, such individuals may profess it frequently with their words. Many abusers and even killers have been known to state adamantly that they "love" their partner, and perhaps in their own minds, they do. But unlike normal love, an abuser's brand is possessive and selfish. In his mind, if he can't have the sole attention and devotion of his partner, no one else will, and she deserves to suffer or even die for not giving herself to him completely.

Because the twisted brain of a batterer is capable of both being attached to and loathing a current or former partner all at once, his proclamations of adoration do not have the same meaning as those from a healthy, nonabusive man. Take for instance the recent case of Ryan Jenkins, a reality TV show contestant charged in the gruesome slaying of his wife. After her body was found in California, he fled to Canada, where he hung himself in a hotel room. Jenkins left a suicide note that said he considered her "the love of his life" but thought she was cheating on him. He couldn't live with the narcissistic injury that idea (likely false) created, and he couldn't let her live because of it.

6. We were meant to be together, so I have to somehow make it work.

It's time to put the "one true soul mate" myth to bed. In reality, the world has nearly seven billion inhabitants and there are many people out there with whom you can find real and healthy love. Don't believe someone who tells you, "You will never find anyone else" or "No one will ever love you like I do." They can't see the future, and they stand to gain from making you feel "lucky" to have them as a partner. Similarly, beware of someone who tells you, "You're the only person who understands me" or "Nobody has ever loved me before you." While designed to make you feel special, these declarations really say more about the "uniqueness" of the person stating them. There may be a very valid and frightening reason he hasn't had successful relationships before meeting you. Maybe the "true love" that he speaks of is the exact kind you should be avoiding at all costs.

7. He is a misunderstood "diamond in the rough."

Are you a natural helper, someone with an open heart who is intrinsically inclined to try and fix wounded souls with troubled minds? This is an admirable and inspiring quality but also one that can make you a prime target for an abuser. Women who are ingrained with a propensity to nurture, comfort, and forgive the people closest to them are also those who manipulative individuals may seek out because they offer care and freedom from accountability. Abusers may offer their psychological issues as an excuse for their actions, saying things like, "I only explode on you because I can't handle my problems. You're the only one that gets me/can help me/has ever been there for me." These statements may actually be true. He may in fact not be able to control his emotions and has perhaps never had a closer relationship with anyone in his life. But does this mean that you are automatically required to dedicate your life to repairing him, sticking around and enduring the abuse while he "works on himself"?

The fact is *You don't need to fix anyone else—it's not your job.* If you were shopping for a new car, you probably wouldn't buy one that had an obvious multitude of problems, thinking you could just repair them later. The truth is that abusive men can change, but often don't, because they never see clearly what they are doing wrong and how it affects other people. In more egregious cases, they may see it but just don't care. If you truly believe he can change, then let him do so alone, separate from you, and then come back later to show you his progress. The proof is in actions not promises. If you find that a new partner has a lot of problems, resolve to remember that they are his, not yours. You have the right to say, "I hope life works out for you but I'm moving on."

If you recognize any of the above lies as ones you have told yourself, please reevaluate your relationship and use this book to learn about other signs of potential danger. It is not your fault that you walked into a spider's web, and you shouldn't feel foolish admitting that your new partner isn't what you thought he was. It may feel like you've been had and you don't want anyone to say "I told you so." But keep in mind that intelligent, independent women get fooled by abusers every day because they don't have the right tools and are up against an abuser who has spent a great deal of time crafting his "good guy" persona. You are far smarter for acknowledging the fact that you were deceived than ignoring it and remaining in a dangerous situation. It's always better to save your life than to "save face."

THE SIGNIFICANCE OF "I'M SORRY"

The first time a new lover does something verbally or even physically abusive, most women want to believe it was a one-time mistake.

Most abusers often blame victims outright, but they also frequently "apologize" for their behavior. The patient, forgiving parts of us reach to accept the excuse that he was drunk, stressed out, or abused as a child because it enables us to keep the romantic dream alive. If we trust that he is a good man at heart, one who simply made an understandable human error, then we can continue to have the positive parts of our partner and cast aside the possibility that we have made a mistake in judgment. So we brush it under the rug and move forward. This process is simultaneously self-protective and self-destructive. It preserves the "love hurts" lie and allows abuse to continue unfettered and unrecognized as it perpetuates its cycles over and over again.

In their linguistic origin, the words "I'm sorry" roughly mean, "I am full of sorrow and regret" about what has happened. They express remorse but are also inextricably linked with a promise not to blithely offend again. Therefore, the apologizer must accept the responsibility to make every effort to avoid repeating the words or actions that caused the victim physical or emotional pain.

If your partner is verbally or physically abusive to you, is it followed by an apology? Far more importantly, is it followed by any sort of restitution, amends, or real change in behavior? Think of a time when you've delivered a heartfelt apology. Did you then turn around and commit the same offense the following week? If so, you probably would have had to change your appeal to gain forgiveness again. You would have had to throw in a gift, a promise, or some other incentive to once again receive their good graces. An abuser does the same in his bid to add credibility to his "remorse" and gain control over the situation again. He may even pledge to "change" by promising to pursue counseling, enter into rehab, or get married. But time and again, they'll be empty promises, or if big actions are taken, they'll end up a smokescreen against which the dynamics of his abusiveness will simply change, not disappear. When uttered over and over in the absence of reformative action, the words "I'm sorry" imply apathy toward a partner's pain. While an abuser may be regretful that he "let himself" get out of hand, he doesn't really have any intention of putting a plan in place to prevent future explosions. To him, the words are simply a Get-Out-of-Jail-Free card in the realm of your relationship. Repeated apologies without real change are like saying "I know I have a problem, but you just have to deal with it, because I'm too lazy to do

Case in Point

When it comes to saying "I'm sorry," abusers often use it to regain control and foster sympathy, not out of remorse. Take the story of my former client, Penny. As a young mother of two little boys, Penny faced a lot of challenges trying to start her life over after leaving an abusive partner. But she was energetic, optimistic, and seemed to have an understanding about her situation that went far beyond her years. She described her relationship with former boyfriend Rob this way: "Rob was like an addiction to me. I wanted so badly to be considered special by someone that when he came along and plied me with sweet-talk, I was ripe for the picking. But a pattern emerged early on for us—he would call me some disgusting cruel name, or push me onto the floor during an argument, and then within minutes, the apologies would start. He would act all repentant, and beg me to help him with his 'sickness,' which he blamed on an abusive dad. Of course I would give in and somehow I'd end up soothing him, with his head in my lap after he punched me in the face. It was so twisted that I even felt bad for 'making him' flip out and causing him such emotional pain. What a master of manipulation. If he felt so bad, then why did he do it again every three to five days?"

the work required for transformation. Instead, I expect the entire world to conform to my erratic moods, self-centered demands, and lack of concern for other people's feelings."

What an abuser wants you to think is that if you just treat him the right way, love him the right way, or change yourself in the right way, he will stop having to abuse you. He wants you to see the error of *your* ways, and conform to his idea of the perfect subservient slave (although this is impossible, since an abuser is never permanently happy with his partner, no matter what she does). In short, he often sees the abuse as *your* problem, not his. Thus, his apologies will always remain just empty words.

THE CONFRONT AND CHECK STRATEGY

The only way to truly stop this cycle is to stop accepting the apologies. Instead of "forgive and forget," women can employ a policy of "Confront and Check" when the first offense is committed. We can store it in our mental books, comparing it against other factors to determine the state of the relationship. We can let our partner know about his offense by using the three-step method mentioned earlier in this book: name the behavior, explain how it affects us, and clarify what needs to change. We can then set up expectations that will measure progress, and if they are not met, we need to consider this failure in relation to everything else that has transpired. If the sequence repeats itself several times, we can establish with certainty that our partner is not someone who made a one-time error but rather a man exhibiting a pattern of abusive behavior.

If this is the case, your partner will have likely provided multiple excuses, most of which put the blame on something other than his actions, beliefs, and decisions. It is possible that he has told you he can change, that he *will* change, that he just needs your help to do it.

Case in Point

When it comes to seeking couples counseling, an abuser may oblige you, but out of a twisted desire to validate his actions not to change his ways. And more often than not, the session itself becomes a trigger for further abuse. Take Erin's case below.

Erin and her husband Keith had been married for four abusive years when he decided they should seek couple's counseling. "I tried to get Keith to do most of the talking because I really thought he went there to get help. But I soon realized that the only reason he brought me there was to get support for his actions and to make me feel like I was the problem. He had been to see the therapist on his own and laid the groundwork by telling him that I was a crazy, nagging bitch. I felt like the therapist agreed with him, like they were ganging up on me, so I started saying all the things Keith had done out loud. I told the therapist how he had pushed me down the stairs and grabbed me around the throat. That's when I got the look: the one that tells me I'm getting my ass kicked as soon as we're alone. Keith denied everything and then shot the therapist a smirk, as though to say, "See what I mean?" The therapist never asked me if I felt safe, and when he said our time was up we left. We didn't even make it to the parking lot. As soon as we got in the elevator at the therapist's office, Keith looked around to make sure there was no camera. Then he punched me in the stomach and brought his knee up to my face when I doubled over. As I picked my tooth up off the elevator floor, I realized I had been set up. After that, I just started doing what he said. Keith actually made a comment that he thought the therapy had worked."

Perhaps, as mentioned above, he has even suggested couple's counseling. Here's why that is a terrible idea in violent relationships: counseling helps couples who are willing to listen to one another, make compromises, and work toward an egalitarian, mutually beneficial, loving union. All those things are anathema to the abuser. His card-house of power and control will always lean toward his own self-interests, and there is little hope that a counselor green to the dynamics of domestic violence will ever be able to convince the abuser otherwise. Most counselors don't receive extensive formal or field training around intimate partner violence and may make mistakes such as unwittingly aligning themselves with a crafty abuser. For the particularly dangerous psychopath partner, therapy is a sickly entertaining game and is rarely effective in regard to the malignant personality disorders that many abusers have. In addition, if you are a victim of domestic violence, then you already know that *everything* has repercussions. Whatever you say in the couple's therapy session will likely be used as ammunition in the arguments that come after, and several women have reported to me that they were assaulted directly after a joint therapy session (see sidebar).

If you are being abused and your partner suggests counseling, you can also use the Confront and Check Strategy, but in a slightly different way. Tell him that you agree there are problems and if he really wants to improve the situation, you should both seek individual therapy. Explain that you've got "things to work out on your own," which will likely fit well into his construction that you are at fault. Try to find separate counselors that are both well versed in domestic violence work. That way, if he's serious about changing, he can demonstrate the drive to do so on his own and come back to show you his progress. If he isn't committed to healing the damaged parts of his personality or is simply afraid of what secrets you might tell a therapist, then he will refuse the idea. If he does, please find a way to go to counseling alone. Then at least you will have begun to work on your own issues and uncover the innate strengths that will help you to exit the relationship.

THE POSSIBILITY OF INTERVENTION

Another beacon of hope to victims and other supporters of change is the Batterers' Intervention Program (BIP for short). BIPs are a series of curriculum-based sessions led by facilitators that attempt to rehabilitate people identified as abusers by either themselves or a court of law. While some attendees volunteer, the vast majority are mandated to participate by judges, often as a condition of probation or as part of a sentencing package.

I used to cofacilitate a BIP, and I still know many dedicated professionals who do this work. They are some of the most patient, Zen-like people I know, and I have a great respect for their efforts to reform some of society's most dangerous perpetrators. While the basic goal of business (even nonprofits) is to stay in it, most BIP providers will admit that the challenges they face in rehabilitating abusers are steep. In regard to the effectiveness of such programs, researcher Julia Babcock states:

> Most highly respected experts agree, change is rare even in world-renowned BIPs. Sadly, most men just learn to abuse without looking bad, using new skills and psychological jargon to avoid responsibility for the pain they inflict. Researchers have concluded, with disappointment, that batterer intervention programs, as currently structured, have scant effect on the behavior of men convicted of domestic violence.[2]

Because the practice of battering is often backed up by patriarchal attitudes about gender and relationships, it is difficult to replace deep-seated, long-held beliefs with new ones centered on equality and nonviolence. Abusers are often deficient in empathy for others or have little insight into their own behaviors. They maintain a self-focus and lack of accountability, while blaming everyone around them (particularly the victim) for their problems.

If he were to change these features, an abuser would first have to acknowledge them and then be willing to put in the necessary work for real progress to take place. He might also have to address any accompanying issues such as anger management or substance abuse (forms of treatment for both are conducted separately, though sometimes in conjunction with batterers' intervention). When a participant absorbs the information and support given by the group's facilitators and his fellow attendees, he has the genuine chance to learn and change. Unfortunately, a multitude of studies show that only a small percentage of batterers who attend mandatory abuse-intervention classes will take these important steps toward totally ending their own use of power, control, and violence. While the numbers for those who attend voluntarily is slightly better, only a tiny fraction of attendees seek help of their own volition. The expectation for those who never attend professional programs is even smaller.

By sharing this information I don't mean to disparage the caring practitioners who commit their lives to repairing the violent soul. They espouse the same belief most of us are taught as girls growing up: showing patience and love to another human being can be transformational. As women, we may have come to believe that we are responsible for keeping our relationships and families together. These sentiments are fine to apply when the people around us are nonabusive individuals. But when we cross paths with an abuser, social mores of tolerance can be deadly.

In all my years of domestic violence work, I have never heard of a looming, lying, and lethal abuser who magically changed to become the ideal loving mate. No one has ever sincerely told me that her husband used to beat her, rape her, and threaten to kill her, but then stopped with the miraculous help of therapy, religion, or jail. Abusers may shift tactics such as switching from physical to emotional abuse to avoid consequences. However, their thought patterns, verbal assaults, and basic regard toward others generally do not change.

The point of this chapter is not to quash the idea that change is possible, but to posit the reality that while a violent partner *can* stop abusing, most do not, and all the work that you put into solving his problems won't change that. Rolling the dice on a glimmer of hope is rarely a safe bet. If your partner is psychologically, physically, or sexually abusing you, there is nothing to "work out" except how you will plan your escape.

Walking away from the dream of true love and the illusions you wanted so desperately to believe is painful. However, it pales in comparison to the regret of staying with an abusive man and wondering what your life could have been like had you decided to rip off the band-aid *before* the infection set in.

Chapter 9

Ending a Violent Relationship:
The Pursuit of Life, Liberty, and Happiness

There is no freedom without courage.
—Eric Schaub

One piece of good news that I can give you after working with intimate partner violence for two decades is that most women do escape. While it is an enormous feat to leave your abusive partner—emotionally, financially, and logistically—it is always the safest outcome. But before that can happen, many abused women need to arrive at what I call "escape velocity." They need to reach a point in their situation where the challenges and pain of leaving outweigh the challenges and pain of staying. They have to be ready to psychologically extricate themselves from what may have been a lengthy and sick (but close) relationship, and be economically prepared to take care of themselves (and often their children) without their partner's support. Sometimes, reaching this level takes several practice attempts. One study on battered women found that most try to leave an abusive partner about five to seven times before they separate permanently.[1] While this final step can bring freedom and security, it's also the time during which a woman is at her greatest risk.

Before I address the safest possible breakup plan, I would like to acknowledge that some of you, for a variety of complex and valid reasons, may not be ready to take that leap. Here we will focus on ways to stay safe until you are. The following section concentrates on living with your abuser and the minefield of concerns it may present. Please use it as a temporary strategy while you prepare for a lasting escape.

Take Action

If you have made the courageous decision to end a dangerous relationship, it is vital to your safety that you develop a well-thought-out plan and accept advice and assistance from qualified professionals. The information in this book is designed to inform and stimulate ideas, but because everyone's situation is different, you will want to create a flexible, individual safety plan. For help, contact a domestic violence advocate through your local service agency or call the National Domestic Violence Hotline: 1-800-799-SAFE (7233) or 1-800-787-3224 (TTY).

LIVING WITH AN ABUSER

Maintaining a relationship with an abuser, particularly if you're living together, requires carefully honed survival skills. In addition to having keen perception, you must constantly monitor their levels of intoxication, their stress triggers, and their minute-by-minute moods. Victims have to use evolving measurements and cautious judgment to stay safe. It is the delicate unpredictability of abusers that lends so well to the phrase "walking on eggshells," but even the unforeseeable can sometimes be presaged by taking note of established patterns. For example, do you notice that your partner is often more volatile when discussing particular subjects or at certain times of the day? For some women, this might be the morning, especially if he has been woken up. For others, it might be when he returns home from work, in the evening after he's consumed a few drinks, or on days of the month when household bills arrive in the mail. If at all possible, try to schedule your activities around these times, planning to be walking the dog at seven in the morning or grocery shopping at 5:30 PM. There is no guarantee that targeted shifts in your action will enhance your safety because many abusers will simply simmer while you are out and then explode upon your return. But removing yourself at key tension points may help to minimize risk in the *moment*. Consider the following strategies for minimizing risk in the heat of an abusive incident.

Defuse the Tension

Victims often talk about the "tension-building phase," the time before an assault when stress is mounting, the abuser's voice is rising, and his face begins to change. During moments like these, there may be nothing we can do to avoid what is coming, short of running out the door. The key tactic in this situation is "de-escalation." Since it is rarely possible to reason with an irrational violent individual, the focus should be on reducing the level of arousal to avoid an assault. To improve your chances of not being physically hurt, use the following techniques to try and calm your partner down.

   1. *Stay calm*—If your tension rises, it will exacerbate his already volatile state. Even if he is screaming at you

and you're feeling frightened or angry, try to speak in a composed, modulated voice.

2. *Increase your distance*—Try to create some physical space between you and your partner, perhaps taking a few steps backward so you're several times your usual distance. Stand at a slight angle so you can sidestep a blow if needed. Be aware of where he is in the room, but don't stare him down. Avoid raising your fists, shaking your fingers, or pointing at him, as these are all natural signals of aggression.

3. *Acquiesce if possible*—If there is something specific the abuser wants, and it is possible but unpleasant to acquiesce, you might want to consider doing so if the alternative is far worse. Short of putting you or your child at risk of physical or sexual assault, if the request is simple, it may be better to comply. Suppose he wants you to make him some food as you're walking out the door to work. You know that if you refuse, an argument will ensue. Is his demand rude and insensitive to your needs? Of course. But if stopping to prepare a sandwich saves you from a beating, it's worth it. Is there a particular dress you wear that he hates, or a certain friend that you always "get in trouble" for speaking to? Let your defiance go for the time being—*this is only a temporary stop-loss measure.* It is intended to increase your safety while you are planning your escape.

Case in Point

Women living in abuse try many combinations of resisting and placating in an attempt to ward off or defuse a violent partner. For example, some victims try to stand up to their abuser while others may reason or plead their way out when they feel an attack is pending. Many can sense the beginning of conflict and will work at calming and satisfying the abuser's demands to avoid being assaulted. While a victim's methods are as unique as her own situation, some techniques are downright dangerous. A woman named Leslie once told me that her way of staying safe was by doing cocaine. Her abusive boyfriend would often bring home a gram of cocaine, and Leslie knew that if he snorted the entire thing by himself, he would become enraged and violent. But if Leslie shared the drug, doing half of it herself and leaving only a portion for him, he remained in control. While I would certainly never recommend Leslie's strategy to anyone, it serves as an example of the desperate lengths some women will go to avoid violence.

If you think conflict is imminent, the only real protective place to position yourself is out of the abuser's presence, or at best, near a door. Although it makes sense to stay out of rooms (such as the kitchen) where weapons are readily accessible, most victims know that an assault can happen anywhere and abusers will make weapons out of just about anything, particularly their own bodies.

Call the Police

If you think your abuser is going to come after you in a violent way, you should call 911. The cell phone is an important tool to have when

Take Action

Even before the threat of violence occurs, you should be familiar with the "breakout avenues" in your home. Do a walk-through when he is not around, noting the quickest escape routes for each room, should an interaction become dangerous. Which rooms have windows that face the street so neighbors might see what is happening and call the police? Is there a room you can lock yourself into with a phone? What areas have decks, fire escapes, or ground floor windows you could exit through? Try not to become cornered in an area from which you have no flight path.

living with an abuser. If possible, it should be clipped to your belt or nestled in your pocket. Any charged phone will dial 911, even if it has no service carrier. Having a charged cell phone at your reach will increase your ability to call for help if the regular phone has been disabled or you are trapped in a room without a landline. It will also allow you to call 911 while you are on the move.

Find an Escape

Your next (and perhaps simultaneous) option when under physical attack is to escape. Grabbing my car keys and literally running out the door saved me from assault more than once during my own abusive relationship. If you are able to flee the home during a moment of danger, where will you go? The time to think about this is not when you are behind the wheel or standing on the side of the road. It is *before* an argument even happens, so that your plan is more likely to be successful. Having a plan can also make emergency choices less stressful. Does your car have an extra set of keys attached to its undercarriage

Take Action

If you cannot afford a cell phone (or need an extra, secret one) please contact your local domestic violence organization. Many shelters and assistance agencies have programs through which you can receive a free phone that only dials 911. If your abuser controls your access to the main telephone, consider getting a secret, inexpensive prepaid phone.

Stash your prepaid or 911-only phone in a special hiding place, such as under the bedroom dresser or inside a box of tampons in the bathroom cabinet (he'll never look there!). The best place for a cell phone to be is where he can't find it or get to you while you're using it.

in a magnetic box so you can drive away when you flee the house? Do you have some money stashed under the floor mats or the dashboard so you can get food, gas, or lodging? Perhaps an overnight bag hidden in the trunk, your attic, or cleverly stashed at a friend's house? Many women don't have access to a car at all. If this is your situation, decide which neighbor's house you could run to and which one will be your alternate if they aren't home. Carry a bus schedule (with one-way fare) or money for a taxi (but keep in mind that your abuser could learn your destination by calling the cab company). If you live in a secluded area, is there a hiding place on your property where you can hole up until you can escape to find help? Consider where you would go if you had to leave for a few hours—maybe a coffee shop or the mall. If it is the middle of the night, fast food restaurants can be a good choice, but hospitals and airports are even better because of the built-in security. What if you have to leave for a few days? Could you stay at a shelter, a friend's house, or a motel? What is your Plan B if that friend is not home or can't have you there for some reason? If you have been with your abuser for a while, it is likely that he knows where all your local friends and family live. In that case, an undisclosed or public place is a better choice. If you do go to a private home or a motel, request that no confirmation of your stay be given to callers or visitors.

Establish Code Words

Another tool that victims living with their abuser can use is the code word or code signal, which is a way of telling someone you need help without saying exactly what is happening. A woman I once worked with named Jennifer had a great example that may have helped save her life. She told me that her estranged husband would often show up at her home unexpectedly, sometimes breaking in to threaten and assault her. On one occasion he got in through a window, and stood before her in the living room, armed with a knife. "You're coming with me," he growled. "Go to the goddamn truck." Jennifer was terrified but she kept a cool head. "No problem," she said. "I'm certainly willing to talk. Just let me call my mom first and tell her I'm not bringing the kids over for pizza tonight. If I don't call, she'll expect me and might notify the police." Her abuser relented and Jennifer dialed her mother's number. When she picked up, Jennifer said calmly, "Hi Mom. I just wanted to let you know I'm not bringing the kids over for pizza tonight, I've got something else I have to do." Then she said, "Okay, goodbye," and hung up the phone. Jennifer stalled for a couple more minutes, which was just long enough for the police to arrive and take her abuser into custody. Months earlier, Jennifer had laid the groundwork for this plan by telling her mother, "If I ever call you and say I'm not bringing the kids over for pizza tonight that means *he is in my house*. Call the police." A bit of preparation goes a long way.

Even if you haven't had the chance to do advance work, you can still use codes to communicate. Luisa, another victim I interviewed, told me a similar story to Jennifer's—except in her case, a call from her best friend, Raquel, came in just as her abuser was gearing up for an assault. When the phone rang, she convinced him to let her answer it because not doing so might give the caller a clue that something was wrong. One thing abusers don't want is to get caught in the act, so they may agree to let their victim take measures they assume will prevent the discovery. When Luisa picked up the phone, an unsuspecting Raquel began asking her simple questions like, "What are you doing tonight?" Luisa answered, "Oh, hi, Monica. No, that folder is on top of my desk." When her friend replied, "This is Raquel. What folder are you talking about?" Luisa said, "That's what Tina from corporate told me." Her friend knew about Luisa's abuse situation and instantly understood that something was amiss. "Are you okay, Luisa?" she asked. "7:30 AM," answered Luisa cryptically. The next question made the situation clear: "Are you in danger right now?" her friend asked nervously. "Yes," said Luisa. "Goodbye." The exchange triggered a call to the police from Raquel who was sharp enough to know a code when she heard it. They arrived six minutes later and arrested her abuser on the spot.

Codes don't even have to be verbal. I have heard ingenious ideas from women who came up with codes for their neighbors such as a porch light flashed three times or a knock on the adjoining apartment wall. Anything that tells the outside world you need help can be a life-saving device. Just remember to change your code if the abuser ever learns about it or hears it used.

Defend Yourself

If de-escalation techniques, code words, and escape attempts fail, your only alternative during a violent incident is to bear it out and survive. If you are facing imminent assault, try to ascertain if this is an "everyday" abusive moment where he wants to give you a quick shove and walk away, or a particularly vicious attack designed to seriously injure you. Remember, the first can easily turn into the next. When your abuser is bigger and stronger than you are (which is most often the case), concentrate mostly on blocking his blows and protecting your head. Curl up in a ball if you must, bringing your knees up to a fetal position and using your arms to cover your face and skull. I'm not suggesting women lie down and allow themselves to be beaten day after day, but *in the moment,* the path of least resistance may reduce the length of the assault and allow you to stay alive and make your escape after the assault.

Deciding to fight back is a serious resolution, the wisdom of which will depend on your circumstances. To swing at an enraged abuser has the potential to inflame him even more and may in fact be just the green light he has been looking for. Some abusers will push or take insubstantial shots at their victim until she hits back, at which point even a slight scratch can provide the justification he needs to brutally assault her, later claiming "self-defense." However, if the beating is intense and your life is at stake, you must fight with everything you have. Give the battle 100 percent of your strength while focusing on momentary opportunities to get away and get help. Every situation is different, so please use your best judgment when deciding how to react to an attack. Remember that the way we *think* we will react or plan to react is often not the way it turns out in reality. Stay vigilant and flexible, while considering all of your options.

Prepare the Children

Often, the abuser's primary victim is not the only one who lives in the home. Sadly, children get caught in the crossfire of abusive households, and if they are old enough to understand what is happening, they must be taught what to do when a fight breaks out.

As a mother, it's natural to be concerned about talking to your children about abuse—particularly if it involves someone they're either afraid of or someone they love. But the good thing to know is that having a plan—and sharing it with them—can bring the opposite effect, lending confidence and a sense of security to scary scenarios. Just as you would talk to your kids about what to do if the house catches on fire, teach them what to do if violence erupts.

A primary message to teach your children, particularly older ones who are tempted to help you if you are attacked, is to *stay out of the fight*. Instead of trying to intervene, teach them how to both keep themselves safe and seek immediate help. Depending on their age, that might entail a number of options. Children between the ages of toddlerhood and elementary school can be taught to hide in their rooms or a bathroom, perhaps assisted by an older sibling who can then dial 911, call a grandparent, or slip out the back door to the neighbor's house. Kids need to know who to trust and who to contact if their first attempt fails.

Most importantly, children in abusive environments need to know that their situation is not permanent and that you as their parent and protector are working to make things better. It might be best to leave out specifics because children can be pressured by an abuser to disclose exit plans, thus putting the whole family at risk. Older kids will of course understand more, and teenagers can be apprised of the safety plan you will make after reading the following chapters.

Anyone who is close to your children such as a teacher, nanny, or other care provider should be told the basics of what is happening. Although you may be afraid or ashamed to reveal the inner turmoil of your home life, it is vital that the people around your kids understand the risk they are in, and why they might be behaving in withdrawn, self-harming, or disruptive ways. Additionally, there should be someone you can call to take the kids for a few hours if needed, someone who appreciates *why* you might have to drop them off at odd times or why you might not be able to explain things out loud over the telephone.

Case in Point

Debby had four kids whom she felt were trapped between childhood innocence and harsh reality. Ranging from ages one to nine, some of the children hadn't even learned to talk yet, but they understood well the terror of their father.

Debby brought them in to the shelter where I worked, and together we met with a children's counselor who specialized in family violence. The conversation was tailored to their various levels of understanding, and they all had the chance to share, in their own ways, the fear they felt when conflicts took place. An action plan was developed, in the event another fight broke out before they had the chance to permanently escape. Debby's nine-year-old daughter was assigned the important task of gathering her younger siblings and ushering them to the basement where they could lock themselves in with a deadbolt. A 911 cell phone was stashed behind the washing machine, and the two oldest kids were trained to use it for summoning help. They even crafted a plan to stand on a chair and get out of the basement window if needed. Later, the kids practiced making pretend 911 calls and knocking on imaginary neighbor's doors. They even came up with songs to sing for the toddlers to keep them calm while help was en route.

Although kids can make a game out of anything, Debby's seemed to know that this rehearsal was serious. But they liked having jobs and ideas, especially ones they had acted out in a safe environment. "It's like the earthquake drills at school," her six-year-old said.

Debby didn't like putting her kids through such a dark play, but she felt much better knowing they would be safe if she became unable to stop what was occurring in the home.

Thankfully, in the end Debby and her children were able to escape without having to employ such measures.

⚠ **Take Action**

Children living in an abusive home need a safe place to vent the feelings of fear, sadness, and anger that often accompanies it. You may be able to find referrals to counselors through your pediatrician, child's school, or your local battered women's service center/shelter. If cost is a concern, please note that many schools have onsite counselors who can meet with your children.

Keep in mind that therapists are usually "mandatory reporters," meaning that they are required to report any signs of abuse to your county's child protective services. In some cases, abuse of the mother can be considered a risk to children even if the kids themselves have never been hurt. This should not dissuade you from seeking therapy for your child, but it is important to be aware of, particularly if you have an abuser who has made threats around the discovery of the family's secret. For maximum confidentiality, counseling sessions can often be arranged during the school day so an abusive partner won't become suspicious. Chapter 10 includes more information on keeping children safe through the assistance of your local schools and child protective services.

Children don't have a choice regarding their environments, and it's up to us to make their lives as safe as possible. We owe it to our kids to fight for a better life, and even though the logistics of that journey may be hard for them to understand now, they will be grateful adults for the sacrifices you have made in its pursuit.

Prepare Your "Go Money"

Many women find themselves trapped in abusive relationships simply because they don't have enough cash to leave. That same lack of resources is often behind the choice to stay with (or return to) an abuser, rather than face life on the streets.

In order to ensure that you retain independence in a relationship, every woman, regardless of her age, should have a cache of "Go Money." This is a sum of money that you have stashed away (as much as you can afford, but preferably at least $1,000) expressly for the purpose of escaping a bad situation. It can be used to cover hotel, plane, or bus fare, first month's rent and deposit on a new apartment, a new cell phone, or anything else that will help you stay safe.

Getting Started

While you are biding your time, waiting for the right moment to leave (as soon as your plan is in place and ready to be executed), open a secret bank account, sending a portion of your income to it each week. Be sure to have paperless statements sent to a private email address or divert hard copies to a P.O. Box or a friend's home. If you are married, have children, or hold any financial/property ties to your abuser, you will need to make an appointment with an attorney to learn about your rights, responsibilities, and choices. Legal-aid options are available in most places if you cannot afford representation. Try to meet secretly with a lawyer before you leave so that you are aware of any legal (particularly child custody) obligations that may pull you back into the situation. Think about where your children will go to school or childcare, and try to set up a budget that reflects the realities of living on your own. Remind yourself everyday that there is a way out and you are strong enough, smart enough, and capable enough to find it.

If you work and have a 401K through your job, you may also have free access to the services of a financial planner. Meet with them to discuss whether you can sell stocks for cash. Some savings plans do not allow any cash conversions, while others have penalties upon early withdrawal.

When He's the Primary Income Earner

If your partner makes most or all of the money (perhaps you are a stay-at-home mother), do yourself a favor and know ahead of time exactly what your financial situation is. Even before abuse escalates to the point where your only safe alternative is escaping the relationship, empower yourself with knowledge. For example, make a list of all the bills, noting how much is paid each month, and to whom. Read bank statements as they come in and know precisely how much money is in each account, including stocks, bonds, life insurance, trusts, etc. If possible, do taxes with your partner or sit in on briefings from an accountant. It can be tempting to let someone else handle all the financial particulars, but that makes you "money-blind" and can cause real problems when the relationship falls apart.

Don't Share Accounts

In general, unless you've been with your partner for several years and know he's not abusive or controlling, avoid joint checking accounts or any other type of money-sharing. On a joint account, both users may withdraw funds at any time, and I have worked with many victims who have had their entire life savings cleared out by an abusive husband or boyfriend, leaving them penniless and betrayed.

> ⚠️ **Take Action**
>
> If you must be out of the workforce temporarily—to raise children, for example—try to maintain a marketable skill or learn new ones while keeping up with your professional contacts. Continuing to network, volunteer, or consult is a great way to keep a foot in the door, making it easier to reenter the job market when you need to.

Giving a new partner your PIN codes or account numbers can also be treacherous because if he turns out to be someone other than you initially thought, he may have access to all of your funds and therefore your financial freedom.

Ultimately, you want to be as financially independent and prepared as you can be, even before you meet a new partner. When escape is your only alternative, especially on a moment's notice, an empty wallet can be a formidable barrier to safety.

Send a Message

Living with an abuser is a taxing exercise in balance and awareness, and women are sometimes so conditioned to a constant position of danger that they become desensitized to what is really happening. Many victims refer to this as a state of numbness, an immobilizing and ever-present fear that prevents them from acting because they can't see a light at the end of the tunnel. They don't think they will ever get away and aren't sure they could emotionally and financially make it on their own if they did. In some of the most dangerous cases of intimate partner violence I have ever seen, victims will actually prewrite their death notice or wills. These women are deeply worried that their current or ex-partner might kill them, and they want people to know who was responsible in the event of their murder. Sometimes, these communications come in the form of a diary, a whispered concern to a loved one, or a note they carry in their wallet. If you were to suddenly disappear or be harmed, would anyone know what happened or where to focus their search and investigation efforts? It is terrifying for anyone to think about planning for their own homicide, but the truth is that abused women are sometimes kidnapped, beaten unconscious, or killed and hidden. Despite the discomfort you may have with this idea, it is important that someone or something, even a tiny piece of paper, can document your experience and concerns. Consider hiding some

Case in Point

When I was a case manager for battered women, a few of their files contained notes that shared their fear of being killed by their partner. They were given to me for safekeeping by women like Tamara, whose husband had threatened to cut her into little pieces and scatter her body parts across the state so her parents couldn't bury her. I hated taking these notes while not being able to immediately snap my fingers and make the victims safe. But I knew that it was better to file the notes than to see their abusers get away with murder if they did follow through on their threats.

information about your situation somewhere that the abuser will never find it. It is my strong hope that it will never be needed.

While I have seen cases of incredible human despair over the years, I have also seen many of triumph and escape. Ex-battered women are some of the strongest, wisest, and most intrinsically beautiful people I have ever met. Many of them thought they couldn't ever get away either, but now they are basking in freedom—the same freedom that rightfully belongs to you, whether you recognize it at this moment or not. Get ready to reach out and take back your life.

MAKING THE LEAP: THE SAFEST POSSIBLE BREAKUP PLAN

When you do decide it's time to end your relationship, please don't just get up and leave without crafting a solid plan. Making impulsive decisions can steal your valuable opportunity to design a strategy that will minimize your chances of having to return out of economic necessity, emotional weakness, or concern for your safety. Abusive individuals do not accept rejection well, so separating from one requires careful forethought. You must make a firm decision to go all or nothing, and not put your foot down until you know you have the tools and strength to follow through with your escape.

In my work with victims, I have often compared the process of leaving to drawing a line in the sand, one that the victim must vow to defend and not recross. Even if you have been threatened around leaving, you are being threatened every day when you stay. When a woman knows she has to go, that is precisely when her abuser will attempt to bind her to him through threats, love, pity, and doubt. It may be tempting for a victim to want to reconcile, still holding out for change. It may be difficult to financially carry on alone and she may consider giving in for the sake of the children. But remember this: If you negotiate with a terrorist, the manipulation, the fear, and the violence will never stop. It is frightening to stand up to a person who can inspire dread with a single glance, but staying with him to endure endless punishment is far worse. The following suggestions will help arm you with knowledge and options before taking the leap out of a risky relationship.

Guard Your Secret

Once you have decided to leave an abuser, guard that secret as though your life depends on it, because it very well might. Many women who are killed are murdered in the exact moment they announce to their partner that they are leaving or divorcing him. Because that's how he sees it—they aren't leaving the relationship or the home, they are abandoning *him*. It is something hypersensitive abusers take very seriously, and their reactions to such a declaration are quite unpredictable. The only people you should tell are the trusted individuals whose participation is crucial to your plan. This could be the police, your advocate, your attorney, your best friend, or a relative. Choose people whom you are reasonably sure will not betray your confidence. Even well-meaning individuals can sometimes be tricked, threatened, or otherwise coerced by a clever abuser into giving away information about you. Just make sure they understand the importance of keeping the secret as well.

Choose Who Will Move

If you're married or live together, who will move out? Some restraining orders include provisions that require an abusive person to leave the family home, even if they are the sole owner or renter. Still, there is no stopping them from putting the house up for sale or initiating eviction procedures, but it does allow you a reasonable amount of time to find another home. In many cases, however, this can be a dangerous chess move. Having the police force an already unstable individual from his home can cause major problems, and if you remain there, you may be vulnerable to a revenge plot. Thus, leaving is the better option. Even if you are the sole owner of the house or the primary tenant on the lease, you may still want to be the person who departs. Landlords are often required to let you out of your lease if you are a victim of reported violence that perpetrated on the property, and you can initiate legal activity to evict him from your home, usually within a few months time. I understand that an angry abuser may resort to damaging the property, skipping out on the mortgage payments, or otherwise causing problems when he finds out you have left. You may suffer financially and wonder why he should get to stay in the home while you have to find other accommodations. After all, he's the one who's wrong, right? Right. But that doesn't mean your life is worth arguing over it. The steps in this section are not always easy and they are not always just.

Having to change your life in response to the tactics of an abuser is an unfair necessity. After all, if he is in the wrong, why should you have to spend time, money, and attention on adjusting your life to

> ## Case in Point
>
> A woman who I once worked with named Amy was at great risk for becoming a victim of domestic homicide. Of all the cases I have worked on, hers was among the most frightening, and all signs pointed to an impending fatality. I believed her best bet was extreme relocation (moving to an undisclosed, faraway place), and I told her as much during a frank and intense discussion. But to my surprise, Amy refused assistance on the grounds of her daughter's social life. "All of her friends are in that school. If I pulled her out during senior year, she would never forgive me," she told me. "I won't let him ruin my relationship with my daughter." I couldn't help but imagine her teenage daughter, hysterically crying and yelling—not at her mother, but at her mother's funeral. I don't believe Amy thought her daughter's senior prom was more important than her life, but her response indicated three things: her fear of change was greater than her fear of him, she was angry that he was pushing her toward that change, and she didn't really think he was going to kill her.
>
> In the end, Amy did move, but only after her teenage daughter begged her to, after seeing a death threat spray painted on their car.

increase your safety? Your anger is both warranted and understood, but remaining in a state of stubborn scorekeeping won't help you or your loved ones stay alive. A sign on the desk of legendary threat assessor Gavin de Becker reads "Don't Come Here For Justice." He knows that people arrive with indignant resentment for the situations they have been put in, but that they must see beyond it in order to achieve the true goal, which is always safety.

Security doesn't come cheap, but freedom is priceless.

Decide What to Take

Knowing that you will most likely be going through a major (but worthwhile) downsize, you'll need to decide what's essential to take with you when you first leave. Furniture will probably have to stay, at least for now, along with many other clothing and personal items. Remember, material possessions can be replaced, you cannot. However, if you can safely and secretly remove personal items from the home first, definitely do—you want to avoid having to contact him again after the breakup, particularly to argue over a box of your stuff. Going back to the home after he is angry about the separation can be a very risky time. It is best to put nonessential belongings in storage or leave them for civil court, and just have a bag packed and ready to go the moment you leave. Your escape pack should contain the following:

- An extra change of clothes or two for you (and children if applicable)
- Important documents necessary to start a new life, such as driver license, passports or green cards, social security cards, birth/marriage/divorce certificates, and immunization records (if you have children)
- Cash, credit cards, keys, cell phone
- Small first aid kit, including a few days worth of any medications you (or the children) are prescribed
- Contact information for those who will be helping you on your journey
- If you have children, a special toy or blanket to ease their anxiety
- Your laptop, if possible, since it likely contains information on what you've searched, who you contacted, and where you might be going

- Photographs, including up-to-date ones of your abuser and kids. Pass copies of the abuser's picture to shelter staff, coworkers, new neighbors, police, etc., so they can look out for him. Hold onto the children's current images in case he abducts them and you need to get information out to police and the media quickly

Decide Where To Go

It's important to settle on a destination, even a temporary one, far in advance of your escape. Do not choose a place that will be obvious to your partner, such as a known friend or family member's home. This may put you or other people at risk, since he'll try and find you there

Case in Point

"This may sound materialistic, but the hardest thing for me to leave behind wasn't my boyfriend. It was my grandmother's antique furniture. I had it all set up in our apartment when I moved in, but I couldn't get it out when I left. My abuser knew I wanted it and he made it so hard for me. It came down to the clear message that if I wanted my furniture, I was gonna take a beating trying to retrieve it. The police wouldn't help because it was a civil matter. I said I'd sue him for it in small claims court and his reply was 'All you'll get is a box of ashes.' He may have destroyed it at this point or all my beautiful family heirlooms could be sitting in his living room right now. All I know is that I had to give it up to make a clean getaway from a violent man, and I think my grandmother would have approved of that choice."

—Alexis, age thirty-three

first. If you cannot afford a hotel or permanent housing right away, or have nowhere else to go that you believe will be safe, use the shelter system (please see Chapter 11 for more info on shelters). Lack of stable housing is a major reason why some victims end up returning to a dangerous relationship.

Protect Yourself Financially

Close all joint bank accounts and credit cards, reroute direct deposits elsewhere, and cancel all open lines of credit on jointly-held property. If you have access to an attorney or an accountant, use their services to inform your decisions, but make sure they understand the confidential and risky nature of your situation.

When you have decided to implement your plan, you must make a mental shift into the understanding that you are moving into a different and often more dangerous phase. You may need to begin thinking like "a woman on the run" or a hyperaware soldier on guard, because once you make the leap, things will never be the same again. The system of protective boundaries you must establish starts right away and continues from here on through. Be sure you are stepping out on the right foot.

Time Your Escape

Choose a moment when the abuser is not home to make your exit. If that is not possible or you are unsure when he will return, request an "officer standby" from your local police department. They cannot stay long in many cases, and cannot help you move items, but they will stand guard for about thirty minutes or more to increase everyone's safety while you are leaving. This is safer than doing it alone, or possibly endangering a friend or family member by asking them to

Case in Point

Several years ago, I sat in a child-abuse evaluation center, across from a thirty-year-old woman named Patricia. I was her advocate and had accompanied her to the center that day to have her two children interviewed by police detectives regarding the cigarette burns their father Marco had made all over their little bodies. After the kids confirmed the abuse, Patricia was furious to the point of tears. We had been talking about her plan to break up with Marco for months, but up until this point, her fear of leaving him had outweighed her fear of staying with him. Marco made a point of telling her she'd be shot if she left, and had even threatened to kill any police officers that came to the home. Patricia decided that she would not only leave Marco that day, but she would also help the police safely bring him into custody to avoid the risk posed by the many handguns he owned. We sat together with a telephone between us and rehearsed the script. During a call that we recorded, Patricia told Marco that she wanted to end their fourteen-year relationship. He was at first angry, shout-

accompany you. Call your local nonemergency police number for more information. Take an untraceable means of transportation (such as a bus, not a taxi) to your destination. As soon as you get there, put your target-hardening plans into place (see Chapter 12). If you are headed to a shelter, the police may be able to give you a ride or shelter workers can meet you for pick-up.

End It from Afar

After you are a safe physical distance away from your abuser, announce the end of the relationship through the phone or by letter. Your abuser

ing obscenities and blaming Patricia for their problems. But then when he heard the icy tone of her voice, Marco realized she was serious and he started to cry. "Don't do this to me baby. I know I've been wrong, but you are the only thing I've ever cared about since we were sixteen years old." For a moment I saw Patricia's hand shake, as though her conviction were softening. But then she said slowly, with precision, "I'm outside in the car. Come talk to me if you want to work this out." As Marco stepped out his front door, he was tackled by a half dozen police officers and taken away in handcuffs.

Patricia ended up moving to a new apartment with her kids and going to school to become a dental hygienist. She and her children both received counseling.

"When I look back on that now," said Patricia, three years later, "I'm sure that if I'd broken up with Marco in person, he would have killed me, just like he always said he would. I'm just happy I got to help put that son of a bitch behind bars at the same time I made my break."

will probably be upset by this strategy, claiming that after all you've been through, you "at least owe him a face-to-face conversation" (in which he will inevitably try to talk you out of your decision). The fact is that once someone has shown themselves to be a danger to you, you owe them absolutely nothing, and you have every right to depart in whatever fashion you choose that ensures your safety and that of your children, if you have them. If you absolutely must do it in person, the breakup should take place in public where the presence of others can temper an emotional reaction (or at least provide witnesses). Make your verbal or written announcement quick and practical, and low on emotion and drama. Avoid consuming drugs or alcohol before or during the conversation since it can cloud your judgment and make you more vulnerable to him. The language you use should be direct, indicating that your decision is final. Trying to let an abusive individual down easy by gradually tapering off your involvement with him is often a futile and dangerous idea. Convey plainly that you are not "taking a break" or anything else that will give him false hope for the future—you are ending the relationship permanently. Dangerous people often do not interpret exchanges in the same way that others do, and even when they receive a clear and unambiguous message about the end of their relationship, they may continue to believe that they can restore their control through manipulation and fear.

When you have made your decision to disconnect, tell him with all your communications and actions that he is not permitted to cross your line in the sand. Establish your boundaries and stick to them, whether it is a firm no-contact command supported by a protection order or a very structured coparenting plan that does not leave you open to abuse, emotionally or otherwise. Do not be pulled into discussions about what went wrong or how he can change. And for everyone's sake, please don't continue any sexual connections. This may seem obvious, but some women think they can maintain the physical part of their relationship while ending the emotional side. Remember that "intimacy equals ownership" for many abusers, so resist the desire to perpetuate that link.

When you reach your new destination—whether it's a hotel, shelter, or other temporary housing—you may call trusted friends and family to tell them you are safe, but don't tell them where you are. This reduces the possibility that the abuser can threaten or trick them into disclosing your location. Let your loved ones know that they may not be able to see you for a while or may have to do so in a secretive fashion, away from where you are staying. If you do not have a child that is connected to your abuser's family, seriously consider cutting off contact with his inner circle. Even if this is difficult because you have a healthy relationship with them, keep in mind that your safety is more important than your friendship with his sister or coworker. Additionally, do your best to avoid involving others in the split. For instance, do not send your brother over to threaten the abuser or "set him straight" by "giving him a taste of his own medicine." This may trigger violence against you and/ or others. Leave the enforcement work to the police and courts, who have the legal authority and training to handle it. Carefully weigh the pros and cons of using potentially provocative tools such as protection orders. They can be effective at ensuring your safety, but only if used properly in the appropriate situations (see the next chapter for more information on protective orders).

Stand Your Ground

After you leave, your partner will likely try a variety of ways to suck you back into the relationship—from sweet talk to threats of violence. It is vital that you stand your ground. If you return, he may try to punish you for leaving or increase his abuse as a way to ensure you will not attempt separation again. If he is the kind of person who will put you at risk no matter when you split, why prolong it with repetitive cycles of leaving and returning, increasing your chances of harm? After the breakup, he may try to demonstrate improvement by taking actions such as attending batterers' intervention or other counseling, becoming clean and sober, working full-time, or owning up to his abusive behaviors. If these actions are present, resist the temptation to reconcile. Think carefully about the reasons you decided to leave in the first place and seek group or individual counseling to help you see the situation in an objective light. If you feel at some point down the road that you absolutely must give your partner another chance, try laying out a test boundary first. Use the three-step model to assess his intentions using a statement like the following:

When you call me several times a day, it makes me feel uncomfortable. I would prefer if you would call me once and let me return the call if and when I think it is necessary.

If he adheres to these limits, you can try putting out other more serious ones, setting up careful rules around interactions and conversations until you feel assured that a change has taken place. However, if your partner tramples these boundaries, then it is a clear sign that his "transformation" is based in words, not reality. While you can't control his actions, you can state that you refuse to participate in manipulative or otherwise emotionally abusive communications.

Following a separation, it is possible that your abuser may decide to move on with his life and allow you to move on with yours. I sincerely hope that this is your outcome. But unfortunately, we must remember that we are probably not dealing with a logical, stable, and reasonable person but rather one who may now be consumed by a sense of humiliated fury that he feels he must appease through vengeance. If your abuser decides to take a darker route, you must prepare yourself for what could be a drawn-out and dangerous battle. Please see Chapters 10–12 for guidance on how to proceed when your partner does not accept the demise of your relationship and refuses to leave you alone.

Chapter 10

Building Your Cavalry:
Getting Help from Police,
Courts, and Victim Services

There is always strength in numbers. The more individuals
or organizations that you can rally to your cause, the better.
—Mark Shields

Now that you've decided to leave your abuser and pursue a healthier, happier life free of anguish, fear, and violence, there are several considerations. First, this is not a battle you have to fight alone. If you're like most victims of domestic abuse, you've probably remained quiet about the life of torment you've been living behind closed doors. As you learned in earlier chapters, an abuser's level of control over his victim is insidious and purposeful. Abusers thrive on the assumption that you will keep quiet about what is happening, and remain cowed not only by misdirected shame, but also by the greater fear of retaliation. Your silence allows him to maintain his veneer, operating in a shadow world as you become further confused and isolated. But when you open the doors and let the light in, you may see some of his abusive behaviors scurrying away like a cockroach. Enlisting help forces him to face a cavalry instead of a single "powerless" victim. Suddenly, you're not the only one who's telling him to leave you alone—you are now backed by professionals with the knowledge and authority to make him accountable and enable your freedom. However, it is important to keep in mind that just because normal law-abiding citizens might respond with compliance to intervention by the criminal justice system, that does not mean your abuser will do the same. Personal safety expert Marc MacYoung explains:

> Most abusers lack respect for rules, social standards, and the feelings of others. Because of this sense of entitlement, they are often not responsive to the deterrents that keep the rest of civilization in line. Therefore, trusting them to follow laws or conventions can be a deadly mistake.[1]

When you're trapped in a violent relationship, calling the police or seeking other types of help and intervention can set in motion a powerful and lasting chain of events. Abusers regularly warn victims that they'll face terrible retribution if they attempt to leave or summon police. They'll think nothing of threatening to hurt or kill the victim, her family or children, themselves, or even the responding officers.

Whether you call the police, request a restraining order, or begin working with the courts, once you start the process, you are blowing the lid off a very personal and dangerous secret that your abuser does not want exposed, particularly if a crime has already been committed. Tread carefully, but don't let fear prevent you from living safe and free. The following sections will help you understand what to expect when you "turn the lights" on domestic violence.

WORKING WITH THE POLICE

For victims of intimate partner abuse, 911 is a lifeline, but there are considerations you must be aware of before using it. To begin with, most people today have a cell phone, and many have given up their landline altogether. Cell phones are great for calling for help as you leave the premises, but in most cases your location will not automatically connect as it does on a landline, so if you say nothing else, you must state where you are. In some places, cell phone users will not be connected immediately but told to "press any key," at which point you will reach an operator. Keeping these factors in mind may help to increase your safety.

Often, an abuser will try to stop you from calling 911 by pulling the phone out of the wall or out of your hands. Having a regular cell phone or 911-only cell stashed somewhere in a lockable room is your best bet. If you've only got a second to spare, be aware that you can also make incomplete 911 calls by simply stating your location as soon as you reach an operator, and then hanging up or setting the phone down so they can hear what is happening through the open line. If you hang up, they may call back; in which case, you might be able to answer and use a nonsensical communication code to help the operator understand what is occurring if you cannot explain it outright. If you do not answer their call (or the abuser answers and tells them everything is fine), chances are that the dispatcher will send police to your home anyway, particularly if they've had reason to go there before. Despite the stress of the moment, try to remain calm enough on the line that you can tell the dispatcher what is happening. Police need to know if there are weapons involved and who is in the home with you. Remember that 911 tapes are often used in court later on, so be as clear and honest as possible about the situation you are experiencing.

When your abuser knows that the police have been called, be prepared for some potentially desperate and dangerous behavior.

Many abusers will take one of several unsurprising routes: Some will backtrack and apologize in an effort to gain your forgiveness before the police show up, while others will go into cover-up or threat mode to conceal their crime. In the latter scenario, your partner may begin with the denial, minimization, and blame process to make you believe you were overreacting by calling 911. But as it advances, an abuser's "arrest avoidance plan" may move toward more anxious measures. For example, a frantic and pressured abuser may concoct a story about how his partner became injured and force her to go along with it. Abusers will often do whatever it takes to avoid being discovered and held accountable, and commonly enforce the code of silence by threatening to hurt or kill his victim or those she loves, such as in the case of forty-one-year-old Jenessa.

"As soon as I started talking to the operator, Greg grabbed the phone out of my hand and hung it up. We both understood that the cops would be arriving soon. That's when he became more desperate than I'd ever seen him. He started listing off all the ways that my calling the cops would ruin our lives, from him losing his job to all the neighbors finding out about our problems. He even suggested that child protective services would take our kids away. Eventually, he said what I knew was coming: 'This is all your fault. If I go to jail, you're gonna fucking pay for it!' I knew it was probably all talk but part of me couldn't help wondering if I'd just made a terrible mistake."

Another tactic is for the abuser to attempt the cultivation of a twisted alliance, in which he asks for pity and solidarity ("It's you and me against the world, baby!"), and then turn his anger toward the "invading" police response. When trapped in a metaphoric or literal corner, some dangerous and unstable individuals may even create a barricade or hostage situation, endangering their victim(s), the police, and neighbors/bystanders alike. The safest way to summon help is through concealing your 911 outreach by using secret cell phones,

Take Action

If your abuser tells you he doesn't care if you call the police, that he's not afraid of them or of going to jail, you may be dealing with a very dangerous individual. Such statements may be designed to project an image of bravery, or to make you feel as though there is no one who can help you. But regardless of purpose, a lack of respect for authority indicates an extreme level of impulsivity and lack of concern for consequences, both of which are high-risk traits. If you have seen your partner fight with officers, tear up court papers, or display other belligerent behaviors, you will want to forewarn police and take extra safety precautions in your situation.

hang-ups, and open lines or prearranging for someone else to call through codes.

The following sections will provide insight into what to expect when the police do respond to your 911 call.

On The Scene: How to Deal with the Police

With some exceptions, most police officers in America chose their field because they have a strong sense of justice and want to help other people. Their job is far more difficult than most of us would imagine because often they are dealing with situations and individuals that no one else can (or wants to) handle. They can save your life if you trust and allow them to help you. That being said, law enforcement officers are human beings and are therefore subject to the same frustrations, stressors, and weaknesses as the rest of us. While most officers will try to communicate efficiently and civilly with you, there may be situations in which fear, anger, or simply personality type may make it difficult for you to interact with an officer. Maintaining controlled, honest, and articulate communication with police is imperative to being believed, sympathized with, and assisted. Although police will help even uncooperative people, your chances of getting an officer to go above and beyond the call of duty will increase if you are generally polite and responsive. Appearing composed and compliant in a police report can benefit victims in the courtroom down the line as well. I understand there will be situations in which victims might be panicking, injured, and terrified when they encounter officers, and in those circumstances it would be understandable for anyone to react in a frenzied manner. There may also be cases in which a woman feels she has been treated unfairly by officers, such as if she's arrested when she was only defending herself. No matter what happens, be assured that you can deal with it later through the proper channels.

When police arrive at a location, they have several jobs to do. Some of these include securing the scene, determining the predominant aggressor, documenting evidence, taking reports, interviewing witnesses, perpetrators, and victims, and determining if an offense has been committed. They also make sure people get the medical attention they need and make any necessary arrests. This amounts to a great deal of work on their part, and incoming calls may limit how much time they can spend doing it. With all these tasks comes an added layer of safety concerns: 30 percent of all injuries to law enforcement officers, and one quarter of all on-duty deaths happen during domestic violence calls.[2] But there are ways you can help officers, and hence help yourself, by remembering a few key points:

- If you've made a 911 call, be clear about who and where the perpetrator is, and if he has weapons.
- When officers arrive, you may request to speak with them alone, out of earshot and sight of your partner. Hope-

fully, they will separate you anyway (as proper protocol dictates), but if they do not, you may remind them.

- If you don't feel safe talking to them because your abuser is there or you feel threatened, ask the officers for a business card or contact info, and follow up later with more information.

- If you would prefer to talk with a female officer, see if one is available, but don't expect it. Seasoned officers have heard and seen everything, so don't feel embarrassed about disclosing difficult details, such as a sexual assault. It's their job to listen and offer assistance.

- Sometimes you may have to communicate nonverbally with officers. For example, if they arrive and the abuser hides somewhere (which they often will), you can nod, gesture, or point to help police understand where he is.

- Provide evidence to responding officers. For example, if your abuser has broken something in a rage, ripped your clothing, written a threatening note, pulled out some of your hair, or thrown food at you, request that they document it through photographs or written descriptions.

- If other people were abused as well (particularly children), or witnessed the assault, let the police know. It demonstrates your commitment to protecting your children, should child services become involved, and adds strength to your claims if the case goes to court.

- Be sure that when the police take your statement, the reporting officer includes direct quotes from you about what happened, such as "My husband Michael kicked me in the stomach and pushed me onto the floor." In some cases, they may ask you to write out a first-person narrative of the events.

- You may state that you are afraid of your abuser and would like him arrested, but the decision is not yours to make. Victims don't press charges, the state does, so once police arrive the situation is largely out of your hands.

If the perpetrator has left and you have some idea where he may be, police may go look for him. Otherwise, they may issue a warrant for his arrest and officers can pick him up later.

Police should ask you if you want medical help. If you have been physically or sexually assaulted, it is important to be seen by a professional—particularly if you're pregnant or have a pre-existing medical condition. You may not think you need a paramedic or doctor's attention or believe you can "tough it out" with some Tylenol and an ice pack, but any marks or DNA samples on your face and body are considered evidence, and they paint a dramatic and convincing picture during trial. Request that police or medical personnel take photos of any injuries you may have, particularly in the days following the assault when bruises emerge and swelling is most evident. If they don't, you can take them yourself, but nonofficial pictures may not be admissible in court. Another reason to accept medical help is that the extent of

⚠ Take Action

If the police respond to a domestic call between you and your partner, be sure they do not leave without giving you a report or file number, their name and identification/badge number, and details for future contact. These particulars can be essential to creating a paper trail and building a court-worthy case for the future. If applicable, they may also give you information about options such as protection orders, shelters, and advocacy resources.

your injuries may be more than you realize, especially with crimes like strangulation and rape. When in doubt, get checked out.

How Your Partner May Talk to Police

When police become involved in a "domestic disturbance," abusers generally divide themselves into one of three camps. The first and smallest of these would be the men who confess their abusive actions and understand completely as officers cuff them and lead them to the squad car. They apologize profusely, state that they need help, and cry on the way to jail. They are likely few and far between.

The second group is the opposite—a collection of abusers who will see the police as an invading army and attack with everything they've got. These individuals often end up in fights, stand-offs, car chases, and hostage situations with law enforcement. They are very dangerous people.

The third and probably largest faction divides into two subgroups. The first of these includes the abusers who are generally cooperative with police and may admit they've hurt or threatened a partner but act as though they were justified in doing so. Excuses include "self-defense" and classic pretexts like, "She attacked me, I was just holding her down" and "I caught her in bed with someone else." These stories may in fact be true, but that doesn't mean the abuser is justified in brutally beating the woman involved. The second subgroup contains men who deny, minimize, and blame directly to the responding officers. They may say the victim's account of events simply never happened, or didn't happen the way she described. They may tell officers that their victim is mentally ill, intoxicated, or lying for no reason other than jealousy or spite. Abusers may even try a male sympathy ploy with officers, making sexist statements like, "You know how crazy women get when it's their time of the month."

Fortunately, most police hear this bullshit all the time and are well prepared for it. They sometimes even appear to agree with the subject in order to solicit a confession of illegal behavior. "Mandatory Arrest"

Case in Point

Many abusers are surprisingly clever and convincing when it comes to dealing with the police. Some abusers are simply twisted, and my ex-boyfriend was a perfect example. One afternoon, I found myself standing across the room from him during one of his many staged suicide attempts. I told him I was calling the police, and just as the 911 operator picked up, he began screaming that he was going to kill himself if I didn't hang up the phone. I pretended to hang up but actually just laid the receiver down so the phone line stayed open. As I tried to talk him out of hurting himself, the police were en route to my home. As soon as the doorbell rang, we both leapt up and raced downstairs to the door. He pushed me out of the way and opened the door just a crack to see two male officers standing in front. At first he tried to stammer something about an accidental 911 call, apologizing for wasting their time, but by then I was right behind him. "I want to talk to you!" I shouted over his head at the police.

laws state that police must make an arrest if they have probable cause to believe that a crime of physical or sexual assault (or the imminent threat of such) has been committed. However, this does not mean your abuser will always be arrested for abusing you. There may not be enough evidence for officers to meet the standard of proof required, or the abuser may just be particularly adept at manipulating police and anyone else who comes in contact with their behavior. Some abusers project an image of being above reproach, upstanding, and influential citizens who deserve special treatment. They may even be law enforcement officers themselves.

While there are any number of ways your partner may interact with police, remember that there is no *normal* domestic violence incident

They asked him to step outside, which he did, and then motioned for me to come toward them. In that instant, I saw my partner's face change. He became eerily calm and then conjured up a sad sort of expression as he turned to the tallest officer. "Sir," he said. "I didn't want to tell you this, because I know Lynn wants it to stay private. But I'm so glad you arrived when you did. She has been upstairs for the last hour and a half telling me she is going to kill herself." I stared at him in disbelief. "Me?" I asked. "You're saying that *I'm* the one who is suicidal? What?" My now ex-boyfriend looked me right in the eyes, cool and sincere, and said, "You know you have a problem, Lynn. The officers are here to help you. They can take you to the hospital and you can get the psychiatric care you need." Then he added intently, "*I don't want to see you end up dead.*"

Fortunately for me, the 911 tape revealed the truth and he was hospitalized for observation. Forty-eight hours later he was out and back at the house.

and outcomes will vary widely. Do not become overly concerned with what your partner says to police. Instead, concentrate on how you can prove what you have reported to them and how you can permanently remove yourself from the situation to avoid repeating your interactions with the law.

What Happens If Someone Is Arrested?

As previously mentioned, most jurisdictions in the United States observe Mandatory Arrest laws when they have probable cause to believe that abuse has been perpetrated. Typically, abuse is defined in the following ways:

- Attempting to cause, or intentionally, knowingly, or recklessly causing physical injury or serious physical injury
- Intentionally attempting to place another in fear of imminent serious bodily injury
- Causing another to engage in involuntary sexual relations by force or threat of force

Under this law, *you* can be arrested if your partner shows physical injury, even if those injuries happened while you were defending yourself. Be aware of this possibility in making your decisions, because your abuser likely has this information as well.

If your abuser is arrested at the scene, he'll usually be taken to the county jail, to the "booking" area, where he'll be fingerprinted and registered. From there, he may be transferred to a cell and released within a few hours by posting money—or "bail"—as security to guarantee his appearance at future court hearings. This is referred to as "bailing out." If the jail is full, and/or he has committed a relatively minor offense (by arrest standards) and does not have a serious criminal record, he could also be released on his own recognizance. Either way, the judge may issue a "no contact" order temporarily forbidding him from contacting you. If he is not released, he will most often have to remain there to see a judge the next business day. At that point, if the district attorney's office has not filed criminal charges, he might be released.

If you have been the victim of domestic violence, you should contact the district attorney's/prosecutor's office as early as possible after arrest to ask about pressing criminal charges while the offender is still in custody. Remember that in reality, the victim doesn't press charges, the state does. All they ask of you is your cooperation and participation in prosecution. While this seems like a terrifying step for victims to take, it can go a long way toward stopping the abuse

> ### ⚠ Take Action
>
> If your abuser is arrested, you must request that the jail contact you *before* he is released so you can prepare for your safety. In most states, you can also use an automated system called VINE (Victim Information and Notification Everyday). Calling and registering the offender's name with VINE will help you find out his status and be automatically notified of his release. The number for VINE is 1-877-OR-4-VINE (1-877-674-8463). Or access VINE online at www.vinelink.com.

and holding the offender accountable to lessen the chances that they will hurt you or anyone else again. Victim-witness coordinators or advocates are usually available to help you through the process, and one can be available to meet with you and the prosecutor. Their role is described later in this chapter.

If the district attorney's office feels that the case can be successfully prosecuted, they will file charges and the arrested person will enter a plea (guilty or not guilty) to the judge at arraignment (see more about navigating the legal system later in this chapter). They may hire an attorney, or have a public defender assigned to them. After making the plea, they may be released and given a date to return for trial. For some prisoners, release will be denied and they must then stay in jail, at which point their lawyer can call for a release hearing and try to get them out before trial.

THE PROTECTIVE ORDER: PROS AND CONS

Protective orders may also be called "injunctions" or "restraining orders," depending on where you live. They are a civil decree issued by a judge that orders one person not to "harass, intimidate, harm, molest, or interfere" with another. In the absence of one, committing some of these offenses is not necessarily against the law.

Protection orders can often be tailored to individual needs and requests, including removing the abuser from the home, restricting his access to his children, and allowing some types of contact, as long as they are "nonoffensive." According to federal law, respondents of a restraining order are not allowed to possess firearms, and the judge can order that any guns in the home be removed.

Protection orders are typically applied for at a courthouse, but in some counties, they're now also offered in satellite offices located within Family Justice Centers, which serve as a one-stop hub to centralize victim resources. Some states even offer forms online through the state's website, where you can fill them out in advance and then deliver them to the courthouse. Protective orders are issued without cost to the victim, are usually activated quickly, and do not require a lawyer to apply for (although you may want a lawyer if the order is contested). In most states, to be eligible, the petitioner (the abused or threatened party applying for protection) must have had one of the following relationships with the abuser (who in legal terms is called the "respondent"):

- Current or former spouse
- Related by blood, marriage, or adoption
- Living together now or in the past, in a sexually intimate relationship
- Shared a sexually intimate relationship in the past two years
- Unmarried parents of a minor child
- Be a minor involved in a sexually intimate relationship with the respondent, who is 18 or older

Typically, the petitioner must have been the victim of abuse or threats of abuse during the recent past (often 180 days) and must believe they are in danger of further abuse. In some states, you may be able to get a protection order for abuse or threats that happened more than 180 days prior to the request, but only if the abuser has been out of town or in jail.

When you apply for an order in person, advocates may be available either on-site or by appointment to help you fill out the paperwork. Be sure to articulate why you are afraid of this person and provide exact details about when, where, and how he hurt you or put you in fear of being hurt. Keep in mind that the respondent and his attorney will get copies of the documents, so ask the court clerk for a form to request confidentiality, which conceals your current address, if needed.

Frequently, applications must be turned in by a certain time on the day you wish to see the judge, who will ask you some brief questions. She'll then reject or accept the petition and grant a temporary order. This entire process usually takes two to three hours midday. If it is accepted, the abuser must be located and served with the order.

The order cannot be enforced until the respondent has been served, so it is important that you have at least some idea where he might be found. In most counties, respondents are served by law enforcement officers or other agents of the court, but you typically must call to arrange delivery or drop the paperwork at the precinct or court office (located either inside or separately from the courthouse). Be aware that they are usually very busy and will only make a few attempts to locate the respondent.

Once served, the respondent has the right to contest the order. Whether or not he does, you will likely have to attend a hearing held several weeks later to decide if the order becomes permanent. Advocates from a local domestic violence shelter or resource center may be available to attend the hearing with you, and you are always welcome to bring along a friend for support (however, it's best to avoid bringing children or "inflammatory" companions, such as a new boyfriend).

If he contests the restraining order—particularly if he hires an attorney to defend him—you should find legal representation as well. If you cannot afford it, please contact your nearest victim services center/battered women's shelter for referrals to local legal aid clinics. The following tips will help you prepare:

1. If you represent yourself in court (through choice or necessity) be informed and organized, because going up against a professional attorney can be brutal. Check out WomensLaw.org for helpful information about preparing for the hearing (www.womenslaw.org/simple.php?site map_id=32).

2. At the hearing, the judge will decide whether or not there is enough evidence to make the protection order permanent, which can mean that it remains in place anywhere from one to five years, depending on what you have requested and what state you live in.

3. If you do not attend the hearing or fail to prove your case, the protection order will be dropped. If the respondent does not contest, or does not show up to the hearing, the extended order will often be granted in his absence, and in some cases an arrest warrant may be issued.

4. In many states, you can request the opportunity to renew the order at the end of its term, providing there is still reason for you to fear for your safety. You must apply to renew it before the judicially imposed period expires.

5. If the restraining order is upheld, you should keep a registered copy and "proof of service" on you at all times and leave copies at places that you and your children frequent, such as with schools or daycare providers.

If the respondent violates the order in a way that makes you fear for your safety, call 911 immediately. In a less urgent situation (such as a voicemail message), you can call the nonemergency number and a report may be taken over the phone. Most protection orders are enforceable in every state, thanks to a law called "Full Faith and Credit," so your order travels with you. But if you move permanently, be sure to register it with the courthouse in your new jurisdiction. Only a judge can dismiss, change, or remove a protection order before it expires, and some courts require victims to take a domestic violence education class or meet with an advocate before requesting such an action.

As an alternative (or addition) to a protection order, you can request a "stalking order" to prevent your abuser from threatening you. This can be issued if there has been more than one unwanted contact that would put a reasonable person in fear of her safety. Usually, you don't need to have had prior assault or even verbal threats of injury. Stalking orders can be useful in situations where no sexual relationship (only a dating relationship) or no relationship at all has occurred. In some states, they have more legal teeth than a domestic violence protection order and often last longer. Oregon, for example, has a lifetime stalking order that never expires, and it's an instant felony if the respondent violates it a second time. You may even be able to obtain both a stalking order *and* a domestic violence restraining order, which offers you double the legal protection. Since the standards of what constitutes a violation may differ with each order, you could potentially hold your abuser accountable with one if the other doesn't apply, or on both if they have been dually violated.

In most cases, you must go to court to obtain a stalking order, but in some states police can issue a "stalking citation," which is a kind of "ticket" that requires the perpetrator to appear in court. At that time, a stalking charge or permanent order may be put in place.

The wholesale recommendation of protective orders is a matter of sometimes intense debate among professionals who deal with intimate partner abuse. On one hand, court orders are a powerful tool for police and prosecutors. That piece of paper allows them to arrest perpetrators for behavior that authorities otherwise wouldn't have much control over. Protection orders can "lay out a trap," so to speak, for abusers because although there is nothing deceitful about arresting someone for violating a court order with which they were served, many abusers are careful to walk the line of legality within their abuse. They will push the boundaries of statute, and sometimes need to be given specific limits to violate before they can be caught and held accountable for doing so.

Another upside of protection orders is that they put muscle and meaning behind a woman's plea to be left alone by her abuser. If you get one, now it is no longer just you trying to defend yourself. When the order is issued, the police and courts now stand alongside you, and create a much more formidable team of opponents for the abuser. They also show him that a civilized society will not tolerate or condone interpersonal violence.

While protection orders demonstrate serious legal protection for victims, there are a number of downsides to them as well. The first is that while they are a powerful piece of paper, they are just that: a piece of paper. A court decree is not a bulletproof shield. In domestic violence cases, protection orders are violated about half the time. In some cases, they may even make the situation worse by exacerbating an already unstable offender. To have a false sense of security in such a situation is a serious disadvantage.

Case in Point

While protection orders and stalking orders can be effective in keeping certain types of abusers away, others will flaunt them outright—even reacting by further intimidating and harassing you. Celeste, a twenty-eight-year-old former client, said: "Every time I told anyone (family, friends, police) about how Brad was abusing me, they all said the same thing, 'Get a restraining order!' like that would solve all my problems. So I did, but it just seemed to ratchet things up a notch. As soon as he was served, he started calling and texting me with all kinds of horrible threats. I told the police, but I didn't understand how to capture the evidence at the time, and there wasn't any proof. When I came home one night to find him sitting on my doorstep I called as well, but he just left before the police could respond. Now I'm constantly looking over my shoulder. In a way, it makes me even more afraid, because if Brad doesn't care about the cops or the courts, what is he capable of doing to me?"

Another reason to think carefully about protection orders is that they are not always well enforced or well prosecuted in every jurisdiction. When an abuser violates the victim's orders, the court's orders, *and* society's orders with impunity, he becomes emboldened and virtually encouraged to reoffend.

With all these points in mind, your choice to request a protection order must be carefully considered. Before applying for one, ask yourself the following questions:

1. Has your abuser been responsive to the criminal justice system in the past? For example, has he paid parking tickets, allowed his vehicle to be searched, or complied with

simple court instructions like attending jury duty? If so, he may be more accepting of a judge's decree—but there's no telling how he'll respond to something so personally directed. If not, it's a good indication that the order may simply inflame him, putting you in greater danger.

2. Have you ever had a protection order against him in the past, or has anyone else that you're aware of (note: this information is easily searched in public court records)? If so, did he abide by it?

3. Has your partner ever specifically mentioned what he would do if you applied for or received a protection order?

4. How do you honestly think he will react when he is served with the order? Based on what you know about him, what might he be thinking as the officers hand it to him? Where will you be when this happens and is your safety plan in place to anticipate and deal with any blowback?

Keep in mind that your abuser will not only see the order as a symbol of you trying to control him, but also as an indication that you have brought the situation into the light and involved "outside" parties, like agents of the government, which he may already despise.

If you choose to get a protection order, there are a few important things to remember: First, your abuser may employ a variety of tactics to convince you to speak to him or see him after the order has been issued, ranging from sweet-talk to bribes to threats. Although you cannot technically "break" your own restraining order, a judge may not respond to violations in which the victim invited the abuser to her home, and some may even lift the order if they feel she is not taking it seriously. In addition, such actions send a powerful message to the abuser that you are not committed to severing contact.

Second, if he does violate the order, be diligent about documenting and reporting violations, otherwise the order may be a waste of everyone's time. For example, if he comes to your home and then leaves before police arrive, it may be your word against his. But if you present a date-stamped digital photo of him standing on your doorstep, the burden becomes his to prove otherwise. Just make sure you aren't putting yourself at risk while you collect evidence. For example, don't open the door to photograph him standing there. Instead, lean out the top floor window and snap it incognito, or call your next door neighbor and ask them to take a picture from their backyard balcony. There are many ways you can document violations of a protection order.

For instance, you can acquire a new telephone number (perhaps on the same phone) and give it to those who you want to continue contact with. Maintain a separate ringtone and voicemail account for the original line and let the abuser call the old number—as much as he wants. You will never pick up the calls (silence the ringer if needed); instead, you will have recorded messages he leaves, proving both the violation itself and any threats or intimidating language that may accompany it. The downside to this tactic is that some abusers may become further enraged when their victim doesn't answer the phone and come looking for her in person. Check messages frequently to get a better idea of where he stands emotionally.

Additionally, if you are concerned that your abuser is a stalker, knowing where he is in proximity to you can be an advantage. Ideally, that information would be disclosed by the abuser, perhaps in a message stating something like "I'm at home, call me back," rather than in conversation. Remember, picking up the phone to find out where he is could be considered "encouraging contact" in the eyes of some judges, not to mention that most postprotection order contacts expose the victim to further verbal abuse, emotional manipulation, and threats.

> ### ⚠️ Take Action
>
> A restraining order is only as powerful as it is enforceable. Be sure to document every instance your abuser violates the order. It gives the courts and police vital evidence to act on the violations. Otherwise, it's often his word against yours. Keep a binder with paperwork such as log or journal entries, phone records, photos, and medical and police reports, all color-coded and assembled by date. This is a prosecutor's dream and can help to prove in court what you've been experiencing in a clear and supportable format. It can also help you by presenting an objective view of what this person is really doing so you avoid the temptation to minimize and dismiss patterns of concerning behaviors.

WORKING WITH THE COURTS

If your case ends up in court, either because your abuser was arrested on domestic violence charges, or he violated a restraining order, be prepared for a complex, sometimes frustrating, but often liberating process. It's not always easy, and sometimes because of bureaucracy and case backlogs, it can be a long and arduous journey. But your safety and well-being, and that of your children, are worth it. The following sections will provide you with valuable information about navigating this phase on your path to freedom.

District Attorneys: The Victim's Representative

District attorneys (DAs)—also called prosecutors—represent the state and your community in criminal proceedings. Therefore, they also represent you as a citizen and victim, but they are not your attorney so no confidentiality exists between you. For example, if you say something to the DA that suggests your abuser may not have committed a crime, that is considered "exculpatory evidence" (evidence showing innocence or detracting from guilt) and must be turned over to the defense. Additionally, even if you do not wish to participate in prosecution and want the charges dropped, the DA may move forward anyway in the interest of the public.

Depending on where you live, you may work with the local DA or with one of many assistant or deputy DAs. If the DA's office in your jurisdiction encourages "vertical prosecution," this means you will stay with the same prosecutor (and judge) for the duration of the case.

As mentioned earlier, if your abuser has been arrested for a domestic violence incident and you want him held accountable, contact the DA's office right away and establish your interest in taking proactive steps toward seeking justice. Important decisions are often made within the first seventy-two hours of an arrest, so it is imperative to initiate and maintain communication throughout the process.

The DA will work closely with law enforcement to prove the case against a defendant, and it is in their best interest as well as yours to win. However, they have a strict set of legal rules they must abide by, and regardless of what they want to see happen, a judge, jury, or obscure legal regulation may affect the outcome of your proceedings. At the arraignment (when the defendant first pleads guilty or not guilty), two important opportunities may coincide: that of the defendant to post bail (and be released) and that of the DA to request a "criminal protective order."

If you feel that there are safety concerns around your abuser's release, you must inform the DA immediately, because he will likely have to appear at a bail hearing and argue why the offender should not be released. The second reason to make your anxiety clear is that the DA can also request the criminal protective order, which covers you and your children, without you having to fill out forms or appear in court. The fact that the DA has enough evidence to file charges is usually enough for the judge to grant it. These are two more examples of why it is important for you to establish and maintain close contact with the prosecutor and his or her team.

Defense Attorneys: The Abuser's Representative

If your abuser has been arrested and charged with "domestic abuse," he will likely have an attorney as well. Some particularly egomaniacal perpetrators may try to represent themselves in court, but most will hire a defense attorney or have a public defender provided to him at no cost. Like the prosecutor, their job is to serve their client's best interests, which means that they will usually portray him as a decent upstanding citizen who has been wrongly accused by you, the police, and the state.

Defense attorneys typically will not ask their clients if they are guilty because confession of a crime can limit the attorney's options in providing ethical representation. Information exchanged between them and their clients is confidential and doesn't have to be reported unless the defendant divulges plans to commit a future crime. Their job is simply to seek release, acquittal, or the least possible punishment according to the law. Unfortunately, in order to support that agenda, it's often the job of the defense attorney to make you look like a lying, scheming, possibly addicted or insane idiot, not to mention a terrible mother and partner. Because you know at this point that a person's livelihood depends upon casting you in a poor light, you should be very aware of what they are doing while at the same time try not to become

Case in Point

When it comes to domestic violence court, it's important to know that your abuser will stop at nothing to make a case in his favor. Take the case of forty-four-year-old Emily: "I thought Todd said some vile things about me during our marriage, but that was nothing compared to what was said in court. He and his lawyer not only suggested that I was lying about the abuse but also inferred that I was crazy because I took antianxiety pills to ease the stress of being abused. When I admitted on the stand that I did have a prescription for Xanax, the attorney tried to turn my occasional use into a drug problem. Todd even convinced some so-called friends of mine to testify that I was the abuser because they'd seen me yell at him once or twice. Of course, Todd made sure no one ever saw him beating the shit out of me. The last straw was when his attorney suggested that my desire to have a sexual relationship with my uncle was behind my claims of abuse. Todd knew my uncle had molested me as a child, and it was unbelievably painful to hear them say that. I knew Todd was evil, but sometimes you don't know just what a person is capable of until you reject and reveal them."

Emily eventually won her case and Todd was sentenced to one year in jail followed by several years of probation.

too bothered by it. The defense attorney may do everything he or she can to ruffle you on the stand and evoke angry, hysterical responses. Even if they are rude and insensitive toward you or your witnesses in court, you must not react by arguing or insulting them. Let the prosecutor and judge do their job of making sure you are treated fairly, and don't take the defense attorney's bitter bait. It's not personal.

Do your best to avoid giving them any fuel to stoke their case. Start by monitoring your social networking activity and other communications. For example, don't post profane rants about your abuser the night before a custody hearing. Cutting loose with verbal venom can make you look like an angry aggressor and an unfit parent, not to mention that it gives your legal opponents ammunition, and risks destabilizing your already dangerous abuser. Lay low and focus on safety during domestic violence proceedings.

Also keep in mind that the defense attorney (or an investigator working for them) may contact you, but you are not required to answer any questions unless you are standing in front of a judge. You may be greeted with an innocuous introduction such as, "Hello, I'm an attorney on the Smith case. Can I ask you a couple questions?" If so, hang up. If any attorney or investigator from the defense comes to your home, you have the right to ask for identification, and also the right to order them off your property. They may even approach you at the courthouse before a hearing, trying to get you to agree to some kind of out-of-court arrangement. No matter how nice they seem, they are *not* on your side and are likely trying to trap you into saying things (on record) that may later damage your case. Report any such contacts to the prosecutor immediately.

While you are waiting for the legal proceedings to unfold, it may seem like the case is going on without your input or awareness, and this can cause a sense of powerlessness in an already frightening situation. Understand that there are many minute legal details you will not be consulted on, but if you are curious or concerned about what is underway you have a right to be heard. Call the DA's office and get updated about your case frequently, using the case number that is now public record. Anyone can inquire about the basic status of a case, such as what charges have been filed and when the next court date is, but your name and contact information as victim will remain confidential. Remember to be polite to the clerks, leave clear and concise messages,

⚠ **Take Action**

The criminal justice process can be very complicated, with many potential outcomes along the way. To view a detailed flowchart of the system, please visit the following link: www.victimlaw.info/victimlaw/pages/justiceSystem.jsp.

write everything down, and return prosecutor phone calls promptly. Being an engaged, informed, and cooperative witness is of utmost importance to the success of your case.

The Role of the Judge

Many of us have only seen courtrooms on TV, and dealing with the proceedings and people inside can seem very intimidating. At the top of that list is the imposing, black-robed figure that runs the show, otherwise known as the judge. While they may seem unapproachable, keep in mind that the judge is a human being just like you, and while they do serve a serious function, they are also there to listen. The main job of the judge (beyond issuing final decisions on outcome and sentencing) is to make sure the case is handled properly and that the attorneys are doing their jobs right. In this sense, they can be powerful allies for victims who feel that their rights are not being respected and protected. You are permitted to write to the judge in a variety of situations, including to request an increase or denial of bail, or provide you with a criminal protective order. Consider the following tips to make sure your request is received and considered:

1. Go through the prosecutor to make your request. Not only do they have a better relationship with the judge and

> ⚠️ **Take Action**
>
> If you are involved in a domestic violence case, particularly one that goes to the police and/or the courts, there is a website that may be very helpful to you. The Women's Justice Center/*Centro de Justicia para Mujeres* (www.justicewomen.com) is full of common sense, user-friendly information, and grassroots strategies for getting your case the attention and service it needs. Please check out and support this valuable resource.

therefore a better chance of having the request accepted, but they won't feel as though you've gone over their head by jumping to the judge. However, if the prosecutor is the problem, don't hesitate to contact the head honcho for assistance.

2. Make sure your letter is concise, easily understandable, and polite. State your purpose in the beginning and stick to the topic at hand. Your communication must include your signature and date of birth, the case number, and the date you are writing or submitting the letter.

3. Indicate to the judge that you are a participating, cooperative witness. This will let them know that you are serious and valuable to the case.

4. Do not mention case evidence in the letter because the judge may be required to stop reading it. Focus on procedural issues and concerns about the conduct of the players.

5. You can send the letter by mail, deliver it to the judge's office, or directly hand the letter to the bailiff or court clerk on the day of your hearing. Be sure you have copies for yourself, and remember that everyone else (including the prosecutor, the defense attorney, and the defendant) will likely receive one too.

The Role of the Jury

Another group of individuals you may encounter in the courtroom is the jury. Some trials do not include a citizen panel, but if yours does, it is important to remember that they too have a strict set of rules to abide by. You may not speak to jury members unless you are directed to do so on the stand. You should dress professionally and groom yourself well. You also should avoid using profanity, displaying outbursts of anger, smiling, sneering, laughing, or making any other overt signals toward the jury because it is hard to interpret how they will react. For instance, I once served as advocate on a case where the prosecutor specifically selected a woman for the jury based on the fact that she admitted to being a survivor of domestic violence. He thought she would automatically sympathize with the victim. However, the tactic backfired when the female juror wrote a letter to the judge complaining about the presentation of the case. She admitted that she disliked the victim, whom she felt "brought the violence on herself" and "deserved to be abused" because she appeared arrogant and self-centered. Although we were all surprised that a former victim of abuse would treat another woman this way, we learned the lesson that jurors are individuals, and thus have personal opinions that can't always be predicted.

Another issue with juries is that they are bound to make decisions based on the intricacies of the law. For example, they may believe wholeheartedly that a defendant is guilty, but that is not the question they are being asked to evaluate. Technically, they are being asked if the state has proved his guilt beyond a reasonable doubt, and that can be quite a different situation from "solid" guilt. While a jury may empathize with you and wish you the best, they may also, by law, be required to set your abuser free.

YOUR RIGHTS AS VICTIM

While it sometimes may seem that our justice system is designed to protect offenders, the victim's rights movement is stronger today than it has ever been. Many states have adopted amendments to their constitutions that guarantee certain rights to victims of crime. Some even have built-in enforcers that penalize officials or state agencies when these rights are not observed. With some legal exceptions and variations, your core rights as a victim include the following:

- The right to attend criminal justice proceedings
- The right to apply for compensation
- The right to be heard and participate in criminal justice proceedings
- The right to be informed of proceedings and events in the criminal justice process, of legal rights and remedies, and of available services
- The right to protection from intimidation and harassment
- The right to restitution from the offender
- The right to prompt return of personal property seized as evidence
- The right to a speedy trial
- The right to enforcement of these rights

Take Action

1. For a full explanation of each of your rights, please visit the following website: http://www.victimlaw .info/victimlaw/pages/victimsRight.jsp.

2. For a breakdown of victim rights by state, please visit the following website: http://crime.about .com/od/victimsrightsbystate/Crime_Victims_ Rights_by_State.htm.

If you feel that these rights have been violated or ignored, begin by letting the prosecutor or judge know. If this does not resolve the issue, you may be able to file a legal "Claim of Violation of Crime Victims' Rights" through your state Department of Justice. If the violation occurred in federal court, contact your state's U.S. attorney's office.

Witness "Influence" and Safety During the Legal Phase

Witness tampering is defined as harming or threatening to harm a witness in order to manipulate their testimony in a court case. But in the realm of intimate partner violence, this abuser tactic often takes on a much more subtle and sinister note. Instead of using the term "witness tampering" or "intimidation," I prefer to call it "witness influence," because this form of pressure often comes wrapped in pretty and persuasive packaging. For example, I was once tasked with reviewing taped conversations between an inmate and his victim in a serious domestic violence case. What I heard from this perpetrator (and from many others throughout the years) was not intimidating or threatening at all. Instead, he asked his estranged wife for pity and understanding. He apologized and told her over and over how much he loved her and their children. At the end, he even threw in the suggestion that he could help pay the rent if he was released, knowing that she was having financial troubles on her own. All of these sweet phrases came *after* he had broken her jaw and chased her through a public park with a shotgun. It was his third domestic violence offense.

While some abusers may use fear to control their victims both inside and outside the relationship, just as many will use other forms of emotional, social, religious, or financial coercion. Depending on victim vulnerability factors including age, race, faith, sexual orientation, disabilities, and substance abuse or mental health issues, some abusers may have more ammunition than others. The only way to help guard against these pressures is to avoid any verbal or written contact with your abuser after he has been arrested. If you aren't communicating with him, he won't have the chance to sway you away from the decisions that will help keep you safe.

Unfortunately, some abusers may resort to using third parties to do their dirty work for them. They may enlist family, friends, neighbors, coworkers, fellow gang members, or even innocent children to try and influence their victim's thoughts and intentions. Just as direct witness tampering is a crime, doing it through third parties is also. In some

⚠ Take Action

If your abuser is trying to contact you himself or through another person, inform the prosecutor and request a civil or criminal protective order. The DA may be able to collect enough evidence to proceed with official witness-tampering charges, which will make the case against your abuser that much more powerful.

states, even attempting to prevent a victim from calling 911 can be considered witness tampering.

Financial Support for Victims

All individual states have victim's compensation programs that may be able to help with some of the financial costs you have incurred as a result of your abuser's actions. These programs typically cover the following types of expenses:

- Mental health counseling expenses
- Medical and hospital expenses
- Eyeglasses, hearing aids, dentures, and other medically necessary devices and expenses
- Rehabilitation expenses
- Loss of earnings
- Funeral expenses
- Loss of financial support to dependents of homicide victims
- Grief counseling expenses for relatives of homicide victims
- Counseling expenses for children who witness domestic violence

Some states also have laws that allow employees to take time off of work for domestic violence related medical treatment, police interviews, or court dates without fear of being fired. If you do have to leave your job or are dismissed because of an abuse related issue, you may be entitled to collect unemployment. Check with your state's Department of Human Services or employment commission to see if such possibilities exist in your location.

> ⚠️ **Take Action**
>
> Applications for crime victim's compensation can be obtained at your county prosecutor's office, and victim advocates are generally available to help you fill out the paperwork. The National Association of Crime Victim Compensation Boards (www.nacvcb.org) can also help you to learn what is available in your area.

While the criminal justice system can be challenging and unpredictable, it still offers victims of abuse their best chance at holding perpetrators accountable. Most professionals who work there have a strong sense of justice and want to help you, but are limited without your understanding and cooperation, so keep in mind that you are all members of the same team. Now that you understand the roles of the players on this field, it's time to search out other people in your life who may be able to assist and protect you in your journey toward freedom. We are all stronger standing shoulder to shoulder than cowering alone, so don't be afraid to ask for their help.

Chapter 11

Strengthen Your Alliances:
Finding Support within the Community

Individually, we are one drop. Together, we are an ocean.
—Ryunosuke Satoro

In the not too distant past, women who were victims of intimate partner violence didn't have many options for help. The law did not protect them like it does today, and until grassroots women's shelters began popping up in the 1970s, they had few choices other than fleeing to a relative's home, entering a convent, or living at a segregated homeless shelter. The assistance they received was usually given by family, friends, or on occasion, the church. For our grandmothers and beyond, there was no class of professional victim-service providers, and without the support of the criminal justice system, victims were largely on their own. Today, the country is filled with practitioners who specialize in advocacy, domestic violence law, victimology, victim's rights, post-abuse therapy, and other feminist-driven, victim-focused fields. Many

> ⚠️ **Take Action**
>
> Everyone's situation is different. If you're not sure where to start, given your circumstances, call the National Domestic Violence Hotline at 1-800-799-SAFE (7233) or 1-800-787-3224 (TTY). They will listen, offer you a multitude of options, and direct you to more local services for continued assistance.

of them are abuse survivors themselves and have received extensive training in their areas. Nowadays, connecting with these informed and caring individuals is as easy as getting on a computer or a telephone or taking a short trip to meet in person.

The following sections will provide an overview of services available to help victims as they navigate the legal, emotional, and/ or defensive territory that comes from fleeing their abuser. From government services and nonprofit agencies, to family, neighbors, and employers, there's ample support out there to fortify your defensive bulwark. Now's the time to activate your network.

VICTIM ADVOCATES

A domestic violence "victim advocate" is a professional (usually a woman) whose job is essentially to serve as a guide in the frightening wilderness of intimate partner abuse. She may be employed by a nonprofit or government organization, a school, an employee-assistance program, or a criminal justice agency. Her training will vary, but for a lot of advocates, experience is the best teacher and many come from diverse educational and societal backgrounds, prepared to help. Some advocates are available to respond 24/7, while others are stationed in agencies or accompany police and district attorneys during interactions with victims. They provide crisis intervention, safety and support planning, court accompaniment, and assistance with paperwork. Many are masters at navigating the social service system and have local resources committed to memory. They can help you find the appropriate kind of support and assistance for your situation and will stand up for you when officials throw red tape in your path. Advocates can even help with logistical issues, such as transportation, arranging childcare, and finding basic resources like food and shelter.

While many of your friends and family may try to help you, they don't have the specialized knowledge and training that an advocate does. An experienced advocate will work closely with you to form a plan for your safety and act as a conduit for communication between you and the other professionals in your cavalry. They are adept at finding answers to seemingly unsolvable problems, and they operate within a huge network of organizations established to coordinate around your situation.

Of all the things an advocate does, perhaps the most valuable is that they *listen and believe*, offering nonjudgmental understanding in a whirlwind of confusion and fear. Good advocates don't push their own agenda on victims and will respect whatever choices you make about your future. They will stand by your side throughout the process and never give up on you, even if you temporarily give up on yourself. Simply put, advocates are the overworked, underpaid backbone of the domestic violence movement, filling shelters, courtrooms, and hospitals everywhere with the incandescent spirit of hope.

A note about advocates: Know exactly who your advocate works for, because if they are employed by a police department or district attorney's office they may have different rules around what can be kept private and what must be reported. Some may also be state-mandated reporters of child abuse. During your first conversation, ask

> ### ⚠ Take Action
>
> How do you find an advocate? Start by calling your local domestic violence shelter, state coalition (see Resources list at the end of the book), or state human services department. If you are employed, check with a human resources representative to see if an employee assistance program is available. If you have a case in the criminal justice system, you may have access to police or district attorney's advocates. Check with local nonprofits as well—community organizations such as United Way and Volunteers of America often have partnerships with victim service agencies.

the advocate to thoroughly explain the parameters of confidentiality regarding your work together.

WOMEN'S SHELTERS

Let's begin with the truth: No one wants to leave their comfort zone and step into a communal living situation with strangers, but for many women who are victims of domestic violence, the alternative means certain mental, physical, or sexual abuse. The idea of bringing yourself and your children into an uncertain and unfamiliar place can be frightening, often because you have no idea what to expect on the other side of that door. But for women who need an immediate safe place to stay, it is an invaluable resource, regardless of its pros and cons.

First, while many shelters are very comfortable facilities, they are not the Waldorf Astoria, and they are not designed for permanent residence. When you enter, probably after having been screened via telephone, you will have an arrival interview and be provided a bed

> ### Case in Point
>
> "The night we arrived at the shelter, my kids and I were terrified. The police dropped us off after a really bad blow-up with Abel, and we had no idea what we were doing in the next few hours, let alone months. As soon as we got in the door though, I felt like we were safe. There was this sense of sisterhood inside, like everyone there understood what we were going through. I spent the next few weeks working with my case manager, talking in the support group with the other residents, and feeling free for the first time in years. My counselor even hooked us up with a Native American healing circle at the reservation, so I could connect with women like myself. By the time we left, I felt stronger than ever. Shelter was the perfect jump-off point to our new life."
>
> —Josephine, age thirty-two

and bathroom that may or may not be in a private room. If you need food, clothing, or toiletries immediately, shelter workers will likely be able to assist you. You may be assigned chores and given a briefing on house rules, including curfew, childcare, and drug and alcohol policies (in most shelters, drugs and alcohol are prohibited, for obvious reasons).

In the days following your arrival, you may meet with a caseworker or attend counseling sessions and house meetings as part of your living agreement. While you can still attend work and your children may still attend school, the shelter location must remain confidential. Of course, there is always the risk that if you show up at places known to the abuser, you may be attacked or followed upon return (as you learned in Chapter 10, restraining orders may not necessarily deter your abuser from doing so).

It's also important to know that there may or may not be a place for you to keep any belongings you have brought, let alone a place to park your car (especially in congested city centers). Sometimes, communal living situations have problems with diseases such as lice, impetigo, and scabies. In fact, some facilities require proof of a TB test to enter.

The complexities of shelter life are many, and some residents may not be able to endure the pressure of cohabitating with a wide range of personalities. Having worked in and visited dozens of different shelters, I can honestly tell you that while they vary in conditions and regulations, they all share some important common features:

- Shelters are created and staffed by people who have genuine compassion and skill for helping women in diverse and stressful situations. They are open and accepting, and in most shelters, you will not be asked to prove your abuse, citizenship, or legal status.

- Shelters are places of support and strength, drawn from both the workers and the residents who lean on one another and foster a sisterhood, encouraging recovery and self-reliance.

- Shelters are havens of resource and assistance, where food, beds, showers, and respite can be obtained without having to trade safety for necessity, like you would with an abuser.

- Shelters are vital sanctuaries where women and children can hide while transitioning to new lives, learning to exist without the shadows of fear that permeate a victim's days.

Some women may want to seek refuge in a shelter but are unable to because they have addiction issues, physical or mental disabilities, or language and literacy barriers. Some cannot go because they have a teenage son with them, which many shelters don't allow. For a lot of applicants, the shelters are simply full. Statistics show that at any given time, one-third of shelters are regularly full and often exceed their capacity.[1] To put that in perspective, consider the annual "single-day" count that the National Network to End Domestic Violence does to reveal the scope and prevalence of victim needs. Their most recent count showed that in 2010, on a single day in September, there were 37,519 people staying in domestic violence shelters and transitional housing programs across the United States. Of that number, more than 20,000 were children. On that same day, more than 22,000 hotline calls were answered, and nearly 10,000 requests for help went unmet because of inadequate funding or staff to assist victims.[2]

In light of such dire statistics, some organizations are looking for ways to make diminishing funding stretch even further. For instance, a program in Portland, Oregon, has developed a model of support that seems to be catching on. Home Free, a domestic violence program established through Volunteers of America, addresses the issue of providing sanctuary to women who can't otherwise use the shelter system. The program not only provides individually tailored long-term support to victims of abuse, it also features a hotel voucher system to house families who are otherwise out of options. This is often followed by participation in a transitional housing program where victims and their children can live in rent-subsidized apartments, continuing to receive counseling and support as they move toward independence.

Although packing up limited belongings and changing everything about your surroundings is not an appealing or fair option for dealing with abuse, it is often the difference between life and death. Not all situations require "going underground," but staying in an undisclosed and fortified location, such as a shelter, is certainly an effective way to reduce your accessibility (and therefore vulnerability) to attack.

> **⚠ Take Action**
>
> For more information on the Home Free program, visit their website at (www.voaor.org/Learn-About-our-Services/Children-and-Family-Services/Home-Free.aspx). For more information on the shelter system in your area, please see the state-by-state coalition guide in the Resources at the end of this book or call the National Domestic Violence Hotline at 1-800-799-SAFE.

SOCIAL SERVICES

While there are many barriers to freedom and safety in intimate partner abuse, one of the biggest, by far, is a lack of cash. One of an abuser's most common tactics for maintaining control over his victim is restricting access to money, and the less financial strength a woman has, the fewer opportunities she has for permanent escape. Fortunately, there are many organizations and services throughout the United States that recognize this need and address it through innovative assistance programs.

The first place to start if you need help is your state's department of human services. Most states have special funds set aside to aid victims of abuse as they set out on their journey. The best example is the Temporary Assistance to Domestic Violence Survivors (TA-DVS) grant. This goes by various names in different places but is essentially an economic safety net, providing a particular amount of money (usually around $1,200–$2,000 dollars) for the establishment of a safer existence. This is typically used for setting up new housing, but it can also be used to pay for expenses such as hotels, transportation, a cell phone, or additional clothing for the women and children who leave with nothing but the clothes on their backs.

In many cases, you will not have to provide police reports to prove that you are a victim, but you will have to answer questions about your situation and make steps toward safety and self-sufficiency. Often, the grant can be linked with other state-sponsored services, such as food stamps, welfare, childcare, and Section 8 housing assistance. One drawback to the program is that in many places it is only offered to women with children. Another issue is that those who do have children may be opening themselves up to state involvement and therefore scrutiny from child protective services (you can read more about this possibility later in this chapter).

In addition to state assistance programs, many national and local nonprofit religious or community organizations have specially designed programs to help victims of abuse, including the YWCA, The United Way, and Catholic Charities, to name just a few. While some residency requirements may be in place, most of these groups will not demand that you belong to a particular faith or ethnicity to be served. Many will not even inquire about your citizenship status. Cast a wide net, but know exactly what you are looking for when seeking assistance.

In addition to programs and organizations that help with fundamental needs, like housing, food, and clothing, there are many others that specialize in very specific needs. Here are just a few:

- For transportation, contact 1-800-CHARITY CARS. They are affiliated with the National Coalition Against Domestic Violence (http://www.ncadv.org/takeaction/ DonateaCar.php).
- For education assistance, contact The Women's Independence Scholarship Fund at www.wispinc.org.
- For women who have been scarred or disfigured by their abusers, corrective plastic surgery is available through the FACE to FACE Program, a free service supported by The

American Academy of Facial Plastic and Reconstructive Surgery (www.aafprs.org/patient/humanitarian/pa_ffviolence.html).

You'd be amazed at the level of help available for a host of economic, physical, and mental health issues related to intimate partner abuse. Contact your advocate to discuss the myriad programs and services relevant to your needs and situation. Remember, help is out there, you just need to ask for it.

OTHER SOURCES OF FORMAL ASSISTANCE

In addition to the primary victim-support resources listed above, there are a host of other less-obvious agencies and professionals that can provide either direct or ancillary aid to you, depending on your individual situation.

Parole Officers

Are you "lucky" enough to have an abuser who's on probation or parole? If so, you have a person in a position of authority who is already charged with monitoring and correcting his behavior. The knowledge they may have about your abuser's activities and emotional state may help protect you, so it's imperative that you contact them. Find out exactly what the parameters of his supervision are, and inform the officer if he's broken them. In some cases, an abuser may have his parole or probation revoked for his abusive behavior, and thus end up back in jail. This may save you from having to go through a lengthy court process. Also, there may be help such as counseling and financial assistance available for you through the services parole and probation offers.

Child Protective Services (CPS)

The tragic stories of children being removed from victims of abuse can strike fear in the hearts of mothers and discourage them from seeking potentially valuable help. But with or without your consent, it's important to know that CPS can become involved in your case (and remove the children) if they feel there are valid safety concerns. The best way to avoid this, especially if your abuser is in any way endangering or threatening to hurt or kidnap your children, is to show CPS you are proactive in protecting them by reaching out to them for help. According to many state and county CPS offices, if you are knowingly putting your children in harm's way (by remaining with the abuser), you may be considered an accessory to their endangerment, which could give them grounds for removing them from you as well. Show them your concern by asking how they can help you with everything from financial assistance (to enable escape) to family counseling (without the abuser). If they have to come to you, it will be more difficult.

If CPS does become involved in your case without you contacting them first (either through a domestic dispute call or a mandatory reporter, like a school teacher), be polite and cooperative with the worker assigned to you. They can be your best friend or your worst enemy, depending on how you interact with them and how well you comply with their requests. This is another area of domestic violence that seems incredibly unfair, but try to remember that their end goal is the same as yours—protect the children by all means necessary.

Therapists

If you or your abuser are in counseling, the therapist working with you can provide help and support. Therapy is not only personally helpful to you in dealing with the anxiety, fear, and depression that comes from living with an abuser, but confronting your demons head on can also strengthen your internal defenses against future abuse.

> ### ⚠ Take Action
>
> Finding the right counselor is crucial and challenging, but there are resources that can make it easier. It is important that you find someone with experience and training in intimate partner abuse cases. The following links can help direct you toward an appropriate referral: www.psychology.com/therapist/ or http://therapists.americanmentalhealth.com/therapistlocator.trust.
>
> Consider also contacting the local shelter or victim services agency, which may have referrals as well.

If your abuser is seeing a therapist or batterers' intervention provider, you should establish contact with that person as well. In most cases, due to confidentiality agreements, they can't tell you what the abuser has talked about in session, but they may be able to tell you if he has been attending and participating. Additionally, they are bound by an obligation called "duty to warn" (based on the famous Tarasoff court case), which dictates that if their client divulges imminent plans to do harm, they must alert the authorities, and if possible, the victim.[3] This is a great reason for the practitioner to have your name and phone number.

Schools/Daycare Providers

If your kids go to school or daycare, you will have to inform the facility about any risks to your children, particularly if your abuser has been arrested and released pending trial, is under a restraining order, or if you fear in any way for their safety. Unfortunately, your abuser may try to contact the kids at either of these places, pick them up without permission or even kidnap them from there, or hurt them

Case in Point

After leaving her abusive husband, a former client of mine named Bernice had been granted a restraining order to prevent him from contacting her and their kids. She thought he would respect it, but just to be sure, Bernice notified her daughters' school of the family's situation and gave them copies of the court documents. Several weeks later, she received a phone call stating that her abuser had been arrested at the school after showing up during recess and trying to coax his daughters off the playground and into his car. "I was so thankful I told the school what was happening," said Bernice. "Otherwise a parent talking to his own kids on school grounds might not have caught anyone's attention."

directly on site. Therefore, as mentioned in Chapter 10, teachers and administrators must have a copy of any protection order that covers the kids, emergency contact numbers, an updated photo of the abuser, and a description of his car. They may also be able to help by offering extra support to your children through in-school counseling sessions, or art and play therapy. Ask if there is a family assistance coordinator available, or speak directly to the principal and teacher.

Even if you do not expect the abuser to show up at the school, they will have to be told not to give out information over the phone and understand why your child may be acting differently. Since they care for your kids an average of six to eight hours a day, they need to be kept in the loop.

Animal Resources

A final unexpected ally in your quest for support and safety can be the local animal control office or humane society. As previously mentioned, many abusers are also violent toward animals and some use threats toward beloved pets as a way to control or punish victims. Contact your veterinarian, local Animal Control office, or animal adoption center to find out about possible temporary shelter programs available for your pet or low-cost treatment for injuries. Pets deserve safety as well, and enabling them get it may help you to find the same.

INFORMAL SUPPORT SYSTEMS

In addition to seeking out help and support from formal agencies and organizations, you are surrounded by a potential network of personal support systems, which were identified when you did your eco-map in Chapter 3. This includes family, friends, neighbors, and coworkers, among others. Gathering them closer, to "cocoon" you in assistance, is a great proactive defense tactic, particularly once you've left your abuser, filed a restraining order, or if you're awaiting legal outcomes. As I mentioned before, this is a heightened time of risk for victims, so it's critical that you take advantage of every source of defense at your disposal. While certain groups, like close family and friends, are obvious go-tos as "buffers" between you and your abuser, you can also approach neighbors and coworkers to help enable your safety. One note of caution: when you approach these ancillary supports, you may be surprised by their reactions. Sometimes, the people you assumed you could depend on may not be receptive to helping you or becoming involved in any way, while other, unexpected resources (perhaps your employer) may turn out to be strong allies.

Family and Friends

As you know from earlier chapters, family and friends provide important emotional support, among other things. Even before you escaped your abuser, they may have intervened in moments of crisis and danger, been there for emotional or financial support, taken the kids, and driven you to appointments. The list goes on. And while we've read about the myriad ways in which they can help, and the true risks such help poses to them, it's worth repeating that they are some of your most important allies. Be sure you've taken the following steps to protect you and them, now that you've taken action toward your independence:

- Let your inner circle know that you have left your abuser and he may be looking for you either in person or by phone and computer (you do not have to say exactly where you currently are). Ask them to inform you right away if he contacts them looking for you.

- Tell them to avoid his number on caller ID, and "play dumb" if they do pick up, and not to provide him with any information about you at all. Forewarn that he may try to threaten, trick, or guilt them into revealing it.

- If you have a protection order, give them copies or at least let them know of its existence. In most cases, the order protects you, your children (wherever you are), and your primary locations, like home and work.

- If the order also covers a relative's home, pass along the information you have learned regarding documentation and reporting of violations.

- If you are concerned that the abuser will try to harm a family member or friend, include them in your safety plan, apprising them of what you have designed (on a need-to-know basis) and encourage them to create one as well.

- While they may feel protective of you, advise your family and friends to let the police and courts handle the abuser—many people close to victims have been injured or even killed when confronting an abuser in their loved one's defense.

Neighbors and Landlord

You know that nosy old woman down the street who always has her eyes on everyone's business? She might turn out to be your best friend after you've left an abuser. Alert and observant neighbors have helped many women stay safe, and those close to you should be informed about what is happening. You don't have to tell them all your private details, just that they should be on the lookout for the person in question. They will also need to know what to do if they see him or hear signs of a struggle coming from your home. Provide them with a photo and

Case in Point

"The first thing I did when I moved to my new rental house was go and introduce myself to the neighbors on either side, in front of, and behind me. It took some courage to explain my situation to strangers, but I wanted them to know my ex-boyfriend was stalking me so they could be extra sets of eyes and ears to keep me safe. It worked: I got a call at my job a month later from the man whose backyard borders mine. He said, 'I don't want to scare you, but there's a chair propped against your fence like someone might have climbed over it.' I called the police and they found my ex-boyfriend there, trying to break into the side door. I barely knew that neighbor, but I brought him and his wife a batch of brownies to say thanks. They said they have an adult daughter, and they would want someone to help her like that too."

—Valerie, age twenty-eight

description of him and his vehicle if they don't already know. Many people believe that domestic incidents are "not their business." Let those around you know that you want them to become involved, even if it means placing an anonymous 911 call. The following is a list of some ways good neighbors can be a tremendous help to you:

- *Neighborhood Watch*—Pull your neighbors together into a "neighborhood watch team," complete with a warning system. For instance, you can create a phone tree, where any neighbor who spies something suspicious and they're not sure if it's 911-worthy, can contact you and each other, so everyone around you—whether it's the floor of your apartment or the houses in your cul de sac—is on alert. Or, if it does look suspicious, they can be instructed to call the police and provide the name of the abuser and any other relevant information, such as if he has a restraining order against him.

- *Provide Signals*—In addition to the above, if you're in an apartment, condo, or duplex, ask neighbors to listen for a signal that could broadcast trouble, such as three hard knocks on the adjoining wall. If you live in a single family home, let your surrounding neighbors know that you will flash your porch lights or trigger your car's panic alarm if you are in trouble. Ask them to call police if they see or hear these signals.

- *Be a Witness*—Ask your neighbors ahead of time if they'd be willing to step up as witnesses, or provide evidence of protection order violations, if your case went to court. If not, do not act resentful or dismissive. Thank them anyway, and kindly let them know you understand their reticence. After all, they're important to your overall safety just by way of their proximity to you, since they can alert you to suspicious activity (add that you would do the same if you saw someone breaking into their house, so they understand the value of neighborhood cooperation).

If you live in a rental property, your landlord may have a legal responsibility to help you stay safe. For example, in some states they're required to change the locks if a crime, including domestic violence, has been reported at the residence. They may be required to add or maintain lighting, trim bushes that the abuser could hide in, or ask for identification when people enter the building. Also, if you are in danger and have to leave, the landlord may be obligated to let you break the lease without penalty. They cannot kick you out because you are a victim of domestic violence and may even be able to evict the abuser, while other family members stay.

⚠ Take Action

Because landlord/tenant laws vary so much from state to state, you will need to know what rules and protections apply in your location. Check out Legal Momentum's State Law Guide on Housing Protections for Victims of Domestic Violence at the website www.legalmomentum.org/assets/pdfs/housing-1.pdf.

You may also be able to find specific information by contacting your state's housing authority, local legal aid center, or domestic violence shelter.

Employers and Coworkers

Because many estranged intimate partners do attempt to contact their victims at their places of employment, it's critical that your employer and coworkers are informed—and warned—about your current situation. We've all read the terrible news stories about innocent coworkers losing their lives or being injured when an abuser attempts to wield retribution against his victim. More often, however, they may be harassed or have their work space or time disrupted by his actions or presence. Here are important ways that you, your coworkers, and/or your company can enhance your safety, and by association, their own:

- *Documentation*—Coworkers can write down what they see and hear related to your case. For example, if you've shown up with bruises, or your abuser has been stalking you in the parking lot after work, the independent account of an uninvolved party can go a long way when you need to prove abuse for a protection order or other criminal justice action.

- *Screening Calls and Visitors*—If there is a front desk/reception area at your job, provide the gatekeeper with a photo of your abuser and specific instructions on what to do if he shows up (call the police, alert you, summon security, etc.). Advise them that he may be overly nice, deceitful, or threatening when trying to see or call you. Your employer may also be able to change your desk phone or office location in order to throw the abuser off your trail.

- *Priority Parking*—Parking a block or more away from your place of work puts you at risk. Ask for a temporary spot that places you closer to the building and the watchful eyes of others.

- *Schedule/Location Switch*—If you work at a job with multiple locations (such as a bank or chain restaurant), ask if you can be switched to a different branch. If you're in management or sales, can they transfer you out of state? You can also request different work hours than your abuser expects, or ask to work during hours you know he's at his job. Perhaps you can telecommute from a "safe" location, as well.

- *Increased Security/Uniformed Escorts*—If you are fortunate enough to work in a building that has security, you need to tell them what is going on and provide them with the abuser's description/photo, copies of the protective order, whether he is armed, etcetera. Perhaps they can post a guard outside the building entrance, or escort you to your vehicle at the end of your shift. If this happens, make sure the security officer is uniformed or clearly marked as such, otherwise the jealous abuser may assume he's your new boyfriend and target him as well.

- *Corporate Protection Orders/Trespassing Orders*—Your employer can also "trespass" the abuser from the property if he has been disruptive or threatening. In some states, they can take out a corporate restraining order, which prevents him from calling or visiting the company location at all.

- *Carpool/Public Transportation Safety*—Because abusers know your schedule well, they will be anticipating those breaks of perhaps just a few minutes when you are alone and vulnerable either coming or going from work. For example, if you stand at a bus stop in the morning or park while waiting for your carpool, it's likely that your former partner knows where these safety gaps are. Consider changing your method, schedule, and route to work if possible.

Although intimate partner abuse has a way of making you feel alone, rest assured you are not. As you have just read, there exists a multitude of allies ready to help if you are willing to seek and accept their support. The following chapter explores how to fortify your environment and enlist the commitment of the one person who will guide you out of this experience alive. You may have met her a long time ago, and then lost touch, but don't worry, she has stayed with you all along, patiently waiting for her time to emerge. She is the heroine who will bring your story full circle, and lead you to a place of safety and peace. Armed with knowledge and strategies, she stands prepared to advance and take control. Your liberator has arrived, and she is *you*.

Chapter 12

Target Hardening:
How to Fortify Your Defenses after Escape

Fortune favors a prepared mind.
—Louis Pasteur

Every woman reacts differently to risk. In working with thousands of cases of intimate partner abuse throughout the years—from subtle to extreme—I have witnessed a vast spectrum of over- and under-reactions to the threat an abuser poses. On one hand are the women who score off the charts on risk factors and share terrifying tales of severe abuse, only to end their session with a statement like, "But I don't think he would ever really do anything to hurt me." Then there are the victims who score relatively low on assessment scales, whose abusers have no specific illegal or prosecutable offenses, and yet they will insist, to anyone who will listen, that they are a dead woman walking. I listen to such voices very carefully, because they are the experts on their abuser, and they know things that outsiders couldn't possibly know. Study after study has shown that a woman's fear of her abuser is usually warranted, and should be acknowledged while planning for safety, but still many women don't truly recognize their position. One study by researchers Alex Heckert and Edward Gondolf found that "women who were uncertain or felt somewhat unsafe were more likely to be reassaulted repeatedly than those who felt they were in great danger.[1] The reason for this apparent contradiction, they posited, was that women who felt in greatest danger took more effective countermeasures to protect themselves. In other words, if women are not certain they will be safe, they err by giving the benefit of the doubt to their abuser.

Strictly speaking, better safe than sorry.

But being over- or underalarmed are both problematic states, so victims need multiple angles from which to assess their situation. A balanced reaction stems from a combination of analyzing facts and trusting your gut; therefore, if your ex-partner has made it clear that he plans to hurt or kill you after you have left him, yet another critical shift in your thinking must take place. At this stage, as unpleasant as it may be, there is benefit in seeing yourself the way he sees you: as a human target. This is a frightening reality, one that you may want to reject because denial makes us feel safer inside. But when a dangerous individual mentally paints a bulls-eye on your head, sticking it in the sand won't help.

Evaluating yourself as a target will help you to develop a better eye for the security weaknesses that make you more vulnerable. Consider this an opportunity for proactive empowerment and self-protection, not cowering. The state of "moving target" is not as helpless as the position of "sitting duck." Taking measures to actively participate in enhancing your safety is what threat assessment experts call "target-hardening." This term refers to efforts that strengthen and increase security, therefore reducing the likelihood of attack. Although you can't stop another person from making you a target, you can stop them from turning you into a victim.

CULTIVATING A SENSE OF HEIGHTENED AWARENESS

Animals in the natural world are keen observers of their surroundings. They are constantly aware of what is in their personal field and not easily surprised by approaching enemies. Yet no one ever refers to them as paranoid, only attentive. As an alternative to living in fear, I suggest a state of "confident awareness" in which women can balance intelligence with instinct to increase their safety. Self-protection begins when you become more alert and responsive to signs of danger in your environment. It's not about being paranoid or living in fear; instead, when you learn to be ready and in control, you will reduce your anxiety and heighten your preparedness. The following strategies will help guide you.

Adopt High-Level Alertness

Sometimes when I'm in public, I like to play "spot the cop," trying to recognize law enforcement by the way they move and behave. Coming from a police family and spending years working alongside officers, I've developed a sense of how to identify one and can often confirm it by speaking to them. One thing that sets police officers apart (and soldiers as well) is that they are trained to never let their guard down, on or off duty. When they walk, they are constantly but subtly scanning a 360-degree circle around their person. When they sit, they put their backs to the wall, not the door. They take notice of who is looking at them or who is not, who is behaving strangely or lurking in the corners. They glance into and around their cars before entering, use windows and mirrors to gain additional viewpoints, and walk with their eyes and chin upward, shoulders squared straight ahead. Law enforcement and other security professionals generally regard strangers with a quiet degree of suspicion because they have learned through their jobs that people are not always what they seem. And most of this they do subconsciously. It doesn't disturb them or cause them anxiety—it's simply their way of practicing the confident awareness that can save your life.

A helpful way to perceive your level of alertness is through an "awareness color-coding system." Developed by Lieutenant Colonel Jeff Cooper (Marines), the system uses a shifting palette of colors—like the government's color-coded terror threat levels—to help you recognize your level of attention to your surroundings. The levels are broken down below by their rank of intensity:

- *Condition White*—You are oblivious to your surroundings. Walking with your head down, talking on your cell phone, or wearing headphones are examples of operating in this low-level state of awareness.

- *Condition Yellow*—This is a state of assertive alertness. You're not expecting to be attacked, but you're aware of the possibility.

- *Condition Orange*—You become focused and vigilant, because something (like an abuser's threat) has given you good reason to be. You will remain at this level until you are satisfied that the threat has been mitigated.

- *Condition Red*—This is when you're in the "fight or flight" mode that accompanies real and present danger.

According to Cooper, the ideal state to remain in is Condition Yellow. For the average person I would agree, but if you are the victim of a violent abuser who has now threatened your safety or life, you should probably stay in a holding pattern of Condition Orange for the time being.

Although not a permanent state, adopting extra watchfulness can add to your protection until the threat has sufficiently passed.

Avoid Ambush Points

Here's something the Secret Service knows that you can apply to your own situation: comings and goings are popular ambush points. If your home is secure, your place of employment is secure, and you're accompanied almost everywhere else, a hunter will pick the transition spots to get at his target. To avoid these traps, glance out the windows before you leave your home or office to make sure that no one is lurking outside. Be on elevated alert as you exit, and glance around, beneath, and in the back seat of your car as you approach. Once you've gotten in your car, lock the doors immediately. Vary the routes you take to places you frequently go: work, the gym, your children's school, etcetera. If you won't be returning home until after dark, leave outside lights on so you can see the area around your front door. As you walk through parking lots, keep your phone in one hand and your keys in the other, ready to call for help if you need it.

Some abusers will stalk in public places, so as part of the confident awareness mindset, you need to think about ways to stay safe when you are not at home. For example, if you should see your abuser in a public place, avoid making contact with him. If you believe you are in danger, first look for someone in uniform—any uniform. If you're lucky, you might see a police officer, a security guard, or a soldier, but any employee with responsibility—such as a bus driver or store manager— will be more likely to help you than the average bystander. Not only will they probably not turn around and walk away like a regular citizen might, but you also know where they work, so you'll know where to send police if they need witness statements. If they do not wish to call 911 or don't have the means, ask them to stand near you while you make the call. Again, independent objective witnesses are prosecution

> ### ⚠ Take Action
>
> If you think you are being followed while in your car, test it out. For example, make three lefts in a row. If you still believe you are being followed, drive to a police or fire station or another public place (such as a fast food restaurant) where you can lock your car doors, or lock yourself in a bathroom, and call for help, all under the watchful eye of witnesses and surveillance cameras.

gold. If there is no one in uniform, and you don't have a cell phone or can't use it in the moment, make eye contact with someone, anyone, and point to them saying, "You—Please call 911 right now!" Gesturing to an individual and giving them a specific directive is more effective than yelling "help" to no one in particular, or trying to fumble for your phone when you're being chased.

Try not to go out alone—there's a reason for the well-worn adage that "there is safety in numbers." Ask friends, coworkers (or possibly store security guards) to walk you to your car or wait with you for public transportation.

Anticipate Potential Incidents

While designing your custom safety plan, draw on your knowledge of your abuser's personality and patterns to ask yourself what to expect from him in a worst-case scenario incident. Many women can give specific predictions of what their abuser's mode of attack will be because they've seen him in action before and know his capabilities. Take Vanessa, a twenty-three-year-old woman with a nine-month-old daughter. She had come to my office to find help from the abuse and threats of her career criminal ex-boyfriend, also her baby's father. When

I asked her, "How do you think he will come at you? We need to know where to focus our resources," she didn't skip a beat: "He's going to shoot me in the head. Three times now he has burst into my home or caught me out on the street. He runs up on me and sticks a gun to my temple, every time. He holds it there and screams at me for a few minutes about how he's going to kill me, then stops and smacks me around a bit. The police don't even know where to find him because he's transient, but he always seems to know where to find me."

Vanessa's situation was terrifying, and she was beginning to run out of hope. With the help of the local police, I was able to arrange for Vanessa to get an alarm pendant, one that would hang around her neck twenty-four hours a day. If she triggered it, a silent signal would immediately notify police dispatch and officers would respond, well aware of the situation they were walking into. Vanessa's fear was that if he attacked her again, she would be too afraid to press the alarm button. "When he does these things, I just freeze," she explained. We walked through it in her mind, trying to prepare her for the anticipated emotions and actions that might occur in that moment. Threat experts call this "preincident visualization" and doing it helped Vanessa to believe that she really could act without letting fear overtake her body. Two and a half months later, Vanessa's ex-partner jumped out from behind a parked vehicle as she was entering her duplex. She ran inside and slammed the door shut behind her, simultaneously locking it and triggering the alarm pendant. She then ran out the back door and across the street, where she hid behind a neighbor's garage. Police arrived and arrested the perpetrator, who was later imprisoned for several years on a multitude of charges and outstanding warrants.

Having a strategy tucked away in your data bank will allow you to react if a situation does arise, because in moments of danger, there is no time to come up with an on-the-spot solution. The thinking must be done in advance, and then warehoused in your mind for instant retrieval.

PREVENT TECHNO-STALKING

While you are considering how to protect yourself at home, work, and wherever else you may be, ask yourself the following question: "Is technology putting me at risk?" The Internet, cell phones, and GPS (global positioning system) are wonderful progressive inventions, but they are also an abuser's dream. Devices like vehicle trackers, hidden cameras, and keystroke loggers have brought techno-stalking to new heights, and their use is becoming more common every day. Once the tools of computer-savvy hackers, this equipment and software is now available to anyone with a computer and a credit card. For example, your abuser can monitor and track you easily using cheap spyware toys or even your phone itself. The following information will help protect you from techno-stalking:

- Most cell phones have a general GPS setting, and when turned on it allows the unit to be tracked from a private computer. Check your settings and make sure your GPS is turned off or better yet, set to "911 only."

- Be aware that "open source" online databases (accessible to anyone) can reveal personal information that might put you in danger, such as your address, phone number, and place of employment. Websites like Intelius, Spokeo, and ZabaSearch allow anyone to go in and scour public records to mine data on where you might be found. Fortunately, there are ways to get off the grid. Run an exhaustive search on your name, like he would, and see what pops up. Then check the removal policies for those services. Some allow removal and some don't. If all else fails, you can go to the source of those records (the local courthouse, county land records office, etc.) and ask to opt out of their system or have your account flagged and concealed, but every county has its own rules.

- Create new, unpredictable usernames and passwords for all your email addresses, online banking sites, and any other important accounts. Consider shutting down your social networking activity for the time being. The small amount of amusement these sites provide isn't worth all the valuable information your status updates and friend's posts are giving away about you. Remember that just because you've "de-friended" or blocked your ex doesn't mean he can't view your page through various loopholes.

- If your abuser keeps mysteriously showing up where you are or always seems to know exactly what you've

Case in Point

"I couldn't figure out how my ex-boyfriend Justin always seemed to know where I was. It was like he had magic or something—I would walk out of a store and he would be sitting in his car in the parking lot staring at me. I would show up at a friend's place, and within twenty minutes we'd see him outside, driving by the house, real slow. Finally, one of the officers that had been helping me with my stalking case asked to look at my car. He crawled underneath and came out holding a small rectangular metal box. I had never seen anything like it and was horrified when he explained that it was a tracking device. I felt sick inside knowing that for months Justin been following my every move."

—Linda, twenty-eight

been doing (online and off), chances are he may have
some kind of tracking or monitoring device on you.
Alert the police to your concerns and ask if they (or
even the local mechanic) will sweep your vehicle for
suspicious equipment. Then have a private investigator
who specializes in computers come to check the insides
and outsides of your laptop, desktop, and surrounding
hardware.

Although cyber abuse has become more common, laws punishing
such action have been slow to catch up. However, there are still options
for dealing with typical internet abuser tactics. For example, if your
abuser is writing fake Craigslist ads that send men to your house, or
he's pretending to be you in chat rooms, you can go for felony identity
theft charges. If he is posting nasty comments about you online, there
may be a cyber-bullying law on the books in your state. Do some
detective work to find out what crimes he may have committed and
retain whatever evidence you can.

⚠ Take Action

For more information on technological stalking, visit
the Stalking Resource Center at www.ncvc.org/src.

BUILD A DO-IT-YOURSELF FORTRESS

Because studies show us that the most common place for a woman to
be hurt or killed by an abusive partner is in her home, it's important
to explore how to improve security in and around your house or
apartment.

When government officials tell citizens about disaster or terrorism preparedness, they often use the term "shelter in place" to describe the act of hunkering down indoors in the event of dangerous outside conditions. When it comes to domestic violence, I prefer to use the phrase "fortress in place," because it conveys that victims of an abuser may need to create a fortified environment that can withstand (or at least slow down) his attempts to breach it. Even if you don't think your abuser would try to break into your home, the world is full of burglars and rapists who might, so in securing your home from an abuser you are also making it safer from other criminal elements as well. Some police departments may offer free "safety walkthroughs," in which they will come to your home to give you tips on keeping it more secure. Some municipalities even have subsidized programs through which citizens can have locks changed, windows repaired, or extra lighting installed around their residence for free. Even if the upgrades aren't covered, you still may be able to get assistance in paying for them through an area victim-services agency. Inquire with local law enforcement and advocacy centers to see if they have programs available.

If such resources are not available in your area, you can still do a "safety walkthrough" on your own. Start outside by facing the front door, and later from the rear of the home. Take a step back and begin to look at your home through new eyes, pretending that you're the potential intruder. What would your first choice for point of entry be? Maybe you'd check to see if the front, back, or basement doors were unlocked. Perhaps then you'd move on to open windows. If there are no unlocked entries, you would have to consider breaking in, and if you did, you'd want to make as little noise as possible. Picking locks, prying screens, or putting a jack under the garage door make far less noise than breaking glass or kicking down doors, but those aren't off the table as a last option. Your job is to think the way the abuser would when he looks for ways to attack.

Upgrade Your Security

Upgrading your security is no guarantee that your abuser will not be able to strike, but the following measures will at least buy you extra time to escape the premises or summon help. Home fortification shouldn't consist of only one barrier that an intruder has to knock down in order to gain access. Rather, it should present a series of stacked challenges, all of which buy the people inside precious time to react. In other words, security should be like a multilayered onion, not a single-crack egg.

- Do you have a fence around your yard? This may seem like a protective measure but really it just serves to slow an intruder down. If its chain link, it can be easily climbed and if its solid wood, it conceals the trespasser from the watchful eye of neighbors. I'm not suggesting you put a fence up or have one torn down, just that you consider the advantages and disadvantages of your environment.

- Are there large, dense bushes or shrubs around your home? If so, consider trimming them back to prevent easy hiding places.

- Can you use landscaping as a deterrent? Cactus and other prickly, thorny plants can be placed under windows, making it harder for an intruder to climb in.

- Is your outdoor lighting sufficient enough to reveal someone standing in the shadows as you approach the house? If not, invest in a cheap spotlight or two and train them on vulnerable areas. Or consider a motion-sensor light. They're energy-efficient, and they may deter trespassers, who think they've been spotted when they flash on.

- Does your apartment or neighborhood have security cameras? If not, consider either talking to your landlord or investing in one for your home. They are more expensive than lights, but they're valuable not only to alert you to suspicious activity but also because the footage can later be used as evidence, should your abuser violate a protection order, or if a crime is committed.

Let's continue our intruder's eye examination, but this time from the inside of the home. Start by making sure all the locks on your doors and windows are working properly. Then begin reshaping your habits to include locking all of them, at all times, whether you are in or out of your home or apartment. I have even trained my two-year-old daughter to lock the exterior doors from inside. You can easily get into the habit yourself within just a few days. As the target of a violent abuser, you can never underestimate your safety. Consider the following when it comes to your interior security:

- Does your exterior door have a deadbolt, or at least more than one long-screw lock? It should, because multiple locks make a door harder to kick in. Skip the chain type though—they aren't very strong and you should not have to partially open the door to verify a dangerous visitor.
- Does your front door have a peephole? It allows you to see who is standing on the other side and is relatively cheap and easy to install.
- Could your abuser still have an entrance key? If you have any reason to believe that he might, or if your situation is high risk and you don't want to take any chances, it's worth spending the money to get the locks changed.

- Do you have a sliding glass door? These are easily pried open but can be secured simply by inserting a bar, broomstick, or wooden dowel in the track. You can also purchase relatively inexpensive security film that keeps the glass door from being easily shattered.

- Do you have curtains, shutters, or blinds? If not, put them up immediately and make it a habit of keeping them closed. It is difficult to see who is looking in, particularly at night, and an open view allows an attacker to know who is in the house, what rooms they are in, and what they are doing.

- Do you have working smoke detectors in your home? Arson is a deadly method of attack, and even if your abuser would never do such a thing, protecting your home from fire is always a good idea.

- Does your home or apartment have a security alarm? If not, there are many companies out there that will install

Take Action

Consider a natural "safety alarm." Dogs are not only proven to be great therapy animals, but even small breeds can act as miniature sentinels. They're naturally territorial and loyal, and have exceptional hearing, so they'll bark up a storm at unusual sounds or suspicious-looking people. Larger animals can be trained to handle defensive tasks as well. There are many well-trained, good-natured dogs available through local shelters and rescue foundations, and many exist for specific breeds. Contact the ASPCA (www.aspca.org) or the Humane Society of the United States (www.humanesociety.org) for local adoption referrals.

them at a reasonable cost. Contact your local Better Business Bureau for reputable companies, and call for estimates.

Create a Safe Room

If the abuser attempts to, or succeeds at, gaining entry into your home while you're in it, you will have to have a designated safe room that you (and your children, if applicable) can retreat to. Safe rooms don't have to be the elaborate, expensive steel boxes you see in the movies, but can rather be constructed quickly, out of simple materials that won't cost you an arm and a leg. Choose one room to modify, ideally one with a viable exit—even if that means you have to jump one floor to the ground if he gets through the door or decides to light a fire in the building. Your safe room should also be equipped with a charged cell phone so that you can dial 911 as you take refuge.

Building a safe room is not as difficult as it might seem. Visit your local home improvement store and select a solid core wooden or steel door designed for exterior use. This will be the new door for your safe room, and you will need to purchase a matching doorframe or lengths of wood to reinforce the existing one. Unless you are skilled in such projects, hire a contractor or trustworthy handyman/woman to install or reinforce the frame and hang the door. They can likely complete this task within a day, and in a way that will not destroy your décor or budget. If you are feeling ambitious, you can find tutorials online, and with the help of some purchased or rented tools, you can do it yourself. Don't forget to change the doorknob to a locking outdoor version, and back it up with a solid deadbolt and/or floor bar. A keypad-style lock can allow you to enter the safe room quickly without a key and can be set to automatically lock behind you once you're safely inside.

284 ✋ STOP SIGNS

DEALING WITH YOUR ABUSER AFTER YOUR ESCAPE

Living under threat from an abuser means that you may have to make adjustments in the way you interact with others. Many people don't want the neighborhood knowing their business, but when you are in danger, the more people who know what is happening the better. Sometimes you have to give them partial details for safety reasons. For example, mutual friends will need to understand that they cannot give the abuser any information about you at all. Your abuser may be cunning and try to enlist others in his campaign to communicate with you. This shows a level of desperation and extreme need for control that could indicate a higher propensity toward violence. Sometimes, well-meaning people may try to help "fix" your relationship but instead expose you to even greater risk, so be selective about which friendships you choose to continue.

Once you have separated from your abuser and he continues to stalk, threaten, harass, or otherwise attack you, I do not advocate contact with him. But life is not black and white, and there may be times when you will have to communicate with your abuser, perhaps over child-related issues. In such cases, you must identify the safest way to do so, perhaps through a third party or an attorney. Consider recording all conversations between you and the abuser after separation so that there is no question of "he said, she said." If you absolutely must meet with the abuser, do so only in a public place, with another person (such as your attorney) there as a buffer. Make sure others know where you are going and when you are scheduled to return. Many women have been attacked, even killed, during postseparation meetings. Sometimes these assaults took place when the victim returned to their shared residence to retrieve belongings after leaving. Sometimes they happened after a victim accepted her former abuser's invitation to see him because he told her he "just wanted to talk" or promised he would leave her alone after a brief conversation. Beware of seemingly harmless or "out of character" requests and persistent begging for contact, as it could signal a dangerous trap.

As a final note on dealing with your abuser after you've left, avoid letting your emotional guard down. As women, we are nurturing by nature—particularly victims of abuse. You may want to find some way to help him "get better," especially if he's employing sentimentality and false acts of remorse. As mentioned earlier in the book, it is not your job to fix an abusive partner's problems. However, if his obsession is contacting, threatening, and hunting you, then it may behoove you to enlist other people in a campaign of "refocusing." Try to pin down what and who really matter to the abuser, and think of ways those things could be leveraged to stabilize his current situation. For example, if he values his job and respects his boss, perhaps that employer could give him some projects or new job-training opportunities that would engage him, helping to alleviate depression and keep him occupied. If his grandfather or pastor has always been someone whose opinion he respected, maybe that individual could talk to him about concentrating on his own life and self-improvement, instead of remaining focused on you and your departure. Renowned threat assessment researchers Robert Fein and Bryan Vossekuil noted:

> *A subject engaged in activities that bring success and satisfaction is less likely to remain preoccupied with a failed relationship. Family, friends, neighbors, or associates may play a role in suggesting and supporting changes in the subject's thinking and behavior. In addition, mental health and social service staff may be of great assistance in aiding the subject to formulate more appropriate goals and develop skills and strengths that are likely to result in life successes.*[2]

Remember, this support is not something *you* would actively execute but rather something that is initiated and performed by others who are in a better position to offer assistance to an unstable individual. For instance, if you are on decent terms with his friends and family, but know you must avoid them for safety reasons, you may want to send them one last communication, telling them in no uncertain terms that their loved one needs help, and you won't be the one giving it to him anymore. Suggest that they try to "talk him off the ledge," steer him away from rash decisions, and help him move on with his life in a positive direction, one that is opposite from the impulsive, vengeful path he may be on. Propose that they encourage counseling for him, and provide him with information on where to receive voluntary batterers' intervention, substance abuse, or mental health treatment. If they love him, they will try to help him, but it is very possible that he will refuse their offers. However, this is not your problem, so no matter what your feelings are postseparation, avoid contact with him entirely.

DEALING WITH AN ABUSER WHO IS THE FATHER OF YOUR CHILDREN

Women who don't have children with their abuser will likely have an easier time escaping him emotionally, financially, and legally than women who do. If you are considering fleeing an abuser with a child or children in tow, I urge you to contact an attorney before you do so. Parental kidnapping laws are quite complex and do not discriminate between the parent who abducts for protective reasons and the one who takes a child for purposes of malicious intent. If you must go before you can consult with a lawyer, at least go to a shelter where you can receive sanctuary and demonstrate that you are seeking safety.

Some mothers may have already received full or partial custody of their children and now have to negotiate coparenting with an abuser.

If you have joint custody, or your former partner has visitation, your situation presents additional challenges but is not without hope. Abusers will often use children, the exchange of them, or communication regarding them as a way to continue abusing their partner after the relationship ends. All too commonly, kids are caught in the middle. Consider the following ways to increase the safety of you and your children:

- If someone who has abused and assaulted a child's mother gets visitation with that child, it should in most cases be supervised, ideally by professionals. Check with the child protective services in your area to see what is available.

- Child drop-offs and pick-ups can be difficult and dangerous moments. Insist that the exchange occur in a public location, preferably a more secure place, like a police or fire station. The best scenario is to stagger arrivals and departures, although this may not be possible, particularly if you have very young children. If they are older (over 10), can you drop them off with a safe, neutral adult like a teacher or in a safe public location (a table in the middle of a crowded fast food restaurant, for instance) for a ten-minute span (as long as they have a cell phone)? If so, that can give you enough time to get safely out of the area before the abuser shows up. Your children can call you if he doesn't show or something is wrong when he does.

- Don't allow lack of or irregular child support payments to become another form of financial abuse. All support arrangements should be ordered through court, and collected through the state. This reduces the need for potentially abusive contacts, makes him accountable to someone other than you, and sets up penalties for noncompliance.

- Use your attorney as a conduit for communication whenever possible. Contacts regarding children should be kept strictly business—resist the temptation to reply to his sarcastic emails and rude messages. Save any text or computer interactions in which he steps out of the boundaries defined by a judge's order.

- Be aware that your abuser may be saying negative things about you to the children, but don't grill them about it or badmouth him back. Instead, set them up with counseling so that they have a place to talk about their feelings and report any unsafe or abusive incidents to an objective adult who knows what to do with such information.

- If things change or he displays any alarming behaviors, go back to court and alter the custody agreement. For example, if he shows up drunk to pick up the kids, threatens you, or hurts the children, let the police and/ or overseeing judge know what is happening. Emergency custody orders can be applied for and received the same day on the basis of immediate danger.

While these suggestions alone might not deter the path of a person committed to targeted violence, they may help when used in conjunction with other strategies for target hardening.

USING SELF-DEFENSE AND WEAPONS

When discussing target-hardening strategies, women often ask me about fighting back as well as the use of weapons. They want to know if it is possible to physically take on an abuser, if self-defense classes are worth taking, and if they should obtain and train with firearms. These are legitimate questions, and while I don't condone the use of violence to stop violence, they are worth addressing here.

Hand-to-Hand Combat

Women's self-defense instructors, like Sara Johnson of Women-Strength, warn that if we choose to fight, we must be completely committed to incapacitating the attacker, and this may not be as easy to do with an intimate partner as it would be with a stranger. Physical self-defense should always be a last option, and if the situation has been pushed to that point, you are justified in assaulting your abuser in order to protect yourself or your children. But be aware of the possible realities. According to one study, 37.3 percent of female victims fought back in the incident in which their male abuser was arrested. However, more than half of those females who fought back found that this made their abuser more violent.[3] Also, self-defense laws vary and it may be hard to prove that you were in a position that necessitated violence, possibly leaving you open to arrest and prosecution.

It is difficult for me to recommend any particular self-defense actions because every situation will be different depending upon several factors, including the size and skill of your opponent, the weapons available (to you and him), your surroundings and levels of intoxication, and previous fighting experience. However, WomenStrength philosophy states the following:

> *Sudden, well-placed strikes to vulnerable body parts are our greatest tools to create an escape with fighting. The downsides of fighting are that it is likely that we will be hit back, and we can only use fighting for very escalated situations. Something like verbal defense can be used at*

> *any stage of an attack, at any level of danger, but fighting is*
> *only appropriate for highly dangerous emergency situations.*
> *Just as with weapons, some people are not comfortable with*
> *the idea of hurting another person and don't want to be in*
> *that position.[4]*

If you do choose to take a self-defense class, do your research and make sure that it offers a safe and supportive environment in which to learn. You do not have to be an athlete or a black belt to successfully defend yourself, but some training is usually better than none at all. There are many formats and methods of training. None of them is a guarantee of safety, but instead seek to increase your knowledge and preparedness in emergency situations.

Weapons

In the case of weapons, remember that any device is useless and perhaps dangerous if you don't have the training and willingness to use it correctly. All weapons have limitations and liabilities, so please think carefully before bringing something into your space that can be stolen, found by a child, or taken and used against you or another family member. In short, do not buy a gun without the training, precautions, and intent you will need to use it to defend yourself.

As you think about self-defense, keep in mind that emotions play into our behavior, whether we want them to or not. In the moment

⚠ Take Action

Check out these guidelines for choosing a self-defense course as created by the National Coalition Against Sexual Assault: http://preventconnect.org/2011/08/choosing-a-self-defense-course/.

of response, it may be a lot easier to hit or shoot a stranger than it would be to injure or kill the father of your children, to whom you've been married for fourteen years. Don't enter that realm unless you have received training and are ready to face the potential physical, emotional, and legal consequences of fighting back.

If your abuser has firearms, you may be able to obtain a protection order that requires his weapons to be removed by police and prevents him from legally purchasing or possessing new ones while the order is in effect. In some states, this is done by checking a provision on the form, and in others you must specifically request this stipulation from the judge, who will then write it into the order.

Additionally, the Gun Control Act of 1968 prohibits certain people from owning firearms. If any of the following apply to your abuser, and he owns a gun, he could face consequences ranging from confiscation of weapons to jail time, depending on which state you live in:

- Has he been convicted of a felony?
- Does he use or abuse a controlled substance?
- Has he been declared mentally ill by a court or institutionalized for mental illness?
- Has he been dishonorably discharged from the military?
- Is he under 18?
- Is he a fugitive from justice?
- Has he been convicted of a crime punishable by more than a year in jail?
- Has he been convicted of misdemeanor domestic violence?

If you answered yes to any of the above, inform the police. They can remove the weapons and may place the abuser under arrest. Guns can also be removed by the police for safekeeping under certain circumstances, but laws vary widely so check out federal and state statutes at WomensLaw.org (http://womenslaw.org/laws_state_type.php?statelaw_name=Federal%20Gun%20Laws&state_code=US).

Finally, some women have disposed of their partner's weapons (or merely the bullets) by themselves, either by turning them over to authorities, giving them to trusted friends or family, selling them, or throwing them away in a postal mailbox or a river. However, this action could potentially cause other problems. You may face violent repercussions from an angry abuser when he finds out his weapons are gone, or the gun could somehow fall into the hands of a child or a criminal other than the abuser. Please work through all other options first.

EXTREME RELOCATION

For some victims of intimate partner violence, there may come a time when they realize they are out of options. They've tried nearly every victim safety and offender accountability tactic available, and it has failed—either because their abuser is particularly persistent, or he is exceptionally dangerous. For these women, the battle comes down to a difficult choice: to relocate. But not just leave, disappear. In this case, it's called "extreme relocation," and it's more than just moving across town or even moving several cities away. Extreme relocation refers to moving one hundred to three thousand miles or more away from your abuser, to a place where he does not have the resources or knowledge to follow you. This was the choice I was forced to make, and while it was hard to leave what was familiar to me, I knew it was the only way my abuser would ever leave me alone. When the restraining order I got was repeatedly violated and he received nothing but a slap on the wrist for beating me up, I had exhausted my legal avenues. Even if he did stop trying to actively contact me, our paths would have crossed frequently in that small town, and I would never have truly felt safe. Fortunately for me, I had something not every victim has: family and friends that were willing to help me financially, emotionally, and logistically with my move.

I was no longer communicating or living with my abuser, so I never directly told him I was leaving the state, although he probably heard through mutual acquaintances. He knew where my family lived (over a thousand miles away) and likely suspected I had headed in that direction, but it was clear he didn't have the guts or money to chase me. Strangely, several months after I relocated a letter arrived in my parent's mailbox addressed to me. It was from my abuser, and it was bizarrely nonchalant, as though nothing had happened between us and we were old friends catching up. It gave me the chills, and I immediately ripped it into tiny shreds.

Like my abuser, most men will not travel across the country to track down their victim, but this is no guarantee, especially if the abuser believes he has a lot to lose by letting you go, or even more concerning, nothing to lose by going after you.

To exercise the extreme relocation option, you will have to choose an area where you have a foothold, but not one where he will immediately know where to look for you. For example, moving back into your parent's home may be risky. Moving into a friend's home or your own place a few towns away from your supportive family is better. Stick with rental accommodations at first, because you do not want to put down roots until you are sure he has not followed or found you there. You may be lucky enough to get a job transfer that will allow you to remain employed, but you'll likely have to find a new way of supporting yourself. It is important to start the process as early as possible, and research all the avenues through which you can get help.

When you leave, empty your bank accounts and for the first year, try to operate on a cash basis in every opportunity possible. The instant you use a credit card or ATM on the run, it will leave a record that can be accessed by a tech-savvy abuser or the private investigator he hires to find you. When you get to your new location, let the local police and some of your new neighbors know what you are running from. They can help shield you from possible contacts and inquiries by the abuser, and let you know if he's been around. At this point, you will have to decide based on signals from the abuser just how secretive your new life will be. Even if you are not sure how to interpret what he has shown you (or perhaps he has given you no indications of his intent at all) it is wise to take precautions, at least for the first year. What to do when you get there:

- Obtain an unlisted phone number with caller ID, call block, and call trace features.

- Get a P.O. Box that's not too close to where you live and check it at different times and days each week. If you use a home-based mailbox, don't put your name on it. Check if your state has an address confidentiality program, which safely reroutes mail to your home.

- Call all your utility providers and banks to request that they flag or pass-code your account, insuring that no one can make changes or receive information about you or your activity.

- If at all possible, trade your car in for a different one, with a different license plate number, should you remain in state.

- Be careful what you throw in the trash or recycling container, as it becomes open to search by anyone once it gets off your property and on to the street.

- Consider getting a shredder for important identifying and financial documents.

- If your situation is high risk, you may want to consider changing your name and social security number and

Take Action

If you're trying to start a new life but have limited resources, there are many service agencies that can help you. As mentioned earlier, the U.S. Department of Human Services (www .hhs.gov) offers temporary assistance to domestic violence survivors, and they can direct you to state-level resources, including help with childcare costs, so you can work.

In most states, you can also sign up for Section 8 housing (which offers priority status for domestic violence victims). You can also apply for temporary food stamp and welfare benefits in your new state.

If you have an open child protection or probation case, request that your caseworker transfer your files to the new state agency.

Assistance may also be available for costs related to transportation. For example, organizations such as Traveler's Aid and Angel Flights (www.angelflight.com) may be able to provide you with bus or plane transport to escape, although requests for these specialized services must often come through an agency.

Remember, your victim advocates are usually well connected and can assist you with accessing additional resources.

that of your children. Contact your local courthouse and the Social Security Administration, respectively. Advocates at your local domestic violence agency may be able to help you with the process.

Escaping an abuser is hardly ever quick or painless, but its challenges pale in comparison to those found in a life of physical, sexual, and emotional violence. If you have embarked on the journey described in this chapter, I applaud your courage and assure you that there are better days ahead. The storm is nearly passed and now is the time to focus on strengthening and healing. Don't turn back and don't give up, no matter what happens from here forward. As Winston Churchill once said, "If you are going through hell, *keep going.*"

Chapter 13

Is It Over?
What Do I Do Now?

Your future depends on many things, but mostly on you.
—Frank Tyger

Most protection experts consider a case closed when the subject is no longer deemed a threat, but what does that mean in intimate partner cases? Clearly, if your abuser dies or gets sentenced to life in prison, you can rest assured that you are safe. But most situations don't end that way and instead fade to menacing shadows that keep women looking over their shoulders for years after the abuse ends. When their relationship is over, some abusers will blow up like a firecracker, killing or attempting to kill their former victims or themselves. Some will want to go after the victim but won't be able to find or get to her due to the comprehensive, effective safety planning she and her support team have engaged in. Some abusers never really go away, but may modify their abuse to consist of emotional assaults that keep them within the boundaries of the law. For example, women who are forced to interact with their abuser because they share children may have to remain in a near permanent state of vigilance, prepared for repeated threat flare-ups every time their ex-partner becomes angry about some small perceived slight.

There are many possible end-game scenarios for an abusive relationship, but most perpetrators will just burn out slowly, deciding after months of harassing you that going to jail simply isn't worth it. They may continue to grumble and gossip about you, but they will likely start moving back into pursuit mode, searching for a new unsuspecting victim to abuse.

If you are a woman who is fortunate enough to have escaped intimate partner abuse, or you're using this book now to prepare for it, you may be wondering how long it will be until you can feel safe again. Is a couple of quiet months enough to consider your abuse experience over? The answer depends on what signs your former abuser is currently showing. After the demise of any dangerous relationship, I recommend remaining on high alert for at least a year, applying all applicable techniques to decrease your vulnerability and accessibility to the abuser. If he knows where you are, and you haven't heard anything from him within that time (or at least anything concerning), you should be able to exhale a bit and start over with a firm sense of self-reliance. After all, your courageous, protective actions may have saved your own life. But don't lose the state of confident awareness you have developed—if the winds change, you must be able to detect that shift and revisit your safety plan. For example, if the former abuser finds out you are dating someone new, will his jealousy come back to haunt you? If he suddenly stops paying child support and you are forced to report him to the court, will that reignite his threatening behavior?

As you read earlier in the book, when a woman exits a violent relationship, her highest period of risk may be the first two months after the relationship ends, and the weeks leading up to and following a divorce or custody decision. These timeframes can be episodes of intense depression and rage for an abuser, and it is therefore important to take note of any emerging or increasing abusive behaviors. Following the protective advice in Chapters 11 and 12 will go far in increasing your vigilance and safety.

Escalations are certainly worrisome, but so might be sharp declines in negative activity. If your former partner goes from a pattern of constantly contacting, threatening, and harassing you, then suddenly stops, you will have to ask yourself what changed to make him back off. For example, if the answer is the issuance of a protection order, that may be a positive response. But if there is no apparent reason for his lapse in abuse, beware. Sometimes this may indicate the targeted violence phenomenon best described as "the calm before the storm," in which a subject appears to cease his terrorist tactics but is actually lying low, simmering, and plotting his attack. Usually this phase doesn't last long before he either acts out or changes his mind, so be sure to adhere to your security plan during this potentially risky period.

Although it may not seem like it now, the time will come when you can start healing and begin to consider your abuse experience a dark but fading memory. The nightmares will become fewer and farther between, and eventually you will be able to refrain from jumping when someone raises their hand near your head. If you have gotten out of abuse alive, be grateful but remember to stay awake. There is no shortage of abusers in the world, and as you have learned, they don't always come in the packaging one might expect.

Though it is of some debate among language scholars, many people believe that the Chinese character for "crisis" is a combination of the terms for both danger and opportunity. Even if it isn't linguistically true, the idea is that hidden within chaos is the chance for growth and positive change. While it is unfortunate that you may have found yourself in an abusive relationship, there is still a chance to learn from your experiences and advance in understanding to help others as well. If you have found freedom, I applaud you and wish you luck for a safe, happy future. But if you are still suffering quietly, let this message ring loud and true: There *is* a light on the other side and we, the survivors, are here waiting for you. It's true that starting life over is scary, expensive, difficult, and uncertain. But the devil you know isn't always better than the one you don't. If you are still being abused by an intimate partner, make a plan with a professional team and run for your life. Freedom is worth the risk of leaving, but he isn't worth the risk of staying. Please don't delay safety one more day. Reach out your hand, and move forward with courage.

Epilogue

Many of you may be wondering what happened after that terrible night when the police found me bloodied on the curb. Just before the patrol car came around the corner, some well-meaning allies presented me with a temptation many victims would jump at. Two male friends had intervened when my abuser physically attacked me, and they overpowered him, holding him down as he thrashed and cursed. When I regained my senses after his barrage of violence, I walked over to where they were and the friends held him up in front of me, pinning his arms back in a "full nelson" wrestling move. "Go ahead," they offered. "Take your best shot . . ."

I would be lying if I said I didn't want to punch him dead in the face. For once, I'd get revenge for all the things he'd done to me and feel what it was like to be on the distributing end of violence instead of the receiving. But I quickly pushed that thought out of my head because I knew I was better than that. I knew I was better than him.

"No," I answered, looking him straight in the eye. And then I addressed him directly: "*You're* going to jail tonight. *I'm* not."

And he did.

In that moment, my whole abusive experience was framed for me, and out of that epiphany came my determination to rise above it. I learned that it wasn't about getting even, or even about getting justice. It was about getting whole and deciding to save myself by walking directly through the fire and out the other side.

Although I had ended my abusive relationship before that final beating, it would be several more months before I left the state. I had to remain for his court case, save money, and muster the courage necessary to take flight—all while my abuser continued to harass and pursue me. But eventually, with the help of a support network, I gathered the remnants of what still held meaning to me, and I drove a thousand miles away.

By following some of the very same advice in this book, I started a new and empowered existence. A *healthy* one. Free of violence, full of love. And eighteen years later, my life is amazing. I married a safe and caring man, bore two wonderful children, and built a fulfilling career out of helping other women escape the nightmare of intimate partner violence. I conquered an abusive relationship and healed.

You will too.

Resources

The following national resources serve as clearinghouses for information and referrals regarding domestic and sexual abuse. Please contact them to find out more about the range of services and assistance available.

Also see the state-by-state listings from the National Coalition Against Domestic Violence to find local resources.

NATIONAL

National Domestic Violence Hotline
P.O. Box 161810
Austin, TX 78716
Phone: (800) 799-7233
TTY: (800) 787-3224
Website: www.ndvh.org

The National Coalition Against Domestic Violence
One Broadway, Suite B210
Denver, CO 80203
Phone: (303) 839-1852

TTY: (303) 839-8459
Fax: (303) 831-9251
Email: mainoffice@ncadv.org

National Network to End Domestic Violence
660 Pennsylvania Avenue SE #303
Washington, DC 20003
Phone: (202) 543-5566
Website: www.nnedv.org

End Violence Against Women International
PO Box 33
Addy, WA 99101-0033
Phone: (509) 684-9800, Fax: (509) 684-9801
Email: info@evawintl.org

National Resource Center on Domestic Violence
(Pennsylvania Coalition Against Domestic Violence)
6400 Flank Drive #1300
Harrisburg, PA 17112
Phone: (800) 537-2238
TTY: (800) 553-2508
Website: www.nrcdv.org

National Sexual Violence Resource Center
123 N. Enola Drive
Enola, PA 17025
Phone: (877) 739-3895
TTY: (717) 909-0715
Website: www.nsvrc.org

Rape, Abuse & Incest National Network (RAINN)
2000 L Street NW, Suite 406
Washington, DC 20036
Phone: (800) 656-4673 ext. 3
Website: www.rainn.org

Resource Center on Domestic Violence: Child Protection & Custody
National Council on Juvenile & Family Court Judges
P.O. Box 8970
Reno, NV 89507
Phone: (800) 527-3223
Website: www.nationalcouncilfvd.org

Violence Against Women Office, U.S. Department of Justice
10th and Constitution Avenue NW #5302
Washington, DC 20530
Phone: (202) 616-8994
Website: www.ojp.usdoj.gov/vawo

The Battered Women's Justice Project Criminal Justice Office
2104 Fourth Ave S #B
Minneapolis, MN 55404
Phone: (612) 824-8768 / 1-800-903-0111 ext. 1

The Battered Women's Justice Project Civil Justice Office
Pennsylvania Coalition Against Domestic Violence
6400 Flank Drive #1300
Harrisburg, PA 17112
Phone: (717) 671-4767 / 1-800-903-0111 ext. 2

The Battered Women's Justice Project Defense Office
National Clearinghouse for the Defense of Battered Women
125 S. 9th Street #302
Philadelphia, PA 19107
Phone: (215) 351-0010 / 1-800-903-0111 ext. 3

Child Welfare League of America
440 First Street NW, Third Floor
Washington, DC 20001
Phone: (202) 638-2952
Website: www.cwla.org

Childhelp USA
15757 N. 78th Street
Scottsdale, AZ 85260
Phone: (800) 422-4453
Website: www.childhelpusa.org

Futures Without Violence
100 Montgomery Street
San Francisco, CA 94129
Phone: (415) 678-5500, Fax: (415) 529-2930
TTY: (800) 595-4889
Website: www.futureswithoutviolence.org

Feminist Majority and the Feminist Majority Foundation
1600 Wilson Boulevard #801
Arlington, VA 22209
Phone: (703) 522-2214
433 S. Beverly Drive
Beverly Hills, CA 90212

Phone: (310) 556-2500
Website: www.feminist.org

The Humane Society of the United States, First Strike Campaign
2100 "L" Street NW
Washington, DC 20037
Phone: (888) 213-0956
Website: www.hsus.org/firststrike

Legal Momentum
395 Hudson Street
New York, NY 10014
Phone: (212) 925-6635
Website: www.nowldef.org

National Center for Victims of Crime
2000 M Street, NW, Suite 480
Washington, DC
Phone: (202) 467-8700
Website: www.ncvc.org

STATE COALITION LIST
Alabama Coalition Against Domestic Violence
P.O. Box 4762
Montgomery, AL 36101
Phone: (334) 832-4842, Fax: (334) 832-4803
Hotline: (800) 650-6522
Website: www.acadv.org
Email: info@acadv.org

Alaska Network on Domestic and Sexual Violence
130 Seward Street, Room 209
Juneau, AK 99801
Phone: (907) 586-3650, Fax: (907) 463-4493
Website: www.andvsa.org
Email: info@andvsa.org

Arizona Coalition Against Domestic Violence
301 East Bethany Home Road, Suite C194
Phoenix, AZ 85012
Phone: (602) 279-2900, Fax: (602) 279-2980
Nationwide: (800) 782-6400
Website: www.azcadv.org
Email: acadv@azcadv.org

Arkansas Coalition Against Domestic Violence
1401 West Capitol Avenue, Suite 170
Little Rock, AR 72201
Phone: (501) 907-5612, Fax: (501) 907-5618
Nationwide: (800) 269-4668
Website: www.domesticpeace.com
Email: kbangert@domesticpeace.com

California Partnership to End Domestic Violence
P.O. Box 1798
Sacramento, CA 95812
Phone: (916) 444-7163, Fax: (916) 444-7165
Nationwide: (800) 524-4765
Website: www.cpedv.org
Email: info@cpedv.org

Colorado Coalition Against Domestic Violence
1120 Lincoln Street, Suite 900
Denver, CO 80203
Phone: (303) 831-9632, Fax: (303) 832-7067
Nationwide: (888) 778-7091
Website: www.ccadv.org

Connecticut Coalition Against Domestic Violence
90 Pitkin Street
East Hartford, CT 06108
Phone: (860) 282-7899, Fax: (860) 282-7892
Statewide: (888) 774-2900
Website: www.ctcadv.org
Email: info@ctcadv.org

DC Coalition Against Domestic Violence
5 Thomas Circle Northwest
Washington, DC 20005
Phone: (202) 299-1181, Fax: (202) 299-1193
Website: www.dccadv.org
Email: info@dccadv.org

Delaware Coalition Against Domestic Violence
100 West 10th Street, #703
Wilmington, DE 19801
Phone: (302) 658-2958, Fax: (302) 658-5049
Statewide: (800) 701-0456
Website: www.dcadv.org
Email: dcadvadmin@dcadv.org

Florida Coalition Against Domestic Violence
425 Office Plaza
Tallahassee, FL 32301
Phone: (850) 425-2749, Fax: (850) 425-3091
TDD: (850) 621-4202
Statewide: (800) 500-1119
Website: www.fcadv.org

Georgia Coalition Against Domestic Violence
114 New Street, Suite B
Decatur, GA 30030
Phone: (404) 209-0280, Fax: (404) 766-3800
Crisis Line: (800) 334-2836
Website: www.gcadv.org
Email: info@gcadv.org

Hawaii State Coalition Against Domestic Violence
810 Richards Street
Suite 960
Honolulu, HI 96813
Phone: (808) 832-9316, Fax: (808) 841-6028
Website: www.hscadv.org
Email: admin@hscadv.org

Idaho Coalition Against Sexual and Domestic Violence
300 Mallard Drive, Suite 130
Boise, ID 83706
Phone: (208) 384-0419, Fax: (208) 331-0687
Nationwide: (888) 293-6118
Website: www.idvsa.org
Email: thecoalition@idvsa.org

Illinois Coalition Against Domestic Violence
801 South 11th Street
Springfield, IL 62703
Phone: (217) 789-2830, Fax: (217) 789-1939
TTY: (217) 242-0376
Website: www.ilcadv.org
Email: ilcadv@ilcadv.org

Indiana Coalition Against Domestic Violence
1915 West 18th Street
Indianapolis, IN 46202
Phone: (317) 917-3685, Fax: (317) 917-3695
Statewide: (800) 332-7385
Website: www.violenceresource.org
Email: icadv@violenceresource.org

Iowa Coalition Against Domestic Violence
515 - 28th Street, Suite 104
Des Moines, IA 50312
Phone: (515) 244-8028, Fax: (515) 244-7417
Statewide: (800) 942-0333
Website: www.icadv.org
Email: admin@icadv.org

Kansas Coalition Against Sexual and Domestic Violence
634 Southwest Harrison Street
Topeka, KS 66603
Phone: (785) 232-9784, Fax: (785) 266-1874
Website: www.kcsdv.org
Email: coalition@kcsdv.org

Kentucky Domestic Violence Association
P.O. Box 356
Frankfort, KY 40602
Phone: (502) 695-5382
Website: www.kdva.org
Email:kdvasac@aol.com

Louisiana Coalition Against Domestic Violence
P.O. Box 77308
Baton Rouge, LA 70879
Phone: (225) 752-1296, Fax: (225) 751-8927
Website: www.lcadv.org
Email:sheila@lcadv.org

Maine Coalition to End Domestic Violence
104 Sewall St.
Augusta, ME 04330
Phone: (207) 430-8334, Fax: (207) 430-8348
Website: www.mcedv.org
Email: info@mcedv.org

Maryland Network Against Domestic Violence
6911 Laurel-Bowie Road, Suite 309
Bowie, MD 20715
Phone: (301) 352-4574, Fax: (301) 809-0422
Nationwide: (800) 634-3577
Website: www.mnadv.org
Email: info@mnadv.org

Massachusetts Coalition Against Sexual Assault and Domestic Violence/Jane Doe, Inc.
14 Beacon Street, Suite 507
Boston, MA 02108
Phone: (617) 248-0922, Fax: (617) 248-0902
TTY/TDD: (617) 263-2200
Website: www.janedoe.org
Email: info@janedoe.org

Michigan Coalition Against Domestic and Sexual Violence
3893 Okemos Road, Suite B-2
Okemos, MI 48864
Phone: (517) 347-7000, Fax: (517) 248-0902
Website: www.mcadsv.org
Email: general@mcadsv.org

Minnesota Coalition for Battered Women
60 E. Plato Blvd., Suite 130
St. Paul, MN 55107
Phone: (651) 646-6177, Fax: (651) 646-1527
Crisis Line: (651) 646-0994
Nationwide: (800) 289-6177
Website: www.mcbw.org
Email: mcbw@mcbw.org

Mississippi Coalition Against Domestic Violence
P.O. Box 4703
Jackson, MS 39296
Phone: (601) 981-9196, Fax: (601) 981-2501
Statewide: (800) 898-3234
Website: www.mcadv.org
Email: dvpolicy@mcadv.org

Missouri Coalition Against Domestic and Sexual Violence
718 East Capitol Avenue
Jefferson City, MO 65101
Phone: (573) 634-4161, Fax: (573) 636-3728
Website: www.mocadsv.org
Email: mocadsv@mocadsv.org

Montana Coalition Against Domestic & Sexual Violence
P.O. Box 818
Helena, MT 59624
Phone: (406) 443-7794, Fax: (406) 443-7818
Nationwide: (888) 404-7794
Website: www.mcadsv.com
Email: mcadsv@mt.net

Nebraska Domestic Violence Sexual Assault Coalition
1000 "O" Street, Suite 102
Lincoln, NE 68508
Phone: (402) 476-6256, Fax: (402) 476-6806
In State Hotline: (800) 876-6238
Spanish Hotline: (877) 215-0167
Website: www.ndvsac.org
Email: help@ndvsac.org

Nevada Network Against Domestic Violence
220 South Rock Boulevard
Reno, NV 89502
Phone: (775) 828-1115, Fax: (775) 828-9911
In State Hotline: (800) 500-1556
Website: www.nnadv.org
Email: nnadv@powernet.net

New Hampshire Coalition Against Domestic and Sexual Violence
P.O. Box 353
Concord, NH 03302
Phone: (603) 224-8893, Fax: (603) 228-6096
In State: (866) 644-3574
Website: www.nhcadsv.org
Email: director@nhcadsv.org

New Jersey Coalition for Battered Women
1670 Whitehorse Hamilton Square
Trenton, NJ 08690
Phone: (609) 584-8107, Fax: (609) 584-9750
In State: (800) 572-7233
Website: www.njcbw.org
Email: info@njcbw.org

New Mexico Coalition Against Domestic Violence
201 Coal Avenue Southwest
Albuquerque, NM 87102
Phone: (505) 246-9240, Fax: (505) 246-9434
In State: (800) 773-3645
Website: www.nmcadv.org
Email: info@nmcadv.org

New York State Coalition Against Domestic Violence
350 New Scotland Avenue
Albany, NY 12054
Phone: (518) 482-5464, Fax: (518) 482-3807
English-In State: (800) 942-6906
Spanish-In State: (800) 942-6908
Website: www.nyscadv.org
Email: nyscadv@nyscadv.org

North Carolina Coalition Against Domestic Violence
123 West Main Street, Suite 700
Durham, NC 27701
Phone: (919) 956-9124, Fax: (919) 682-1449
Nationwide: (888) 232-9124
Website: www.nccadv.org

North Dakota Council on Abused Women's Services
418 East Rosser Avenue, Suite 320
Bismark, ND 58501
Phone: (701) 255-6240, Fax: (701) 255-1904
Nationwide: (888) 255-6240
Website: www.ndcaws.org
Email: ndcaws@ndcaws.org

Action Ohio Coalition for Battered Women
5900 Roche Drive, Suite 445
Columbus, OH 43229
Phone: (614) 825-0551, Fax: (614) 825-0673
Statewide: (888) 622-9315
Website: www.actionohio.org
Email: actionoh@sbcglobal.net

Ohio Domestic Violence Network
4807 Evanswood Drive, Suite 201
Columbus, OH 43229
Phone: (614) 781-9651, Fax: (614) 781-9652
TTY: (614) 781-9654
(800) 934-9840
Website: www.odvn.org
Email: info@odvn.org

Oklahoma Coalition Against Domestic Violence and Sexual Assault
3815 North Sante Fe Avenue, Suite 124
Oklahoma City, OK 73118
Phone: (405) 524-0700, Fax: (405) 524-0711
Website: www.ocadvsa.org

Oregon Coalition Against Domestic and Sexual Violence
380 Southeast Spokane Street, Suite 100
Portland, OR 97202
Phone: (503) 230-1951, Fax: (503) 230-1973
Website: www.ocadsv.com
Email: adminasst@ocadsv.com

Pennsylvania Coalition Against Domestic Violence
6400 Flank Drive, Suite 1300
Harrisburg, PA 17112
Phone: (717) 545-6400, Fax: (717) 545-9456
Nationwide: (800) 932-4632
Website: www.pcadv.org

Puerto Rico Office of Women Advocates
Box 11382
Fernandez Juancus Station
Santurce, PR 00910
Phone: (787) 721-7676, Fax: (787) 725-9248

Rhode Island Coalition Against Domestic Violence
422 Post Road, Suite 202
Warwick, RI 02888
Phone: (401) 467-9940, Fax: (401) 467-9943
Statewide: (800) 494-8100

Website: www.ricadv.org
Email: ricadv@ricadv.org

South Carolina Coalition Against Domestic Violence and Sexual Assault
P.O. Box 7776
Columbia, SC 29202
Phone: (803) 256-2900, Fax: (803) 256-1030
Nationwide: (800) 260-9293
Website: www.sccadvasa.org

South Dakota Coalition Against Domestic Violence and Sexual Assault
P.O. Box 141
Pierre, SD 57501
Phone: (605) 945-0869, Fax: (605) 945-0870
Nationwide: (800) 572-9196
Website: www.southdakotacoalition.org
Email: pierre@sdcadvsa.org

Tennessee Coalition Against Domestic and Sexual Violence
2 International Plaza Drive, Suite 425
Nashville, TN 37217
Phone: (615) 386-9406, Fax: (615) 383-2967
Statewide: (800) 289-9018
Website: www.tcadsv.org
Email: tcadsv@tcadsv.org

Texas Council on Family Violence
P.O. Box 161810

Austin, TX 78716
Phone: (512) 794-1133, Fax: (512) 794-1199
Website: www.tcfv.org

Utah Domestic Violence Council
205 North 400 West
Salt Lake City, UT 84103
Phone: (801) 521-5544, Fax: (801) 521-5548
Website: www.udvac.org

Vermont Network Against Domestic Violence and Sexual Assault
P.O. Box 405
Montpelier, VT 05601
Phone: (802) 223-1302, Fax: (802) 223-6943
TTY: (802) 223-1115
Website: www.vtnetwork.org
Email: info@vtnetwork.org

Virginians Against Domestic Violence
2850 Sandy Bay Road, Suite 101
Williamsburg, VA 23185
Phone: (757) 221-0990, Fax: (757) 229-1553
Nationwide: (800) 838-8238
Website: www.vadv.org
Email: vadv@tni.net

Women's Coalition of St. Croix
Box 2734
Christiansted
St. Croix, VI 00822
Phone: (340) 773-9272, Fax: (340) 773-9062

Website: www.wcstx.com
Email: wcsc@pennswoods.net

Washington State Coalition Against Domestic Violence
711 Capitol Way, Suite Suite 702
Olympia, WA 98501
Phone: (360) 586-1022, Fax: (360) 586-1024
TTY: (360) 586-1029

1402 Third Avenue, Suite 406
Seattle, WA 98101
Phone: (206) 389-2515, Fax: (206) 389-2520
Statewide: (800) 886-2880
TTY: (206) 389-2900
Website: www.wscadv.org
Email: wscadv@wscadv.org

**Washington State Native American Coalition Against
Domestic and Sexual Assault**
P.O. Box 13260
Olympia, WA 98508
Phone: (360) 352-3120, Fax: (360) 357-3858
Statewide: (888) 352-3120
Website: www.womenspiritcoalition.org

West Virginia Coalition Against Domestic Violence
5004 Elk River Road South
Elkview, WV 25071
Phone: (304) 965-3552, Fax: (304) 965-3572
Website: www.wvcadv.org

Wisconsin Coalition Against Domestic Violence
307 South Paterson Street, Suite 1
Madison, WI 53703
Phone: (608) 255-0539, Fax: (608) 255-3560
Website: www.wcadv.org
Email: wcadv@wcadv.org

Wyoming Coalition Against Domestic Violence and Sexual Assault
P.O. Box 236
409 South Fourth Street
Laramie, WY 82073
Phone: (307) 755-5481, Fax: (307) 755-5482
Nationwide: (800) 990-3877
Website: www.wyomingdvsa.org
Email: info@mail.wyomingdvsa.org

Notes

Introduction

1. Callie Marie Rennison, PhD, and Sarah Welchans, U.S. Department of Justice, *Intimate Partner Violence* 1 (May 2000).

2. Karyn Maughan, "Ending an Abusive Relationship Can be Deadly," IOL News, May 3, 2005, www.iol.co.za/news/south-africa/ending-an-abusive-relationship-can-be-deadly-1.240196.

3. Sharon Lamb, *The Trouble with Blame: Victims Perpetrators, and Responsibility* (Cambridge, MA: Harvard University Press, 1996).

Chapter 1
It Will Never Happen to Me: Intimate Partner Abuse in America

1. Thomas, K., Joshi, M., Wittenberg, E., and McCloskey, L.A., "Intersections of harm and health: A qualitative study of women survivors of abuse," *Violence against Women* 14, no. 11 (2008): 1274 – 1294.

2. U.S. Department of Justice, "Violence against Women: Estimates from the Redesigned Survey," *Bureau of Justice Statistics Special*

Report (August 1995), 4, http://bjs.ojp.usdoj.gov/content/pub/pdf/FEMVIED.PDF.

3. Karen Scott Collins, Cathy Schoen, Susan Joseph, et al., "Health Concerns across a Woman's Lifespan: The Commonwealth Fund 1998 Survey of Women's Health," May 5, 1999, The Commonwealth Fund: A Private Foundation Working toward a High Performance Health System, www.commonwealthfund.org/Publications/Fund-Reports/1999/May/Health-Concerns-Across-a-Womans-Lifespan--The-Commonwealth-Fund-1998-Survey-of-Womens-Health.aspx.

4. Irene Hanson Frieze and Angela Brown, "Violence in Marriage," in *Family Violence*, eds. Lloyd Ohlin and Michael Tonry (Chicago: University of Chicago Press, 1989).

5. U.S. Department of Justice, "Intimate Partner Violence in the United States," Bureau of Justice Statistics, December 2006.

6. Stephanie Covington and J. Kohen, "Women, Alcohol, and Sexuality," *Advances in Alcohol and Substance Abuse* 4, no. 1 (1984): 41–56.

7. Jeffrey Edelson, "The Overlap between Child Maltreatment and Woman Battering," *Violence Against Women,* no. 5 (1999): 134–54.

8. K. M. Radtke, et al, "Transgenerational Impact of Intimate Partner Violence on Methylation in the Promoter of the Glucocorticoid Receptor," *Journal of Translational Psychiatry* 1, no. 21 (2011).

9. Sandra A. Graham-Bermann and Julia Seng, "Violence Exposure and Traumatic Stress Symptoms as Additional Predictors of Health Problems in High-Risk Children," *The Journal of Pediatrics* 146, no. 3 (2005): 349–354

10. Frieze and Brown, "Violence in Marriage."

11. Naimah Jabali-Nash, "Kentucky Tragedy: Man Kills Wife, Five Others, in Rampage Over Cold Eggs, Say Cops," CBSNews.com, September 13, 2010, www.cbsnews.com/8301-504083_162-20016224-504083.html.

12. Michigan Department of Community Health, "Violence in the Lives of Michigan Women: Results of a Statewide Survey," Violence Against Women Prevention Program, 1999.

13. http://www.libraryindex.com/pages/2055/Effects-Abuse-Why-Does-She-Stay-WHAT-CAN-WOMAN-DO.html14.

14. Carey Goldberg, "Spouse Abuse Crackdown, Surprisingly, Nets Many Women," *New York Times,* November 23, 1999, www.ny times.com/1999/11/23/us/spouse-abuse-crackdown-surprisingly-nets-many-women.html?pagewanted=all&src=pm.

15. Shamita Das Dasgupta, "A Framework for Understanding Women's Use of Nonlethal Violence in Intimate Heterosexual Relationships," *Violence Against Women* 8, no. 11 (2002): 1364–89.

16. Lisa Larance, personal communication, November 2011.

Chapter 2
Knowledge Is Power: Recognizing All Types and Patterns of Abuse

1. Judith McFarlane, et al, "Stalking and Intimate Partner Femicide," *Homicide Studies* 3, no. 4 (1999): 300–16.

2. Frank Ascione, et al., "The Abuse of Animals and Domestic Violence: A National Survey of Shelters for Women who are Battered," *Society & Animals* 5, no. 3 (1997): 205–18.

3. Judith McFarlane, et al, "Intimate Partner Sexual Assault against Women: Frequency, Health Consequences, and Treatment Outcomes," *Obstetrics and Gynecology* 105, no. 1 (2005): 99–108.

4. Jacquelyn C. Campbell, Daniel Webster, Jane Koziol-McLain, Carolyn Block, Doris Campbell, Mary Ann Curry, Faye Gary, et al., "Risk Factors for Femicide in Abusive Relationships: Results from a Multisite Case Control Study," *American Journal of Public Health*, 93, no. 7 (2003): 1089–97.

Chapter 3
Armor Up: You Are Your Best Defense against Abuse

1. "Intimate Partner Violence: Risk and Protective Factors," Center for Disease Control, September 10, 2010, www.cdc.gov/Violence Prevention/intimatepartnerviolence/riskprotectivefactors.html.
2. Morris Rosenberg, *Society and the Adolescent Self-Image,* revised edition (Middletown, CT: Wesleyan University Press, 1989), www.bsos.umd.edu/socy/research/rosenberg.htm.
3. Nathaniel Brandon, "Our Urgent Need for Self-Esteem," www.nathanielbranden.com.
4. Ibid.
5. Barbara De Angelis, Quotations Book, http://quotationsbook.com/quote/8628.

Chapter 4
Forewarned Is Forearmed: How Abusers Test, Prime, and Ensnare Their Victims

1. David Adams, *Why Do They Kill? Men Who Murder Their Intimate Partners* (Nashville, TN: Vanderbilt University Press, 2007), 139.
2. Patricia Schnitzer and Kruse Ewigman, "Child Deaths Resulting from Inflicted Injuries: Household Risk Factors and Perpetrator Characteristics," *Journal of the American Academy of Pediatrics*, 116, no. 5 (2005): 687–93.
3. Campbell, et al., "Risk Factors for Femicide in Abusive Relationships."

Chapter 5
Turning the Tables: Time to Test Your New Partner

1. Marc MacYoung and Dianna Gordon MacYoung, No Nonsense Self-Defense, www.nononsenseselfdefense.com.

Chapter 6
The Devil You Know: Risk Factors by Characteristic

1. Adams, *Why Do They Kill?* 26.

2. Dr. Frank Colistro, personal communication, March 2010.

3. Terrence Real, *I Don't Want to Talk About It: Overcoming The Secret Legacy of Male Depression* (New York: Fireside, 1997).

4. Minnesota Center Against Violence and Abuse, Barbara J. Hart's Collected Writings, http://www.mincava.umn.edu/documents/hart/hart.html.

5. Lundy Bancroft, "Understanding the Batterer in Custody and Visitation Disputes," 1998, www.lundybancroft.com/?page_id=279.

6. Dr. Neil Jacobson and Dr. John Gottman, *When Men Batter Women: New Insights into Ending Abusive Relationships* (New York: Simon and Schuster, Inc, 2007).

Chapter 7
Clear and Present Danger: Risk Factors by Behavior/Method of Abuse

1. Linda Villarosa, ed., *Body & Soul: The Black Women's Guide to Physical Health and Emotional Well-Being.* (New York: Harper Collins, 1994).

2. Federal Bureau of Investigation, "Crime in the United States, 2000," *Uniform Crime Reports* (2001).

3. Lawrence Greenfield, Michael Rand, et al., *Violence by Intimates: Analysis of Data on Crimes by Current or Former Spouses, Boyfriends, and Girlfriends* (U.S. Department of Justice, Office of Justice Programs, Bureau of Justice Statistics, 1998), www.fbi.gov/about-us/cjis/ucr/crime-in-the-u.s/2000/toc00.pdf.

4. Ibid.

5. Jacquelyn C. Campbell, "Intimate Partner Violence Risk Assessment: Implications for Women's Safety," Domestic Violence Danger

Assessment and Safety Planning Training, Multnomah County, Oregon (December 13, 2010).

6. Campbell, et al.,"Risk Factors for Femicide in Abusive Relationships."

7. Campbell, "Intimate Partner Violence Risk Assessment."

8. Adams, *Why Do They Kill?* 186.

9. Campbell, "Intimate Partner Violence Risk Assessment."

10. Adams, *Why Do They Kill?* 20.

11. Ibid.

12. "Intimate Partner Homicide: Hamilton County, Ohio, 1997–2006," Hamilton County Domestic Violence Fatality Review Team, 2007, www.uc.edu/News/NR.aspx?ID=7415.

13. National Violent Death Reporting System, Centers for Disease Control, http://wisqars.cdc.gov:8080/nvdrsDisplay.jsp.

14. Lee Wilbur, Michelle Highley, Jason Hatfield, Zita Surprenant, et al., "Survey Results of Women Who Have Been Strangled while in an Abusive Relationship," *Journal of Emergency Medicine* 21 (2001): 297–302.

15. Campbell, et al., "Risk Factors for Femicide in Abusive Relationships."

16. Robert Peters, "The Link Between Pornography and Violent Sex Crimes," Morality in Media, March 2004, http://www.morality inmedia.org/full_article.php?article_no=193.

17. Loretta Park, "Pornography at Root of More and More Domestic Violence Incidents," September 19, 2009, www.standard.net/ topics/news/2009/09/19/pornography-root-more-and-more-domestic-violence-incidents.

18. Adams, *Why Do They Kill?* 181.

19. Barbara J. Hart, "Domestic Violence: A Model Protocol for Police Response," Minnesota Center Against Violence and Abuse, January 1989, http://www.mincava.umn.edu/documents/hart/ hart.html#id2369487.

20. ASPCA, "The Connection between Domestic Violence and Animal Cruelty: How Is Animal Abuse Related to Domestic Violence?" www.aspca.org/fight-animal-cruelty/domestic-violence-and-animal-cruelty.aspx.

21. American Humane Society, "Facts about Animal Abuse and Domestic Violence," http://www.americanhumane.org/interaction/support-the-bond/fact-sheets/animal-abuse-domestic-violence.html.

22. Adams, *Why Do They Kill?* 105.

Chapter 8
But He Can Change, Right? Knowing When and How to Make Self-Protective Decisions

1. Gavin De Becker, *The Gift of Fear: Survival Signals That Protect Us from Violence* (New York: Dell Publishing, 1997).

2. Julia C. Babcock, Charles E. Green, and Chet Robie, "Does Batterers' Treatment Work? A Meta-analytic Review of Domestic Violence Treatment," *Clinical Psychology Review* 23 (2004): 1023–53.

Chapter 9
Ending a Violent Relationship: The Pursuit of Life, Liberty, and Happiness

1. Vanessa A. Handsel, "Psychological Variables in Battered Women's Stay/Leave Decisions: Risk-Taking, Perceived Control, and Optimistic Bias," (master's thesis, University of North Carolina, 2007), http://libres.uncg.edu/ir/uncw/f/handselv2007-1.pdf.

Chapter 10
Building Your Cavalry: Getting Help from Police, Courts, and Victim Services

1. Marc MacYoung and Dianna Gordon MacYoung, No Nonsense Self-Defense, www.nononsenseselfdefense.com.

2. National Law Enforcement Officers' Memorial Fund, http://www
.nleomf.org.

Chapter 11
Strengthen Your Alliances: Finding Support within the Community

1. "California Domestic Violence Shelter Facts," California Partnership
to End Domestic Violence, 2011, www.cpedv.org/Shelter%20Facts.
2. "Census 2010 Report," National Network to End Domestic Violence,
http://nnedv.org/resources/census/2010-report.html.

Chapter 12
Target Hardening: How to Fortify Your Defenses after Escape

1. Alex Heckert and Edward Gondolf, "Battered Women's Perceptions
of Risk Versus Risk Factors and Instruments in Predicting Repeat
Reassault," *Journal of Interpersonal Violence* 19, no. 7 (2004): 778-800
2. Robert A. Fein, Bryan Vossekuil, and Gwen Holden, *Threat Assessment:
An Approach to Prevent Targeted Violence* (Washington, DC: National
Institute of Justice, U.S. Department of Justice, 1995).
3. Eve Buzawa, Gerald T. Hotaling, Andrew Klein, and James Byrne,
*Response to Domestic Violence in a Pro-Active Court Setting—Final
Report* (National Institute of Justice, grant number 95-IJ-CX-0027,
U.S. Department of Justice, National Institute of Justice, July 1999),
www.ncjrs.gov/App/Publications/abstract.aspx?ID=181427.
4. "WomenStrength Instructor Training Manual," WomenStrength
(Portland, OR: Portland Police Bureau), www.portlandonline.com/
police/index.cfm?c=35911.

Index

A

abandonment, 170

abuse: abuser's fear of exposing, 216; "confront and check" policy toward, 179–182; cycle of, 50–55, 187; defined, 33; economic, 36–37, 94–95, 287; emotional, 17, 31–33; justifications for, 169–176; legal definition of, 223–224; multi-generational, 20; myths about, 20–22, 25; past record of, 113–114; police documentation of, 219; post-reconciliation, 211; questioning potential mate on, 112–113; red flags for. *See* red flags; and restraining orders, 227; temporary escape routes, 189–192; types of, 34–50; verbal, 17, 31–33, 35–36; victim as blamed for, 179; with weapons, 163; *see also* physical abuse; violence

abusers: arguments as clues to, 90; childhood impressions of, 108; children as covictims of, 17–18; counseling for, 182–184, 258; cycle of violence, 51–52; "debt" to, 59; do the choosing, 81; eventual burn-out of, 298; as father of your children, 286–288; forced relocation of, 203; high-risk traits of, 217; legal representation for, 236–239; living with, safety tips for, 186–201; mindset of, 169; myths about, 20; placating anger of, 50; reaction to 911 calls, 216; red flags indicating. *See* red flags; response to police presence, 221–223; returning violence to, 25–26; secrets and lies of, 121–123; "sorriness" of, 176–179; suicide threats, 151, 156,

Battered Women's Justice Project
Defense Office, 306
Batterers' Intervention Program (BIP),
182, 258
battering, defined, 25
beauty, and self-esteem, 62
Becker, Gavin de, 171–172, 204
behavior: apology plus change in, 177–
178; changes in post-separation, 299;
"confront and check" policy toward,
179–182; controlled via threat, 151;
critiquing unwanted, 100–101;
dangerous, 43–45; hiding negative,
117; lack of personal accountability
for, 131–133; pushing boundaries,
85–87, 90, 102; restraining order
violation, 234; as unaffected by BIPs,
182
Bejerot, Nils, 53
blame: children's self-, 19; as done by
abusers, 52, 114, 137; for suicidal
thoughts, 156; as trait of abusers,
132–133; of victim for abuse, 20–21,
179; victim is not to, 9, 10
body language: aggressive, 102; to
diffuse tension, 188; of liars, 104–
105; of power, 103
boundaries: breaking, 90; drawing,
73, 78–79; pushing, 85–87, 102; of
separation, establishing firm, 210,
211–212; vulnerability of, 87
brain damage, from strangulation, 159
Branden, Nathaniel, 61
Brown, Donna, 101
Brown, Sandra L., 83

bullying, 164, 171
burglary, 153–154, 278

C
Cahill, Sharon, 24
"calm before the storm", 299
cameras, security, 281
Cameron, Julia, 79
Campbell, Dr. Jacqueline, 96, 152, 158
carpooling, 266–267
cell phones: for 911 calls, 189–190,
191, 215; preventing techno stalking
on, 276
Centers for Disease Control, Atlanta, 58
charisma, artificial, 120–121
Childhelp USA, 306
childhood: abusers views on their, 108;
as contributing to abusive mindset,
169; self-esteem as grown in, 62
child pornography, 161
child protective services, 18–19, 197,
255, 257, 287
children: abuser as father of, 286–288;
and advocate confidentiality, 249–
250; as covictims, 17–18, 95, 96–97;
escape packing for, 205; having, does
not stop abuse, 171–172; legal issues
for escaping, 198; lifelong influence
of childhood, 57–58; and multi-
generational abuse, 20; national
coalitions for aiding, 305, 306;
physical abuse of, 161; preparing
them for attack, 194–197; protective
services for, 18–19, 197, 255, 257;
restraining order protection for, 229;

sexual abuse of, 49; in shelters, 253;
social services help for women with,
255; staying for the sake of, 204; as
threatened by pet abuse, 46; threats
to, 150; as witness to abuse, 19–20
child support, 287–288
Child Welfare League of America, 306
choice: abuser as eliminating,
89–90; comfort with personal, 64;
psychological control of, 41; see *also*
decisions
choking, 47, 158
Churchill, Winston, 296
"Claim of Violation of Crime Victims'
Rights", 243
code words, 192–193, 263
"cognitive dissonance", 54
cohabitation: and control, 90–91;
does not stop abuse, 171–172;
maintaining control in, 96; moving
out, 203–204; rushed, 93–97
cold rage, 134
Colistro, Dr. Frank, 122
come-ons, negative, 85
commitment, ultimatums about, 93
Commonwealth Fund, 14
communication: about children,
with abuser, 287, 288; announcing
separation, 208–211; avoiding post-
arrest, 244; limiting friend/abuser,
post-separation, 261; with police,
217–218; post-separation, with
abuser, 284; with restraining orders
in place, 232–233; during a trial,
236–238

compartmentalization, 121–123
confidentiality: for abusers in therapy,
258; of address, on restraining
order, 227; of case specifics, 238; of
children's counseling, 197; DAs as
exempt from, 235; defense attorney/
client, 236; and extreme relocation,
294; of finances, 207; of police
reports, 115; of separation plans,
202–203; of shelter location, 251,
253; victim/advocate, 249–250
confinement, 45
Conflict Tactics Scale, 25–26, 27–28
control: apology as form of, 178;
benevolent to malevolent, 89; of
"choice", 41; cohabitation and,
91; to fight powerlessness, 170; of
finances, 36–37; via jealousy, 128;
lack of impulse, 130–131; lack of
self-, 45; paranoia and, 140; power
wheel, 48; as primary trait of abusers,
125–127, 169–170; reclaiming, 271;
restraining order as symbol of, 231–
233; silence as aid to, 213–214; via
stalking, 42–43; tests for potential
partners, 103; via threats, 149, 150;
violence as means of, 27
Cooper, Lieutenant Colonel Jeff, 272
counseling: about reconciliation
attempts, 211; for abusers, 286;
Batterers' Intervention Program
(BIP), 182–184; for children, 196,
197; dangers of joint, 180–182;
empowerment therapy, 60; for past
trauma, 19; referrals, appropriate,

242–246; myths about, 20–22; notifications of arrest release for, 225; prevalence of, 253; reconciliation as tempting for, 202; renter's rights for, 264; restraining order filing, 226, 230; self-defense by, 25, 27, 28–30; silence of, 213–214; social services money for, 254–256; socio-economic statistics of, 14–16; susceptibility of, 58; traits of, 83; witness tampering with, 243–244

VINE (Victim Information and Notification Everyday), 225

violence: continuum of increased, 35, 161; Cycle of Violence, 50–55; diffusing, 187–189; "equal use of" theory, 25–26; and extreme mood swings, 130; following external stalking, 43; Intermittent Explosive Disorder, 131; intoxication as increasing, 152; invisible, 26; is not love, 172–173; as lack of empathy, 130; lack of personal accountability for, 131–133; maintaining un-involvement with, 211; and mental health issues, 124; obsession with, 137–138; paranoia and, 140; physical, 33, 46–47; preparing children for, 194–197; rationalizing, 52; returning, 24–25, 27, 28–30; self-deception about partners', 170–171; against women, 8; see also abuse

Violence Against Women Office, U.S. Department of Justice, 305

violent pornography, 161

Volunteers of America, 253

Vossekuil, Bryan, 285

W

Walker, Dr. Lenore, 50

"walking on eggshells", 50, 136, 187

weakness: arguments as clues to, 90; early assessment of, 85–86

weapons: abuse with, 163, 189; fighting back against, 290–292

witnesses: asking for, 273–274; children as covictims of, 19; tampering with, 243, 244, 245

women: abuser's disrespectful views on, 135; as "fixers", 175–176; as owned by men, 141; statistics on violence against, 8; testing partner's view of, 112

Women's Justice Center/Centro de Justicia para Mujeres, 240

WomensLaw.org, 228

women's rights, 11

women's roles: abusers as holding dated ideas of, 135; abusers as rigid on, 103; misogynistic myths about, 20

WomenStrength, 73, 100, 289

Women Who Love Psychopaths (Brown), 83

Y

young women, as high-risk, 14

Z

zero tolerance policy, 78–79

Acknowledgments

I would like to thank my family and friends for their unwavering support throughout my creative process, especially my amazing husband, James, and our two beautiful daughters, for being the sunlight of my existence. I would also like to extend my gratitude for the assistance of my agent, Rita Rosenkranz, who took a chance on a new voice, and the expert team at Seal Press, led by Executive Editor Brooke Warner. Particular thanks go to my developmental editor, Merrik Bush-Pirkle, without whose brilliant guidance my book would never have become what it is. I am also grateful for having had the opportunity to serve and work alongside the infinitely courageous souls I have crossed paths with in the movement against intimate partner abuse. Lastly, I want to acknowledge the people who have made my life challenging, those who have disparaged or hurt me, and specifically my abuser. Although neither of us knew it at the time, your words and actions did something wonderfully irreversible. They made me even stronger. And while that transformation was not of your doing, I wouldn't be who I am today without its defining experience.

About the Author

Lynn Fairweather is an abuse survivor who has specialized in domestic violence response and prevention for nearly twenty years. She operates Presage Consulting and Training, a threat assessment and management firm dedicated to the prevention of intimate partner homicide. Lynn holds a bachelor's degree in social science and a master's degree in social work. She travels the country providing specialized training and consultation for law enforcement, prosecutors, judges, advocates, and private employers on assessing and managing domestic violence cases. Lynn has served on several successful interpersonal violence task forces and response teams, facilitated victim support groups and batterers' intervention programs, and writes professionally on the subject of domestic violence. *Stop Signs* is her first book.

Selected Titles From Seal Press

For more than thirty years, Seal Press has published groundbreaking books.
By women. For women.

Getting Free: You Can End Abuse and Take Back Your Life, by Ginny
NiCarthy. $16.95, 978-1-58005-122-4. This straightforward and motivational
book provides all the tools and advice you need to help yourself recognize,
respond to, and overcome domestic violence.

Helping Her Get Free: A Guide for Families and Friends of Abused Women,
by Susan Brewster. $13.95, 978-1-58005-167-5. This straightforward and
compassionate book offers the information needed to help give strength to
women who are trying to break free of harmful relationships.

Invisible Girls: The Truth about Sexual Abuse, by Dr. Patti Feuereisen with
Caroline Pincus. $16.95, 978-1-58005-301-3. An important book for teenage
girls, young women, and those who care about them, that gives hope and
encouragement to sexual abuse survivors by letting them know that they're not
alone and that there are many roads to healing.

*What You Really Really Want: The Smart Girl's Shame-Free Guide to Sex
and Safety,* by Jaclyn Friedman. $17.00, 978-1-58005-344-0. An educational
and interactive guide that gives young women the tools they need to decipher
the modern world's confusing, hypersexualized landscape and define their own
sexual identity.

When the Piano Stops: A Memoir of Healing from Sexual Abuse, by
Catherine McCall. $16.95, 978-1-58005-267-2. A true survivor memoir
poised to change the face of literature on the topic of sexual abuse.

*In Love and In Danger: A Teen's Guide to Breaking Free of Abusive
Relationships*, by Barrie Levy, MSW. $12.95, 978-1-58005-187-3. Updated
with expanded resources, this revised edition continues to speak directly to
young adults about dating violence.

Find Seal Press Online
www.SealPress.com
www.Facebook.com/SealPress
Twitter: @SealPress